P9-BAT-545

Already Home

Stories of a Seeker

Aruni Nan Futuronsky

COLD RIVER STUDIO
NASHVILLE, TENNESSEE

Cold River Studio is an independent press committed to introducing fresh, exciting voices to the reading public. It is our mission to take a chance on deserving authors and achieve the highest quality when bringing their words to the marketplace. We believe in the power of words and ideas and strive to introduce readers to new, creative writers.

Published by Cold River Studio, Nashville, Tennessee

No part of this publication may be reproduced, stored in retrieval system, or transmitted in any form or by any means, electronic, mechanical, photocopying, recording, or otherwise, without written permission of the publisher.
www.coldriverstudio.com

First Edition: August 2010

All rights reserved.
Copyright © 2010 Aruni Nan Futuronsky
Cover Design © 2010 Cold River Studio
Cover Photo: © 2010 Jupiterimages Corporation

Printed in the United States of America
ISBN 978-0-9828146-1-1

My Abounding Gratitude

*I remember being a little girl and cuddling into my daddy's lap,
hopelessly frightened about something that happened at school that
day. He held me close, as only he could do, and said, "Honey,
everything is going to be okay. You'll be able to do anything you want
to do in your life. Don't worry."*

*I didn't believe him, and I did worry.
Time, however, has proven him completely right.
To Dad, to Mom—time and circumstance have proven you both so right.
Missing you, loving you, forever grateful.*

Author's Note

This book is a work of creative non-fiction. My intention has been to protect the privacy of all the people who have blessed my life while portraying my life accurately. Some characters are composites and certain timelines have been altered. The events described are filtered through the lens of time, space, and those funny tricks memory sometimes plays. I offer them to you as an honest reflection of my experiences.

Contents

Already Home: Stories of a Seeker

Part One: What Was

"I knew I was different." Waiting for Hebrew School.

1

Heaven, Hell, and Hebrew School
1956-1961

I always knew I was Jewish. It was a deep and wordless knowing, yet another mighty divide that separated me from so many other kids at elementary school and summer camp. It seemed to set me apart from most people in my world. Like my stuttering or my wanting to kiss girls, being Jewish was a heavy load and one to keep secret. Secrets were the way to go. Mommy and Daddy never actually said that, but confidentiality, a sense of holding your breath, of holding your cards close to your chest, was surely the attitude in our house. Although a less obvious burden, being Jewish took a containment and focus in order to hold its essence close, to keep others away from that place of deep silence and concealment inside. On a very real level, I knew it just wasn't safe to be a Jew. That was a cellular knowledge that lived in me.

And I knew I was different.

One snowy late afternoon around Christmastime, the daylight just darkening as a soft snow fell over downtown Scranton, I said goodbye to my friend, Gladys, at the bus stop. We had just seen our Saturday afternoon movie, and now, climbing on different buses, we began to make our individual ways home. The wispy snow fell gently, softening the glow of the Christmas lights from all the department store windows. "Little Drummer Boy," that endless, evocative carol, was playing on an ongoing loop in the Globe Store window display; the Christmas shoppers bundled up and hustling from store to store with gifts in arms. And there I sat, watching from my seat next to the steamy bus window, the outside world such an essential Christmas moment, the little drummer boy never, ever ceasing his caroling. The Christmas of it was so palpable. And it was *not mine, not mine*. I would go home to a house without lights, without presents. I would go to sleep without the fantasy of a Santa Claus bringing me gifts. I would live in a family where Jesus Christ was not our Lord. I was an outsider, an observer of this dominant culture's phenomenon. A sense of doom settled over me as we proceeded up the incline of Mulberry Street to the Hill Section where we lived. As the day darkened, so did my heart.

Nevertheless, I was clandestinely proud of being Jewish, too. The holidays were somewhat cool to my child's eye, Chanukah always dovetailing my birthday with the bright lights of the menorah, the candle holder. Passover offered my mother's remarkable matzo balls, made with the perfect, never-to-be-duplicated-by-another-human-being consistency, floating in chicken soup yellowed with rich taste and deliciousness. I never understood why we couldn't have matzo balls any other time of year but at Passover time. I guessed it was just one of those things we had to live with because we were Jewish. There were many of those unseen and silent stipulations.

There existed some unspoken conflict between my parents in the arena of religious observance. My mother's family was comprised of observant Jews, while my dad's family hardly had any connection to religion, and didn't officially even belong to a synagogue—quite the shameful truth. My mother, as with so many other things, "gave it up" for my dad. He was always,

throughout our lives, the one to whom we all compromised—
he was the one we all gave in to. This religious divide between
them was a silent current of hushed comparison and almost-
disparagement in our house. My sister and I wobbled in between
the two, landing in a reform temple, the less observant system
of Judaism.

Madison Avenue Reform Temple was part of the compromise
to meet my father's needs. Here prayers were translated into
English, to accommodate his lack of Hebrew skills; a choir sang;
and the religious school focused on holidays and traditions
rather than just Hebrew. However, for me, this was a problem,
since the cool and popular Jewish kids went to Temple Israel,
the conservative temple. In my eyes, our temple was inferior, part
of the angst I had to wrestle with: wanting to be cool, knowing I
wasn't, wanting to have friends, being too frightened to speak out
to others. Temple became yet another arena of disadvantage.

We would go as a family to synagogue only on the High Holy
Days, Rosh Hashanah and Yom Kippur, in the fall of every year.
We had our reserved seats, always in the same place, on the side
of the altar, or bema, up front, facing the rabbi's side. This meant
two very painful things to me: first, we were always the last people
out of the service, which tried my already stretched patience; and
secondly, everyone could see us, another opportunity for my self-
consciousness to run wild. Suffice it to say, synagogue was not a
place of renewal and connection. For me, sitting on that plush,
mink-colored velour seat, in that blond pew, seeing the stained
glass windows with confusing religious images on them, made
me itchy, restless, and shy. Was that Moses up there in the stained
glass, carrying the Ten Commandments? Was he in heaven?

The services were long, endlessly long, longer than bearable
in my child's world. Our rabbi, Milton Richmond, black eyes

flashing with passion, wore his black flowing robe with great theatrical dignity. His voice was sonorous and deep and rang throughout the open cavernous space as he orated and prayed and taught and preached. I would be lost, lost after the first few pages. I restlessly attempted to stay tuned in, to stay attentive, but sleep played heavy on my eyes, my petticoat itched my thighs, and I was simply bored. Time was hollow and warped.

One warm September day, my father closed his little grocery store as he did only two days each year for the Jewish holidays. We all sat together, our little tribe of four, huddled in our pew for all to see. Several hours had passed during this service. We had no breakfast, and no lunch was coming, since it was the Day of Atonement, the day of fasting. I sat between my parents, my usual spot, their legs pressed warm and heavy against mine. It was a marathon of words, an epic of endless page-turning, hymn-singing, and atonement—asking God for forgiveness for our actions during the year.

Suddenly something felt wrong, some balance around me altered, as if the barometric pressure had shifted. I looked at my mother, and the impossible was happening. Her head was swaying, heavy with sleep, her eyes closed. Horror swept through my body. First her head rolled down toward her chest, a reckless bowling ball out of control, then somehow, miraculously, it righted itself on her quivering neck, only then to sway precariously backwards. To my dismay, this rotation began to repeat itself again. I felt a chill of sweat, the sweat of humiliation, trickle down my neck. *No! Not this. Not again.* My mother, who worked next to my father in their little grocery store from early morning until dark, was tired. Oh, she was tired, and she deserved to sleep. She worked for me, it was all for me, for me. But here she was, drooling now! Her head was rolling, for all the not-even-so-cool Jews to see.

If I could have hidden under the carpet, if the burning bush that Moses saw could have consumed me, if the Red Sea could have swallowed me up—it would have been easier. To sit there, to wait, to watch, to allow her to be, to feel my shame...there was no God in that pew. Not for me. Not yet.

If Jews believed in hell, this would be it.

And where was this God of Abraham, Isaac, and Jacob?

My religious education stalled and lurched forward, based more in protocol than on my specific needs. I had to attend Sunday school, morning classes held on Sundays to learn about traditions, customs, and holidays. Year after year, I was force-fed crafts projects, coloring books, stories, and hymn-singing to acquaint me with my heritage. My fourth year teacher, Mrs. Schecter, was an over-enthusiastic, blue-haired citizen of the Jewish community, her laughter too shrill, her words emphasized strangely on the first syllable. Was that a Jewish way of teaching? She was talking yet again about Judas Macabee, the brave leader of the revolt against the oppressors.

"*Mac*abee *fo*ught and *fo*ught against the *op*pressors," she said, smiling broadly.

What was an oppressor? I really didn't understand, and I knew I couldn't ask her my question; I couldn't say the words. I couldn't risk it. My stutter would humiliate me. Her smile was too bright, her gaze too gay—I knew she couldn't quiet down enough to receive me. So I continued sitting in the short, red chair, my jumper itchy, pretending that I understood. I wanted to go home. In the arts and crafts projects, in the clay molding of the candle holders, I couldn't find a thread to hold onto, a thread to relate to, to understand. I was in a cloud of lonely confusion.

Snacks would come soon, my only consolation, at 11:00— escape from the classroom, all ages together now in the auditorium for the organized bedlam they called community time. I sucked my orange drink mightily out of its wax container while folk songs and dancing boisterously exploded around me. Every Sunday I would drink that orange drink. Every Sunday at 11:30, I would run, liberated, to my mother's car waiting for me outside, in the line of parent cars double-parked in a patient and tidy line outside Temple. I would slide inside and slam the powder blue Buick's door behind me, my head aching, throbbing. Was it the pressure of the classes, the too-cheery teachers? Was it the wax carton? I wanted to go home, to put on my play clothes, to ride my bike in the park and pretend that I was a Canadian Mountie, on his horse, out to save his damsel in distress.

"How was it?" she would ask, eyebrow raised slightly as she held the steering wheel at three and twelve o'clock, with her strong, distinctive, and competent hands.

"Good," I'd lie, knowing there was no room, no avenue, no road to a deeper response. I couldn't say it, and she couldn't hear it.

But protocol dictated. I continued my Jewish education halfheartedly, Sunday school classes anchoring my weekend with dread and boredom.

But the ante would be upped. It was soon time for me to go to Hebrew school. All kids my age did this in conjunction with learning about the Jewish traditions and culture. My Hebrew education had been delayed, gratefully, due to my stuttering. My grade school classes at John James Audubon School were scary enough. But somehow, after great discussion, it was decided: to my ten-year-old self's dismay, I would be enrolled in the Madison Avenue Temple Hebrew School.

My career as a Hebrew student was brief, doomed, and painful for all involved. The first level teacher was Miss Tischman, an erratic middle-aged woman with a beehive of disturbed dark hair trembling on her crown. I recognized her as a concentration camp survivor, the tattoo on her forearm similar to the parents of my best and only friend, Gladys. I understood about the Holocaust and was secretly furious about my people's plight. I tried so hard to be a good student, especially because of her tattoo. But her questions were too garbled, her accent too different, the sounds too confusing, the alphabet too squiggly, the pressure too intense. I was doomed.

Somehow I realized that, if I acted out and got silly, I didn't have to answer questions and risk the exposure of my stuttering, unreliable voice. Thus my formula for survival unfolded. One day during my third week, we were going up and down the rows, reciting the alphabet. For me, that was like waiting for the firing squad to execute me. To get myself off the recitation hook, I jumped fully into my new assumed role of the class clown. I took Alan Shinkman's ski cap—he sat in front of me, and it was easy enough to yank it out of his dirty brown corduroy winter coat pocket. I covered my entire face with the red, smelly wool, and began pantomiming and singing Alvin and the Chipmunks' latest song, in my most successful falsetto. "*Christmas, Christmas, don't be late,*" I sang from the dark, itchy incognito of the mask with all my heart and soul.

In a storm of fury, summoning up the power of the generations stolen from her, Miss Tischman literally threw me out of class with a hefty shove and, to my astonishment, threw my red rubber boots after me. The door slammed behind me, leaving me and my boots to ponder my Hebrew-less future. I was destined to be a Jew without the key to unlocking God's secrets. What had I done?

My parents were quiet and non-confrontational about it. The situation just disappeared from my life—I never returned to

Hebrew school. The humiliation of being a class clown expelled from Hebrew school was diminished by my profound relief and liberation from the shame-filled classroom. Yet my guilt for disturbing Miss Tischman, who had already been disturbed by Adolph Hitler and his master plan, plagued me endlessly.

But my Jewish education, though thwarted, could not end here. My Sunday school classes put me on the track for confirmation, my entryway into the community of Jews. There was no real discussion—I was on the track. The years peeled away, Sunday after Sunday, grade after grade. At age thirteen, along with thirteen other students, male and female, we would be confirmed in a ceremony that we orchestrated on a Friday night before the entire congregation. My greatest fear hovered on the horizon—public speaking. Private speaking was horrifyingly hard enough. But to speak in front of the congregation? Unthinkable. Yet I was on an unstoppable Jewish locomotive, delivering me toward confirmation.

Rabbi Richmond was our teacher that year, the culmination of years of endless Sunday school sessions—we had stayed long enough in school to have gotten the jackpot, the head of the faculty. Our curriculum covered the range of the Jewish experience, culminating in Holocaust studies and the creation of the state of Israel. Sundays were certainly more interesting now…but my mind and my heart jumped unwillingly to June, the time of our official confirmation service. I was still slightly interested in the concept of God, but didn't know where to look for road signs, suggestions, hints of His Presence. It was hard to keep focused, my interest waning, since doom hovered on the horizon of June, molding the texture of the classes, painting them with a tint of growing panic. Confirmation approached. Public speaking was my burning bush—the hoop that I had to jump through to find God.

There was one, single brass ring, one gift in this process that held me captivated, to propel me through my terror. Our temple had a tradition. As each confirmee completed her speech, she approached the rabbi. He put his hands on her head, and offered a specific benediction, suited especially for that individual, welcoming her into the congregation as an adult. This was much played up by all involved. It was all I had to hold on to. It was my only hope. Oh, I needed a prayer.

Spring came with unfortunate swiftness during that, my thirteenth year. Our confirmation class planned the ceremony with great detail. Each of us thirteen drew an area of interest, in order to write our presentations. Mine, drawn with great misfortune, was "the role of the rabbi." I was pretty confused about that very subject, but framed my written speech with awareness of the words I could and could not say. I framed a hopefully easy opening sentence, "*The rabbi is our teacher.*"

I needed a prayer. I needed a benediction. Life was pretty uncomfortable—no boys liked me, school was terrifying. Things were getting worse all the time as high school approached. Camp was the only good part of my life, and that was not enough to get me through. Maybe the rabbi's special prayer would help me find God, and the pain would go away. It was my dream, a blessing that soothed my heart and kept me safe.

June came. I felt like a sleep-walker, sightlessly moving through the days. My mother made an appointment for me at the beauty shop, for a wash and set for that day. As usual, she attended to the details well, getting my flowers all arranged for the service, buying me soft, white leather ballerina flats that would work with my white robe. My dad, following the dictates of the early 60s, didn't call attention to my speech defect. If you didn't speak it, it didn't exist. No fuss was made, no mention of my challenge passed their lips as I approached this challenge of ultimate challenges. I was just Any Kid, headed toward the pulpit. I mistook their loving silence for denial, and held it closely wrapped around me in my aloneness.

The day dawned with a humid, fuzzy light. June 10th, 1961. It had actually arrived. I lay in my bed with my pride-and-joy green, purple, and white plaid bedspread tucked around me, watching the light filter into my room. No matter how much I willed it away from me, the day came just the same.

June 10th, 1961.

I had taken the day off from school, to get my hair done and practice my speech some more.

"The rabbi is our teacher..."

The morning was hollow and empty, the minutes clicking loudly on the big clock in our kitchen. My parents were at the store, working, always working, working for me, always for me. I sat at the Formica kitchen table, running my fingers over the specs of white in its green base, sipping on a glass of milk.

"The rabbi is our teacher."

Could I will the words out of my mouth? *Maybe I'll die before tonight. Maybe the beauty shop will burn down with me inside. Maybe the temple will disappear.* I lay on the sofa, crunched my knees into my chest, and tried to see how small I could get. How tiny could I scrunch up? Knees and legs one, arms squeezing me close to myself. I just wanted to disappear.

"The rabbi is our teacher."

At 1:00, my mom took me downtown to Helen Gazda's Beauty Shop, on Lackawanna Avenue. She dropped me off there, since she had to return to the store for the busy afternoon. I sat moodily in the chair while Miss Helen put sticky, hard pink rollers in my hair, and chatted aimlessly away. I played with the hem of the plastic cape, picking at it.

"The rabbi is our teacher...our te-our-te-a-cher."

As Miss Helen lowered the drier around me, it roared with a fury that enveloped me into itself, like a metal spaceship. *Maybe the dryer will explode. Maybe I'll break my leg on the way home.* I closed my eyes and tried to die. It didn't work. The rollers jabbed at my scalp, heating up with the intensity of the dryer. Finally, after an interminable thirteen minutes of roaring heat, Miss Helen deemed me dry, and lifted up the great metal contraption, returning me to reality.

As she teased out my pageboy hairdo, Miss Helen continued her chatter, chewing gum noisily, her blue eye shadow sparkling in the strange light of the shop. She sprayed my hair, over and over again circling my head with a fine misted halo of smelly chemical sweetness. *Maybe I'll die from hairspray poisoning. Death by hairspray.* I fingered the pageboy—it felt sticky and unnatural. I didn't recognize myself in the mirror.

"The ra-bi-bi-the rabbi."

At least I'd get my benediction. At least I'd get the entranceway to God. At least.

I called my mom to tell her I was ready. I stood outside on Lackawanna Avenue, the day now steamy and damp, traffic crawling by, and waited and waited for the pale blue Buick, my father's pride and joy. *Maybe I'll run away. Maybe the sidewalk will break.*

It didn't. Mom picked me up, complimenting me on my helmet of plastered hair. I said nothing.

Nighttime did come to Scranton, Pennsylvania that evening, of its own accord. I didn't eat any dinner, my stomach achy. My parents benignly drove me to temple, wishing me luck, patting me on the back, telling me they loved me, sending me off with my white robe on a hanger—plastic bag cautiously covering it—to the dressing room, while they went to find their proud, parent seats. The other girl confirmees giggled and busied themselves. I dressed myself quietly. I was numb, legs wooden, the non-stop locomotive steaming me forward on the tracks of Judaism.

Eventually, robes on, flowers in our hands, and with much tittering, we stood in place, waiting to march into the sanctuary. I was silent, titter-free, and breathless.

"The rabbi is…the rabbi is…"

My inane mantra hummed, soared and echoed throughout my body, almost taking me over.

I had my tiny note card with my speech on it in my hand, sweat softening it, bending it. I found myself ripping at its sides, for no particular reason. I watched myself doing it, and strangely, I had no capacity to stop myself.

The organ struck up a frighteningly loud chord as the chorus burst into song. Our procession. Left step. Left step. Left step. Left step. I willed my eyes forward, forbidding myself to look at any of the faces of the people sitting in the pews as we marched down the aisle and made our way, one by one, to the steps. Up the steps on wooden legs I went. No matter how many times we had practiced, this ascent was surreal. I found my position, second from the right, next to Karen Jano who seemed completely aglow, and turned to face the horde of observers. I didn't raise my eyes—I couldn't. My eyes acted on their own, separate from my will, frozen downward, with a life of their own.

I was freezing. Despite the heat and humidity of the night, I was shivering with some foreign sense of cold. My hands were clammy and damp, icy. My bouquet of spring flowers looked foreign to me, resting in my trembling hands.

The rabbi's voice boomed a welcome, startling me out of my inner ruminations. I held my flowers close to my heart, a protective shield from the reality of the moment. The service unfolded—the lighting of the candles by the Sisterhood's president, the welcoming of the families. The rabbi's sense of drama was great. He flourished, he waved, he gestured— he was flush with the excitement of thirteen new souls. My awareness faded in and out, hearing a word or two, a snatch of a phrase, and then literally leaving my body, floating up into the stained glass floating high above the heads with Moses, Moses in heaven. I merged into the stained glass and floated with Moses in that stained glass heaven. I could still hear the roar of the hair dryer from Miss Helen's beauty shop, like a space ship delivering me throughout the cosmos. Then—smash—back down to earth, to the pulpit, to the flowers, to the moment of ultimate dread.

After eons of breathless standing, time had arrived for our speeches. I was third from the last in this firing squad. I heard nothing, as if sounds were permanently banned from my ears. Time ceased to exist. I stood there forever, forever in my terror, forever in my shame, forever in my banishment from grace and God and goodness. Oh, maybe this would be the moment I would enter, I would be safe, the pain would go away. Oh, maybe.

The time arrived. I did not know how I knew, but my body, on its trembling wooden legs, moved me toward the dais. I automatically put my flowers down as we had practiced a dozen times, reached for my torn and dog-eared index card in my sweaty hands. I didn't recognize it at all. It looked completely unfamiliar to me, as if a stranger had offered it to me in that moment. I looked up momentarily, only to see balloon-headed people floating above their seats. The sight of that terrorized me and I jerked my head downward again.

"The the," I sputtered into he microphone. The sound crackled and echoed all around me.

Silence and a puffy breath.

"The rabbi the rabbi…"

I sputtered and started, stopped and hesitated, started again. Three long minutes unraveled, probably the longest three minutes of my life. If Daniel's lion could have devoured me, if the angel of death could have swooped me up right there, I would have wept with release. But there was no release, only the stuttering through, the stumbling through, the sweaty, humiliating jerking through.

And that was that. It was complete. My last sentence jerked forward, escaping me. I was done, swept with cold sweat, shaky and weak. I retrieved my flowers, clutching them to my broken heart. And now the benediction. I turned spastically toward the rabbi, who stood dynamically in front of the open arc. The Torah, the teachings of my people, beamed down on me. The moment I had lived for now arrived. I would be offered my secret, perfect blessing.

The rabbi put his hands on my head. Oh, how much smaller they were than Stacey the basketball player's, whose hands blessed me before every home game. The rabbi's hands were white and small, dry and strangely warm, denting the helmet of my sprayed plastic pageboy. Oh, the blessing was coming. I was trembling with relief, with possibility, faint with it all. I could have fallen over from the merging of exhausted terror and hopefulness.

His voice was a staged, hushed whisper, surrounding me:

"Nan," he dramatically began. "Stay—as beautiful—as—you are—in—this moment."

What? Stay as beautiful as *what?* I was fully and positively certain that I was not beautiful; that my hair was cardboard, my face pimply, my stomach too big, those white spots on my fingernails too noticeable. I was both outraged and profoundly disappointed. *Stay as beautiful as I am in this moment!* It was bullshit. There was no blessing here. There were lies here. Lies. He didn't know what to say; he made it up. I was not beautiful. I could have collapsed into a pile of disappointment at his feet.

But I did not.

The moment passed. I made my way back to my spot for the concluding prayers and final blessing.

The rest of the night unfolded with hugs and smiles and food and celebration. I said nothing about the experience to my parents, and never told anyone about my insipid anti-blessing, the fake prayer of my confirmation.

God did not come to me that night. God did not bless me nor did he welcome me into his people. God was nowhere in sight, as much as I could tell. God wouldn't have lied to me like that.

He just didn't show up.

I would have to continue on alone.

"I found my position, second from the right."

2

The Scranton Miners
1956-1961

In my entire eight years on earth, I knew that this was clearly the most wondrous place on the planet to sit—between my father and mother, his excitement exploding with shouts of glee to my left, tempered by my mother's neutral, slightly disapproving silence to my right. Strangely enough, their opposite responses seemed to open a space into which I was able to relax. The hard wooden bench beneath us held us fast with a familiar hold, as the unmistakable smell of resin and sweat filled up the entire Catholic Youth Center gym. This was home to me.

I was in bliss. Life did not get much better than this.

It was the second half of a Scranton Miners basketball game. The Miners, a semi-pro team and part of the American basketball league, were a major artery of our lives. My father had "invested" some money toward ownership of the team. Art Pachter, a chubby, rounded guy constantly reeking of smelly cigars, with a shiny bald head that made me giggle, was the official owner; my dad and some of his friends were contributors. Money was always an unspoken issue in our family, each dollar hard-earned by my parents' endless, dawn-to-dark toil in their small neighborhood grocery store. Where did money come from for such a luxury? I didn't know. Like all money issues in our family, my father's stake in the team was shrouded with a vague secrecy. But I knew this was not a luxury. Basketball was the core of our days.

Our Miners were down two points, with less than two minutes left on the score clock. My dad kept muttering under his breath in my direction, "Plenty of time, Itsy. We've got plenty of time here." Itsy was my nickname, one he reverted to in moments of extreme excitement or stress. *Plenty of time?* I thought dizzily. I held my breath as the two teams raced down the court. Our opponents, the Wilkes-Barre Barons, in their unattractive purple and black uniforms, had possession of the ball, aggressively worming their way toward their basket and toward potential victory. I held my breath. *Oh, no.* My entire body was constricting and writhing with the rhythms of the game, protecting the basket from our opponents' potential shot from my bench mid-gym. I was the equivalent of a backseat driver, attempting to control the car from afar. I was fully participating in defending against the Barons' full court press. I was one with the Miners' defense.

And then, out of nowhere, Marty Satalino, my hero, number 6 in the beautiful golden Miners' uniform, stole the ball! Nothing short of miraculous, he flowed like a gazelle unencumbered down the court, stopped, and leapt gracefully into the air, defying gravity, the ball leaving his hands in an arc of grace and perfection. Two points! The game was tied. And the referee's whistle—Marty was fouled, calling him fourth to shoot for two extra points. Ecstasy. My father jumped to his feet howling with happiness, as I mirrored his movements. I clapped until my palms ached. With three seconds left, Marty, my hero, stood innocently and unfazed on the four line. Be still, my pounding heart! With face flushed, I breathed Marty's breath. With forehead dripping, I felt his sweat. With fingers compulsively crossed on both hands—toes, too—I willed the ball into the hoop. Marty entered his typical foul shot routine, one I knew and would duplicate in my mind's eye time after time: three bounces, stop, deep breath in and exhale, three more bounces, bend knees, fixate on the hoop, and let go.

The ball flew effortlessly out of his hands, a guided missile not to be deterred from its goal—into the net it swished. The Miners were ahead! Second free throw, Marty repeating his three bounces, deep breath, three bounces, fixation, and another shot good! We were two points up, with three seconds left. The Barons grabbed the ball, threw it in bounds. One of their tall, lanky, awkward players flung the ball down court, randomly and hopefully in the direction of a tied game. The ball fell short at mid-court. The home crowd erupted in hysterical jubilation. I had fully participated, emotionally, energetically, and physically, in manifesting another Miners' victory. We had won.

Our Sunday afternoons found us at basketball games at the CYC on Jefferson Avenue. My sister L., too old to be bothered, disdained the ritual, and made her way to the Jewish Community Center instead, for boys, dancing, and possibility. Some Saturday nights found us three—Mom, Dad, and me—tracing the narrow highways of Northeast Pennsylvania, weaving our way to Sunbury, Allentown, Wilkes-Barre, and other grey, nondescript cities bustling with hoop mania. We followed our guys. In the car, I sat between my parents again, my habitual position in the front seat. My mother was quiet, not unusual; remote, her familiar stance. My father was gabby and animated, me, his daughter, the apparent heir of his voyeuristic athletic delight. The away games were different, night casting strange shadows over the unfamiliar gyms, our voices a drop in the sea of the hometown roar. Clumped together with a handful of

Miners' fans, we were quieter, more reticent in and protective of our zeal.

And the players...oh, the players. Such warriors, such athletes, such gods in my awed and youthful eyes. There was the coach, my dad's friend, Hank Rosenstein, taller than any man I had ever seen, rail-thin, dour, and practically speechless. I never heard him say anything more than a mumble to anyone. His silent height almost frightened me. I became shyer and even more tiny around him, disappearing in his shadow. "A Jew," my dad would say, with inflated pride, his voice rising. "A Jew who used to play for the New York Knicks!" I never saw any Jewish kids play sports very much, except some occasional, lame, boring kickball after Sunday school. It was good, good for our people, good for our family, that Hank was a Jew. This I knew to be true. I didn't know any tall Jewish people at all, just Hank.

If Hank's presence pushed me into awed retreat, Marty's brought me forth. Handsome Marty Satalino, smaller, fluid, dark hair and eyes flashing, white skin consistently flushed with potential victory. Marty from Seton Hall's esteemed college team, my dad said, Marty who fascinated me, Marty whose every movement I followed, memorized, made my own. My dad kidded me once, joking that I had a crush on Marty. No, I didn't. Not at all. I wanted to *be* Marty. I wanted to dribble with such effortless flow, to shoot with such consistent, fluid precision, the ball a mere extension of my movement, my hand, my arm. I wanted his grace for my own. But I never said this to anybody, never told. I knew this was wrong. A crush for a girl was right. But to want to become a man, a strong, fluid man...that was wrong, so wrong.

And then there was Stacey. Stacey Arsenik. He was the only black man I had ever seen. He was built like a wall, his gold uniform taut over his rippling chest. Hair cut to his scalp, feet and hands massive. Although he was less interesting and distinctive to watch in play, he developed a fascinating athletic superstition, a ritual he performed at every home game, a ritual that, strangely enough, involved me. After warming up, before the first huddle, he would sprint up the bleachers to where we sat, usually mid-court, a few rows up. He would rub his giant hands up and down my head, from my nape to my forehead, from my left to my right ear, my pixie haircut offering him some talisman, some unseen, little-white-Jewish-girl mojo. Complete, with a giant smile, now infused with the energy that I so innocently and passively offered him, he trotted off, readied and only now able to join his team.

I loved his attention—and yet it made me so uncomfortable. I was giggly with glee that he knew me and needed me. Yet I didn't want to be noticed. A lifelong pattern emerged: see me, love me, notice me—no, not really, don't see me. My ambivalence, too, was linked to my physical contact with his huge hands. Both the size of his hands and the pink of his palms were like nothing I had ever known before. Black people were not real in my world. He was of another pigmentation, literally of another planet. My child's sense of racism and empty self-esteem intersected with Stacey. A voice inside my head whispered, *If he were white, I wouldn't have been good enough for him.* His blackness and my worthlessness united.

His touch made me slightly squeamish; my reaction to it confused me. I knew that my mother didn't approve. She tightened when he approached, her body language radiating her disapproval. My dad characteristically shrugged it off, and, as Stacey lumbered away, my dad hugged me close, squeezing my shoulders toward him. Stacey continued this ritual throughout all the many years that I attended the Miners' games.

And the parties! At the end of every season, my parents would open our home to the Miners. My mom would go hog wild in preparing a lavish affair for them. She would cover the dining room table, used only for holidays and the most special of events, with a snow-white, embroidered tablecloth graced with my grandmother's intricate needlepoint. Mom would cook at night to prepare, for days and days. Pigs in blankets, wimpies with hamburger buns, all sorts of cheeses that never graced our table, red, ripe roast beef, breads of all sorts, olives and pickles in their special plate, baked goods—all were perfectly lined up, next to the "good" china, with the white pattern with the fake (or was it...could it be...real?) gold leaf, and the fancy silverware. My dad would open the Canadian Club bottles, typically hidden in the breakfront—oh, I had discovered where—and buy bottles of mysteriously clear vodka and dark, glorious rum. The drinks were on the kitchen table with a sweaty, squat ice bucket that only emerged for this event and nothing else.

And they would come, my heroes, in twos and threes. The unthinkable would happen—these impossibly large human beings whom I knew only in their golden shorts and tanks would wander casually into my house, MY house, wearing suits and jackets and ties. Seeing them in clothes was almost embarrassing, so intimate was my knowledge of their bodies—their legs, muscles rippling; their arms, biceps so remarkable. They filled the air in my house, space never inhabited by human form. The sky of my house was alive with their words, their heads, their gestures. They filled it up with body, with laughter, with maleness, with presence. It was ridiculous and impossible, the incongruity of it—my familiar, contained house so opened up to these huge men. So intense was it for me that it magnified my already powerful shyness. I retreated in the shadows, sitting on the steps to the second floor watching hungrily, gathering data silently. My sister L. mumbled about the noise, about the attention Mom paid them, as she pushed past me and retreated upstairs. The noise went on long into the night, both fascinating and distressing, long after I floated to sleep in my bedroom, my beloved Miners downstairs, eating at my table.

But the games were the gift, the joy, the reward to my child's heart. To watch the current of the play, the ball magically flowing from player to player, the shift of body, the brilliance of beings running in symmetry, astonished me. It took away my breath. Although I might not have understood all of the rules—Daddy always filled me in—I knew the movements, the shift of energy, the ultimate flow of basketball in my cells. I was of that flow. It was my birthright.

But some of the lessons learned were less than glorious. One dark November evening in Wilkes-Barre, at the season's end, we hovered before the playoffs, the Miners and the Barons in a hot contest. On the ride to Wilkes-Barre, there was some whisper between my parents about the game possibly "being thrown"; if we lost this game, there would be another—not jeopardizing our participation in the playoffs, while adding another paying game to the players' coffers. I didn't understand and I didn't want to—I was running up and down the court that night with the Miners that night wholeheartedly, ignoring the adult-talk, focused on the purity of play.

And then I understood deeply, my heart sinking to my feet, my belly dropping. I watched Marty throw the ball toward the basket, almost half-heartedly. It slithered with a *woosh* into the net—not unusual. But as I studied his response, I saw the unusual. His face was washed with a sudden surprise, with a new and momentary astonishment. He had intended to miss!

23

He had purposefully intended to miss the basket. I gasped audibly and swung toward my father. His eyes met mine with a kindness and a gentle compassion I will never forget. The rest of the game was a blur of intended defeat. In the car, driving the fifty minutes home through the November drizzle, my parents were quiet. "Sometimes it's like that, Nan," he said quietly. "Sometimes life is just like that."

And on the games went, season after season melting into themselves. Once I entered Central High School, although my heart pulled me toward the CYC, my already precarious image of myself forbade my participation in Miners' basketball. It just wasn't cool. My Sundays were filled, like L.'s, with the Jewish Community Center's teen events, which left me emptied, ashamed, and so lonely. My parents eventually lost their interest once Hank retired, once the bulk of our team had moved on.

And in all this time, nobody once offered me a basketball. In all this time, I had never once felt the rough perfection of the ball rolling in my hands. I had never once dribbled, or shot the ball, or felt myself actually running down court. It was the '50s and the '60s. Girls didn't play real basketball. I only watched, the play going on in my inner world. It wasn't unusual or wrong. I never expected it. It was not mine to have.

Once in high school, I hoped and waited for our gym class to offer some expression, some form in which I might channel, if not my basketball passions, then at least my athletic potential. But no, our sessions were limited to marching—somehow a prerequisite for coordinated, good girls of Central High School—and the assorted and boring gym apparatus. The classes humiliated me. The bloomers we had to wear chafed my thighs, the public and mandatory showers untenable. The marching embarrassed me, my rhythms static and self-conscious. The horse, the pummel—all daunted me. I needed to run, to fly, to dribble, to dunk. I did not need to march.

Yet march I did, to the tunes of the early '60s as Mrs. Reese, the undying gym teacher who had taught my parents and my every aunt and uncle, stood agelessly in that dismal high school gym, her mousy brown hair framing her head, legs widely planted, hands on hips, her beady eyes scanning our ranks for slackers. I somehow was identified as a slacker, which brought me great shame. A slacker I was not—I was actually a contender waiting to explode onto the invisible basketball court of life. But alas, in those pre-Title Nine days, there was no court for me. Not until 1972 was a law passed decreeing that federal funding for intercollegiate athletics could not be gender-biased. In the years that followed, the world of women's athletics would begin changing in drastic ways.

In the meantime, my dad and I hunkered around the television set. His sports voyeurism was contagious. I sat next to him, game after game, sport after sport, season after season, watching, soaking up both his company and his delight in the events. As I grew older, I would only join him for the last few minutes of the game, my patience thinning for the endless early innings or quarters. But together we sat, in silence or in small, shared comments, logging hundreds, perhaps thousands of viewing hours, on couch after couch, in home after home, witnessing the glory and the joy of movement. Throughout our lives we sat together before the god of the television, before the god of sport.

Finally, my freshman year in college approached. As I studied the course offerings with growing anxiety, my heart leapt. As an option for physical education, women's basketball was available! Was it possible? Not only would I get away from Scranton, from the limitations of my embarrassing social standing of no boyfriends, of stuttering foolishly in classes. But I would play basketball! I was almost more excited about this possibility than any other aspect of my transition to college.

The day arrived. After the trauma of leaving home, moving into the cinder-block dorm room, and bidding my parents farewell, I faced my first basketball class with excited expectation. The modern, upscale gymnasium in Monmouth College seemed vast to me; it echoed with the teacher's hollow whistle. Soft light filtered in from the high windows. My freshman year, first semester, had arrived. Perhaps with it came hope. I wore my gym clothes awkwardly, and put on the red colored singlet over my jersey, which distinguished our two teams, red and yellow. I was shaky with possibility.

The teacher was Miss Holiday—young and lithe and all-business. She lined us up, and my ears hummed with the sound of my own pounding heart. She began explaining the rules. But as her words unfolded, my heart began to sink. "Women's rules prohibit the crossing of the mid-court line," Miss Holiday explained. *What?* "You choose to be on either the offensive or defensive team. After three dribbles you must pass the ball. It is illegal to dribble a forth time. Stay on your half of the court."

It made no sense. It broke the flow of the game. I was outraged, betrayed, shattered. I chose defensive position, offense providing too much stress, another pattern I repeated in my half-hearted attempts at adult sports. Avoiding the ball became my strategy of play. The rest of the semester disappeared in a blur of disappointment. That first semester in 1966 served as both the beginning and the ending of my basketball career.

The budding feminist inside of me was outraged. Three dribbles! Did they think we would break into spontaneous menstrual flow if we dribbled a fourth time? Why were we so limited, so restricted? But eventually these disappointments faded away into the haze of marijuana, a freshman sport that seemed more fitted to my personality. College unfolded, class by class, semester by semester, disappointment by disappointment, in its own rickety, imperfect way.

And that child of basketball, that child of flow and movement and grace, that child of body and breath and bravery, receded further and further away, diving into the silent recesses of my own heart.

"The Miners, a semi-pro team and part of the American basketball league, were a major artery of our lives."

"He was a car guy, my dad.
This black Chevy Impala convertible was his newest mobile passion."

3

Exit—This Way Out
1960

"Can you imagine—and on Passover?" my mother groaned, sliding into the passenger's seat and resting a large Tupperware of charoses, a traditional holiday dish made of apples, nuts, cinnamon, and wine, on her lap. It was as eerie and uncanny a fluke of nature as Northeastern Pennsylvania could provide that April: snow. Long graduated to the back seat with my older sister, L., I peered out of the window of my dad's black Chevy Impala convertible. He was a car guy, my dad. Without much money, he still managed to prioritize his cars, hyper-vigilantly attending to their every squeak and moan, polishing each one to a brilliant and dazzling shine, and trading them in early to reap value toward his next purchase. This cool convertible was his newest mobile passion. Through the fog on the inside window, I could see the snow spitting down onto the April pavement. My dad grunted his response as he worked his baby, the Impala, out of the parking place in front of our house. He turned up the Arthur Avenue hill, carefully climbing his way up the street and making a left on Mulberry Street to track his way down through town to the Madison Avenue Temple.

For a series of reasons related to my parents' untenable work schedule and a sense of obligation they felt toward temple participation, we would be attending the communal Temple

Seder, the traditional Passover ritual/meal. I was skeptical about our involvement. All previous Passovers found us at my mother's dining room table, one of my grandmother's soft and snow-white embroidered table cloths creating the mood of solemn dignity. At home, I had the illusion of control over my verbal involvement in the collective reading of the Haggadah, the service that preceded the meal. This evening, however, we would be sharing the Seder with other members of our congregation, and throwing control to the winds. The ritual would be led by Rabbi Milton Richmond, the enthusiastic yet erratic spiritual leader of our synagogue.

I had a headache, a nagging pain chewing at the tissue behind my eyes. It wasn't an unusual occurrence for me—Dr. Eisner, our family doctor, bald head sweaty in the examination room's light, told my mother it was "stress," ignoring me as I sat miserable and embarrassed on the examination table. "A stress headache," he said, clucking his tongue in pity at both the injustice and the incomprehension of the malady. How could a twelve-year-old possibly have stress? The wordless question floated between them. I shamefully knew it was my fault, all my fault. I caused the headache, just like I caused the stuttering, just like I caused my wanting to kiss Leslie Goldberg, that cute girl in our class. All issues somehow wound their way back to me, threaded their way back to my sole responsibility. There was something wrong with Me. Hence, I should be able to change all of these situations. I tried to keep still in the back seat of the Impala, and monitor my breathing. Limiting my movement and breath intake was a strategy that sometimes worked to control the buildup of pain, but it was hard to do in a moving car.

I adamantly wanted to stay home, and felt whiny and cranky about my parents' decision to go to Temple. Our home Seders were memorable from year to year, my mother's beyond-perfect cooking at its zenith at Jewish holiday time—chicken and matzo-ball soup, charoses, horseradish (only the good, red kind), perfectly cooked chicken that was crisp on the outside, moist and tender on the inside—all were very familiar, normalizing and comforting to me. All week I tried to stall and affect the decision. But alas, with no time for my mom to cook that year, we were off to be part of a community of worshipers, the last thing on earth I wanted to do. I didn't want to be part of a community of anything. I was filled with the same dread I'd felt before my confirmation service, though I never spoke the reasons for my resistance, not to myself, not to my parents—my job was to push the feelings away, to ignore the pull of resistance. Insight into the root of my hesitancy was unthinkable: *I can't read aloud. I can't read aloud.* The act of reading aloud caused emotional, physical, energetic, and spiritual terror in me.

Lulled by the car's movement and our heavy, shared silence, I closed my eyes and imagined I was in a space ship, lifting off, heading toward the Milky Way for grand exploration and adventure. Far from the limitations of Madison Avenue Temple, I found myself floating through the cosmos, untouched by human constraints, the great explorer and adventurer that I was.

The car slowed its pace, interrupting my daydream. Through the murky dusk speckled with wet snowdrops, I could see the outline of our temple. My heart dropped. *We're here.*

My dad somehow managed to park our car despite the many already parked cars, breathing heavily as he backed up, straining to look over his shoulder. Once parked, we struggled our way out of the comfortable black leather seats. The dampness of the night seeped into me. I hadn't known what to wear, and decided on a school outfit: brown leather Weejun loafers, blue tights, my blue pleated skirt, a madras shirt (not tucked in, but bloused out, to camouflage my self-perceived oversized butt), and my circle pin, initials scripted upon it, clasping my collar closed. Although my winter coat felt ridiculously bulky as we trudged toward the entry, my loafers were inadequate to keep the wet cold away from my feet. I felt instantly dampened by our three-quarter-block walk.

The next few uncomfortable, awkward minutes found us hanging up coats on the wire hangers in the hallway metal rack and wandering into the big auditorium, site of my religious school's weekly "community events," now transformed into a meager-looking faux dining area. My mother headed to the kitchen to put her charoses into one of the temple's serving dishes. As we waited for her, the three of us hovered uncomfortably at the mouth of the room, surveying the scene. A series of long tables were strung together, covered with table clothes that clearly belonged to nobody's grandmother—starchy and white, they folded at the sides of the table in severe right angels, like tiny soldiers at attention. The folds in the table cloth mesmerized me with their unappealing perfection. I couldn't stop looking at them. Some people were already seated, while some stood in small, tight circles near chairs. Our family unit lingered, indecisive and incomplete without its matriarch, the bones of our family. She returned with a somewhat forced smile on her face, followed by several volunteer "waitresses," one of whom was carrying my mother's offering in a glass bowl.

A PA system crackled into place, a familiar voice urging us forward. "Okay, everybody," came Rabbi Richmond's deep voice through the ancient microphone. "Please find a place to sit, so we can begin our Seder."

We seemed, our family unit, both individually and collectively frozen. My mother finally broke the spell with a decisive stage whisper. "Come on," she said, shooing us forward. My sister and my father seemed just as reluctant as I was, I hoped and imagined. We, like a fused unit of primal biology, worked our way to a section of the table, barren of people. We were not ones to easily socialize.

"Oh, come down here, Sid and Tillie," Sheldon Schwartz beckoned at us from two-thirds down the table, with the flourish and wave of a pink, fleshy hand. Without a choice, we murmured our acquiescence and lumbered together, making our way toward the Schwartz clan. Sally Schwartz, a blazing pageboy of red hair capping her head, was my sister's age at sixteen. Sammy Schwartz, annoying and puny, with uncharacteristic and seemingly non-Jewish freckles covering his entire face, was my age and a real pain. Mrs. Schwartz, elegant and fancy in her black evening dress and pearls—"putting on her airs," as my father would say—smiled weakly in our direction. And Mr. Sheldon Schwartz himself, driver of his always-changing big, fancy Cadillacs, spoke a bit too loudly, perpetually seeming a little too flushed in the face. The whole family frightened me.

We scraped our seats back and settled into the uncomfortable folding chairs I was too familiar with from "community events." Mom and L. sat on the other side of the table, my dad and I facing them. We endured a flurry of Schwartz introductions. A gaggle of their relatives from Long Island surrounded us, with many names and professions collapsed together as one: "Freddy-the-podiatrist—his-wife-Lauren-the-legal-aide—Manny-the-chiropractor—his-wife-Sandra-the-geometry-teacher." It was overwhelming to descend into, to be submerged by so many Schwartzes. The four that I knew of were plenty enough. I took my napkin off the table and put it on my lap, a tiny protective shield, prematurely hoping for the release of food.

Unfortunately, much more had to transpire before food would release me.

Rabbi Richmond's voice boomed again. "And we'll open with our traditional blessings of the candles and wine." His voice was so familiar, deep and resonant, a Jewish Charlton Heston, our very own black-robed Moses leading us through the desert into the Promised Land. The prayers he sang were profoundly familiar to me, prayers we practiced in religious school, prayers I heard in services, prayers that did touch me somewhere deep inside. I relaxed for a breath. Upon completion of his opening prayer, however, his words of inevitable doom crackled through the mike system: "And now we will share our reading of the Haggadah, the service before our meal. Please speak nice and loudly so everyone gathered can hear you." The hair on the back of my neck spiked involuntarily to attention. Although I knew it would happen this way, that we would share the reading, still, the actual unfolding of my life's worst fear was surreal. Sweat instantly broke out on my forehead.

The man sitting on the rabbi's right, Mr. Fishbaum, who owned the discount shoe store on Lackawanna Avenue, began the reading:

"On this night, long years ago, our forefathers hearkened to the call of freedom. Tonight, that call rings out again, sounding its challenge."

His voice was confidant and booming. It passed to his wife on his left, who was quieter and less dramatic:

"We have dedicated this festival tonight to the dream and the hope of freedom, the dream and the hope that have filled the hearts of people from the time our Israelite ancestors went forth out of Egypt."

And around the table it snaked, this living doom, this weaving worst-case-scenario that haunted me from the first bell of school in the morning until the last, from the first day of September until the final instant in June, from sunup in the morning when my eyes opened, essentially until they closed at night. It was my own particular haunting, this reading aloud. This talking.

I wanted to spontaneously combust, to evaporate like the man did in the science fiction movie Gladys and I had seen the year before, *The Blob*. It didn't happen. I continued to sit in my folding chair, awaiting my destiny.

Since my parents' philosophy about my speech impediment was to not call attention to it, I felt alone. Stuttering was a heavy burden, their silence adding to its weight. Every moment of my life presented the rupturing of that family denial—any time I opened my mouth, answered the phone, replied to a question—I threatened their collective denial. And there I sat, waiting for the firing squad, for every single Jew gathered here to celebrate our liberation from bondage to see my stuttering, stammering, un-liberated Jewish self.

There wasn't any way to count ahead, to gauge how many people sat before me in order to count the potential readings so I could scan my reading for landmine initial consonants. This was a strategy I used fervently in school. But here, since the reading was taking its own, erratic path down the table, meandering down toward the Schwartz-and-Futuronsky area, I was unable to measure my potential paragraph. I sat with a bulls-eye on my heart, waiting, stilling myself, steeling myself present.

"And now the first cup of wine," said Susie Sontheim, the next reader/participant, a sweet, dark-haired eighteen-year-old home from college for the holiday—I always liked the soft flip of her dark hair and her hushed, kind voice. I had a quiet little crush on her.

"Blessed art Thou, oh Lord, our God, King of the Universe who has brought forth the fruit of the vine."

Like everyone around me, I reached for my wine glass and brought it to my lips. The sweetness of deep purple Manischewitz wine startled me awake. I gulped at it, swallowing a little too much and choking. Sammy Schwartz snickered, while my dad put a warm hand on my shoulder. As I put the glass down, I noticed a subtle change deep inside of me. I could feel the seeping of warmth into my frozen, tight belly. Some soft fingers of tingling played at the corners of my mouth. The sensations were pleasant—a shift away from the rigid tension that held me fast.

The readers continued, the service winding its litany of bondage and liberation, slowly snaking its way toward me. My attention was a bit compromised now, the warmth of the wine captivating my attention. My head felt a little swimmy, my fingers warmed. I reached for the glass again, drawing the warmth of the liquid into me. I could trace its flow down my chest, releasing, relaxing, all in its wake. I emptied my glass in the guise of spiritual and religious symbolism—*I am a Jew celebrating liberation!*—but deriving a deeper, more intimate satisfaction from it—*I am escaping from my own, personal suffering.* I innocently reached for the communal wine carafe, pouring myself another glass to be ready for the story of the Jewish people's miraculous escape from bondage.

The reading did eventually make it to me, a cup and a half of wine later, mercifully short and with relatively pronounceable words, a strange anti-climax to my terror. I stumbled on the words nevertheless, but my caring was duller, my tongue looser, my heart protected. It just didn't matter in the same way.

We had the traditional four cups of wine that night, representing the four-fold promise of redemption that God pledged to Israel:

I will bring you forth.

I will deliver you.

I will redeem you.

I will take you.

I had my four glasses that night, plus a few more subtly snatched refills. I liked how I felt very, very much.

After an interminable length of reading, singing, and rabbinical-inspired silliness, my head heavy with sensation, my face alive with heat, the traditional meal was finally and blessedly served. It all tasted inferior to me—even my own mother's charoses seemed compromised by being out of her house, a shadow of its former self. We made our way through the too-hard matzo balls, the dried chicken, the matzo and charoses sandwiches. It was a long, disappointing, and bland meal. The Schwartzes jabbered amongst themselves, Sheldon Schwartz at the center of the lively disagreement/discussion.

We Futuronskys picked uncharacteristically at our food— we were hearty eaters under more normal circumstances. We survived the sugary, boxed macaroons, the hiding of the afikoman, the matzo game that followed the meal. We did it—we sat through—we paid our spiritual dues. Finally, as other people began to say their goodbyes, the signal was given: it was appropriate to leave. We bid our farewells to the Schwartzes, whose pale complexions, pitiful red hair, and fancy airs seemed more amusing to me now. My legs were rubbery, my knees weakened. As we headed toward the coat rack, I felt as if I were walking on somebody else's legs. But I was aware enough of my non-habitual feelings to keep my behavior contained. Despite the swimming inside my head, I walked steadily toward our coats, never so happy to see my tired old winter coat awaiting me. We stumbled our way out into the pathetically damp slush-snow of April, the very air in this un-Passover-like night wet and soggy. Liberation from bondage. Freedom from oppression.

Driving away from the temple, we were a tribe of four, silent Jews. My father drove carefully through the slushy streets, the car projectile-shooting sprays of snow and slush to the sides of the road. After a few blocks, he said randomly to nobody, "Let's not do that again." He was met with more silence.

His words sounded to my ears like a benediction, and made me snicker silently into my palm. My sister, L., sitting next to me, seemed not to notice. She stared out the window, watching the giant flakes of April snow cover the grey streets.

I slept poorly and fitfully that night in my single bed, green and purple and white plaid bedspread tucked protectively under my chin. I dreamt of revengeful angels of death, of seas that did not part, of drowning in vats of Manischewitz. I awoke headachy and strangely and wildly thirsty, yet liberated from school. It was a weekend. No more demands on me.

My parents never spoke to me of my "conduct" that evening—perhaps they didn't notice either my terror or my loose-lipped release from it. As usual, all was status quo.

For the moment, I was free.

That evening, however, a tiny, invisible exit sign was planted inside my consciousness. I had discovered a way out of the pain. This more effective invisible shield had revealed itself to me, whose power I could not even imagine.

Manischewitz had opened the door.

*"Through the murky dusk,
speckled with wet snowdrops, I could see the outline of our Temple."
Madison Avenue Temple.*

4

Once A Whose-a-tute
1961

I had been carefully studying kissing for years. When the men pressed their lips against the women's, they made sounds and sometimes even moved their bodies. My regular Saturday afternoon movie-viewing provided me with a deep pool of endless and infinite kissing research. When Troy Donahue kissed Sandra Dee in *A Summer Place*, I carefully studied his posture, his attitude, and the formation of the very kiss itself, being born out of his lips and exploding onto Sandra's waiting, open, pouting mouth. I watched the way his arms looped around Sandra, how she seemed to melt into him. I was careful to not give myself away, to not be too conspicuous in my kiss-study, so that Gladys, sitting casually slumped in the movie seat next to me, wouldn't know. It was very important that nobody knew. My shame-filled secret was not the studying of the kissing; it was my perspective about the kissing.

The secret was this: I wanted to be Troy Donahue. I wanted to have Sandra Dee in my arms, moaning her pleasure at my touch. But I really wanted to be Warren Beatty in *Splendor in the Grass*. This movie captivated me in both the power of its romance and the illicit danger involved in the kissing. Natalie Wood was mine—all of my thirteen-year-old self was dedicated to her dark-haired, moody beauty. In this movie, she came from

41

the wrong side of the tracks, a strange and powerful adolescent turn-on for me. I sat, spellbound, as Warren Beatty, acting as Bud, the rich boyfriend, began to kiss her. I kissed her, too, right along with him, practicing, enjoying, reaping fulfillment and pleasure from my illicit, clandestine point of view.

At night in my bed, I wrote my stories of women in distress, of women whom I would rescue, who would love me forever. I was the handsome, smart, strong young hero, saving the day with my bravery. With my pillow carefully positioned beneath me, I practiced my kissing, feeling my love's wet and hot lips hungry for me. Rubbing in just the right way, with just the right frequency, released me into sensations I did not understand, but I knew were wrong. The solution to my adolescent guilt was simple—I called my nighttime adventures "writing." I was simply creating stories, in which I was the hero, the star, the male lead. In essence, I was the guy who got the hot girl.

Growing up in the 1950s, in our family, kissing was either right or wrong. Sex was either good or bad. There was no grey area. Sitting at our kitchen table one night, we were having a usual dinner—lamb chops for my dad (oh, how I hated their heavy, strong taste and felt so sad for the sweet, little lambs) and hamburger patties for us. Our "vegetable" was Birdseye frozen mixed vegetables that Mommy thawed, cooked, and covered with yellowed margarine. As we were eating on the green Formica that came out of the wall, my parents discussing their day at the grocery store, my sister L. interrupted to tell them about a shocking event. She had witnessed the teenage girl in the family of our not-so-nice neighbors, who had just moved into the junky house behind us, kissing a boy on their porch. My mother replied to L.'s comments, "Oh, dear, she's a prostitute." To which I innocently inquired, "A whose-a-tute?" This comment triggered gales of laughter from my parents, a snide smile from my older and more experienced sister, and a lifetime of ribbing. Despite the innocent jesting born of this situation, I knew the truth—that kind of kissing was *wrong*.

But some kissing was good kissing. When a man loved a woman and he kissed her, that seemed okay. Daddy kissed Mommy—not like in the movies, but that was good. Like when they took their Sunday afternoon "naps" after my father closed the store, L. at the J.C.C. and me playing in my room, waiting for them to "wake up." Something was going on in there, I knew, something was fishy. But it was good. It was okay. L. told me it was okay. They were married. And he was a man and she was a woman.

What was not okay was this: that a girl thought about kissing another girl. I, as a young girl in the 1960s, should never, ever consider this, the kissing of another girl. But it was all that I thought about. There seemed only one solution—I had to pretend that I was a man. This, under the guise of writing, made it sanctioned. However, the accumulated shame of years of this secretive internal gender swap was so bundled in humiliation and denial that, during my radical lesbian feminist separatist days, I could not speak of this dominant culture phenomenon, my wanting an organ I did not possess, to my more liberated sisters. But I get ahead of myself.

One Sunday afternoon in 1961, I met Gladys at the Jewish Community Center for Tween Teens Bowling. My luxurious days watching the Scranton Miners were over. I was thirteen—a freshman in Scranton Central High School. It was time, I deeply realized, to "get with the program," to pretend that I cared about the boys, the idle girl-chatter, the ranks of popularity, the hierarchy of cool kids. It was bad news, this teenage thing. The only slightly good news was that bowling almost interested me, enough for my parents to buy me my own maroon bowling ball for my birthday, with my name "NAN" strangely etched into it, eclipsing the finger-holes like some planetary arrangement of three moons hovering above deep craters. The best part, however, was a maroon and white leatherette bag that held the ball perfectly, its zipper keeping it safe, its white plastic handles fitting perfectly into my palm. When I got this gift for my thirteenth birthday, I was secretly elated. I continually fingered the ball and the bag, carefully, cautiously, when nobody was looking.

That Sunday, much of the thrill of bowling had dissipated. Gladys and I bowled a lackluster, apathetic game, the shiny alley almost dangerously slippery beneath my rented, blue and white, never-quite-fitting bowling shoes. The tumult of the slamming pins, the giggles and rowdiness of the noisy almost-teenagers surrounding us were overpowering to me. My wrist hurt, my score sucked—91—a few mid-game gutter balls bringing ruin onto my first initial two strikes and a spare. Another lifetime pattern would emerge—flashes of brilliance, followed by erratic and inconsistent follow-up. I was ready to walk home, a twenty-minute hike up to the Hill Section. Gladys and I sat by the snack bar, sipping our chocolate cokes, discussing our options. She unfortunately lived in the opposite direction.

"Want a ride home?" asked a strange, inconceivable voice. It was Alvin Pinkus, a Jewish kid from the Hill Section. He was short and squat, his madras Bermuda shorts and blue Lacrosse shirt sausaging his legs and his arms in strange, cotton casings. Although he was pimply, short, and nasally annoying, he still counted. He was a boy.

Was he talking to me? Impossible.

"Well, do ya?" he asked, nodding in my general direction.

Gladys kicked me surreptitiously under the chair, goading me into response.

"Ah, well, um," I sputtered. It wasn't a huge yes.

"My brother can drop us off. Come on," he shrugged, and started walking with long strides toward the stairs. I looked to Gladys with bewilderment, as she nodded wildly toward the stairwell. I grabbed my beloved bowling ball and case, and hurried after him, my apparent yet inattentive suitor. I attempted to catch up with him, while still looking casual and relaxed. Neither objective was accomplished. By the time I made it up the steps and through the elaborate main lobby, I was huffing noisily, which was clearly not cool. Alvin was waiting outside, standing next to his brother Melvin's rose-colored Ford Fairlane, its four windows opened to springtime. Melvin nodded a similar, grunted greeting, and gestured to the back door. I opened it anxiously, and tossed my precious bowling ball and bag in ahead of me. The leather of the seats was sun-warmed. I sat back and imagined I could breathe. Alvin sat in the front passenger's seat, talking to his brother in low tones. My bowling ball and I sat, in ignored silence. The car accelerated with a jerk, and we began our journey, the bizarre threesome that we were.

The car made its way up to the Hill Section, leaving downtown Scranton behind. The manicured lawns widened and opened as we made our way up the hills. The grey of winter melted at the touch of spring's color, flowers splattering the lawns and brightening the drab, grainy streets.

I was bewildered. Did he like me? That would be good. He was okay, Jewish, from Temple Israel. He hung out with the cool kids. I didn't like him, could never, ever like him. But that was not the point. The point was: he was driving me home. This was weird. Maybe my luck was changing—maybe everything would be all right.

Finally, after a never-ending ten-minute silent drive, Melvin pulled his car up to the curb on Arthur Avenue and Mulberry Street, across from Nay Aug Park. I lived three blocks down the hill. Alvin got out, slammed his door shut, and opened the back door in one movement. I assumed that meant I should get out. I did, yanking the bowling ball and case after me. He thumped my door shut, as Melvin gunned the Fairlane, which spastically leapt away from us. I gestured a wild and ineffectual "thank you" in the direction of the retreating rose-colored car.

We stood there, strangers, Alan assessing me, while I attempted to keep up with the script in which I appeared to be a main character. I had no clue what was unfolding in my life as I stood on the corner of Arthur and Mulberry, tethered to the earth by my stylish leatherette bowling ball case.

"Come on," he said, and started walking in the direction of my house. I acquiesced mindlessly, going through the role that was written for me.

"So, you like Moffit?" he asked, an obviously feeble attempt at inane discussion, as we headed down the hill. Mr. Moffit was the freshman English teacher that we both shared during fourth period at Central High School, a short, effeminate, dandy of a man who wore elaborate handkerchiefs in his breast pocket, dickeys of matching material, and soft, cream-colored socks. He was a gloriously glamorous and sweetly kind guy, who explained poetry and the elements of fiction with intricate hand gestures and deep, heartfelt passion. Both he and his teachings fascinated me. His class was the one feeble light in my day.

"Not really," I replied, towing the party line. All the kids made fun of him.

"Yeah, he's a fag," Alvin confidentially offered, spitting into the street, as we lapsed into silence for the next long and endless block, the bowling bag handle beginning to eat into my palm. I tried to shift its weight without calling attention to myself.

We got to the quiet corner of Mulberry and Linden, and collectively paused to assess our choices in the moment. My house awaited me just three-fourths of the way down the block. The Haleys' tidy stone house marked the spot for all to see, although there was nobody around. The block was still.

What was happening? Was he walking me all the way home? Why? What did he want? Did he like me? Maybe he liked me? I was clueless.

He turned to face me, bringing his head close to mine, his Aqua Velva shaving lotion stinging my nose. He smiled wickedly, reached down, put his hand clumsily on my breast, and, with the other hand, pulled me close to him. My bowling ball fell to the earth of Arthur Avenue.

He pinched away at my breast for an endless moment, squeezing at it as if it were a cantaloupe being tested for ripeness. I was speechless, dumbfounded, without a thought. Then he unbelievably brought his head even closer to mine. Suddenly, with no apparent warning I could see, his lips were on mine, pressing and pushing their way into my mouth.

I stood in bewildered disbelief.

His lips felt rubbery to me, meaty and thick. I thought of the gross lamb chops my father liked so much, their meaty texture hearty and chewable. In this long, extended moment of the kiss, I had one brief thought: that one could chew upon Alvin's lips, not unlike that lamb chop, with its hearty and beefy consistency. He seemed to be jabbing my lips with his tongue, but I thought it my job to keep my lips firmly closed, like I imagined it happened in the movies. We had a struggle there, with Alan's tongue wildly attempting access to my mouth, my lips fixed and unbending.

I wanted Natalie Wood.

After an eternity of kissing, this single unending and painful kiss finally and mercifully did end. Alan jerked away from me with a deep exhale and a snicker. My lips felt gnawed upon and swollen. He looked at me, raised his eyebrows with a mysterious air, and said, "See ya," as he turned with a jaunt and walked down Linden Street, leaving me in the horror and the wonder and the displeasure of my first real kiss.

Did he like me? Was this a good thing? Boys didn't kiss girls they didn't like, did they? Did I do it right? My thoughts flooded, swamped each other, indiscrete and collapsed together.

I looked around. Still nobody in sight, thank goodness.

I brought my fingers to my lips and assessed and inventoried them. There was a tiny cut near the right corner, with a smidgen of blood on it, which I wildly wiped away with the back of my hand. I rearranged my jean jacket and maroon turtleneck top, righting myself to continue along my journey. Tears for reasons I couldn't understand built up behind my eyes. I willed them away. It was my first kiss. That was a good thing. I picked up the burden of my bowling ball and bag, which had witnessed the whole episode, and continued home.

Maybe he liked me. Maybe we'd go on a date.

Walking down that final street to my house, I realized that I knew every crack in the pavement, had every tilt of incline deeply memorized. I felt conflicted. I wanted to be home in my room, but never wanted to enter that house again. It seemed as if I couldn't enter my childhood home, that I was that changed.

I was completely miffed.

My breast was sore where he'd pinched it. It didn't feel good. None of it felt good. But wasn't it supposed to be good only for the boy, not for the girl? I didn't know.

The door to our house was thankfully unlocked, making my entry slightly unobtrusive. I stepped into the quiet of our living room, its soft brown rug so familiar to me. I felt another rush of tears flooding my eyes, and dashed upstairs.

"Is that you, honey?" my mom called from the kitchen, where she was preparing dinner, waiting for my daddy to come home from the store.

"Yes," I barely grunted.

"How was bowling?"

"Fine."

I sat in my room, in the awe and the revulsion of it all. I looked in the mirror. My lips looked red and funny to me. I touched the little cut. It stung to the touch. I lay on my bed and waited, wanting to hear my father's comforting steps on the porch, the door to open, and his steps to echo throughout the house. My bowling ball and bag sat unmolested on my white shag rug, my only witness, silent and non-judging. I heard my dad's truck pull up outside, his footsteps on the porch, the sound of him opening the door. I gathered myself, no longer the child who went bowling that long-ago afternoon, and went downstairs for dinner. Unbelievably, the evening progressed with a mundane normalcy.

I never told anyone about the kiss, not even Gladys. Alvin never called, never asked me out on a date, and ignored me completely in English class. My confusion was thick with shame. Somehow I probably hadn't kissed right, and repulsed him. I tried vainly to forget the entire episode, to read my short stories in English class, to listen to Mr. Moffit's ramblings about poetry, to go to the movies with Gladys, to enjoy my "writing stories" in bed at night. I attempted to forget all about the kiss.

But this clandestine affair was not over yet. Several weeks later, my sister L. came into my bedroom one night after dinner. I was practicing my guitar lesson and concentrating, her intrusion both unusual and unwanted. She sat down on my prized white rug and stared pathetically at me, her eyes burning.

"What?" I said, and stopped practicing the F chord, the one in which your hands were spanned over several strings. My fingers ached from the attempting.

"What did you do?" she hissed at me.

"Nothing. Why?" She was scaring me with her fanatical intensity, her eyes burning into me.

"Susie Meyers said that Alvin Pinkus's sister said you were a prostitute."

OhmyGod. Alvin told his sister who told Susie Meyers who told L., that I was a prostitute! I felt my thirteen-year-old world come crashing, smashing down upon me. That, I knew for certain, was a bad, a really bad thing.

"No, no, really. It wasn't that," I stammered, putting my precious guitar to the side, sparing it the indignity and shame of this discussion.

L. was silently accusatory, eyes burning beneath her tidy, tended bangs.

"No, really," I continued pathetically, trying to prove a point I really didn't know or understand.

"Well, did you kiss him?" she hissed again.

"Well, sort of. I mean, not really. Well, yes, kind of." I didn't even know myself what had happened that day.

Her eyes narrowed, as she lapsed into a wordy and windy big sister's explanation of Morality, 1961, Scranton, Pennsylvania.

As she lectured and explained, my eyes felt teary again, my head full. Her words faded out and faded in, as if someone was playing with the volume dial on my little plastic, purple transistor radio. I did my very best to sit upright, and not flail at the floor in desperate confusion. She eventually left my room with a righteous air, leaving me alone with my chaotic thoughts.

What had I done? I thought you were supposed to let boys do that, if they liked you. How did you know if they liked you? I had so hoped that he liked me. I guessed, lying there on my rug with my guitar facing me dispassionately, that if they liked you, the kissing was good—if they didn't like you, it was bad.

I was shame-filled, and heartbroken.

But eventually, the excitement seemed to pass. L. forgot about it, as I hoped and prayed Susie Meyers did, as well as Alvin's sister. Alvin continued to ignore me and, as our high school years progressed, he became bigger, stockier, and louder. No more real lips were placed on mine for many years, only the lips of imaginary strangers, beautiful women, damsels in distress.

Time did manage to pass, leaving me both dateless and kiss-less. That was mostly okay with me.

The lips of a stranger, a black man, were the next to meet mine. I was at a fraternity party in 1966 in West Long Branch, New Jersey, my freshman year in college, and he was a member of the varsity basketball team. This kiss was a long, marijuana-exaggerated mental journey into difference and consequence, completely devoid of bodily sensation. I never saw that man before the kiss, nor did I see him after it.

I continued to be perplexed by this kissing thing.

5

Cauliflower—The Person
1956–Onward

She was small and wiry, with lots of dark hair cascading around her face. In the sheer innocence of that blue-hued summer morning of 1956, she stood before the entire camp, assembled and waiting for morning flag ceremony, and led songs with all her heart. The grass was alive and wet with dew beneath us as she led those songs with a vengeance, a fervor, an intensity that awed me. She was fully, in body, mind, and spirit, committed to the leading of those camp songs:

Girl scouts together,
That is our song.
Winding the old road,
Rocky and long.
Learning our motto,
Living our creed.
Girl scouts together
In every good deed.

Her every gesture was an invitation to drop inhibition and unabashedly join her, hands rising and falling with the melody, the rhythm alive in her skinny girl-body.

We were both eight years old and in the chronological second unit called "Forest" at Girl Scout Camp Archbald. We lived in wooden bunks with nine other girls, sleeping on cots that moaned and squeaked beneath our tiny bodies. The mattresses were yucky, I thought on Sunday check-in day, the first of my camping experience. They were old, striped, and smelly. My mother carefully covered mine with a plastic drop cloth to keep me safe and hygienically free from all infectious diseases during my two-week stay.

Cauliflower's bunk was three down on the left, by the big screen door. Her parents dropped her off quickly with a mysterious air, not lingering like mine till the last moment, prolonging the painful yet excitement-filled separation.

Her style of fully embodied song-leading continued to mesmerize me that soft morning, her hands illustrating, punctuating, and tracing the melody, as if making it possible for all in Susquehanna County to see and involuntarily burst into song. I was many years away from leading songs. Sitting on the grass with my unit—the other twenty-two girls my age—with the rest of the camp around us was enough of a challenge to my limited social skills. I was shy, my stutter an invisible shield that I used to keep me apart from others. I was the observer. Cauliflower was obviously the full participant.

The song fest ended as we all wiped off our damp bottoms and lined up with sniggers and feigned seriousness for flag ceremony, a daily ritual at Camp that was fraught with tradition and wonderful, unique connection. We filed silently into our lines to march in and witness the hoisting of the flag onto the blue sky of another day.

She appeared anything but shy, this girl, my bunkmate. As I watched her from afar, and watch her I did those first few days, she would approach our tanned, healthy-looking counselor/goddesses without hesitation, with questions, with comments, with the willingness to interact. It astounded me. She seemed to be in the middle of whatever was happening, living at the apex of its activity. My life strategy, on the other hand, was to go to any lengths to avoid interaction, to exist invisibly on the margins of things. She, my apparent opposite, fascinated me.

People called her Cauliflower, or Cauli, due to her inclination—or lack thereof—toward the vegetable. She, at our young age, already had a camp name, even if it were a variety of cabbage. That in itself placed her high in my heart.

During those first few days of Forest, tucked in that shady grove beneath the lovely fir trees, air fragrant with the smell of warm pine, I kept to myself as we worked on our badge projects. Outdoor Camper was the name of the group I had selected, since it supported my Royal Canadian Mountie fantasy of living in the wilderness while rescuing women in distress, women who would love me and kiss me forever. We played kickball in the mornings, had swim lessons at the waterfront every mid-morning, no matter the weather, free swim in the afternoons, and arts and crafts in the cottage that smelled like glue and gimp—the multi-colored, twine-like nylon used for weaving—and delicious, sweet old wood. The days were rich and alive with possibilities, all of which seemed to relax me, seemed to soften the barrier between myself and others. Perhaps it was what kids always felt: connection and ease and potential adventure around every twist of the path. But for me, it was new—new and rich and remarkable was this Girl Scout camp.

Cauliflower and I first officially came together to plan an evening flag ceremony, our names randomly picked from the different Forest bunks. Morning flag was a lighter, more informal experience at our camp. However, evening flag ceremony, held religiously after dinner throughout our camp lives, was expected to be formal and proper, with a certain Girl Scout dignity and ceremonial air. Cauli took instant and effective leadership of our group of eight, organizing roles and responsibilities. She would be the "caller," a role she held consistently for the next ten years of our camp life. I would be one of the color guard, standing in slot #4 with limited responsibility, yet involved. The role of the flag retriever was too much pressure, too much spotlight for me. I began to eek out these roles for myself in activities where I was involved, but not center-stage, not in a position to fail for all to see. Making my way cautiously in from the margins, I poked my toe cautiously into the waters of connection. Cauli seemed to stir the waters, to turn up their flames to a rolling boil.

Ours was a formal flag ceremony, in which the whole camp wore dress uniforms to participate, upping the emotional ante. That afternoon, we laid out the skeleton formation with twine and stakes for the camp to march into—a traditional horseshoe, with Cauli leading the ranks of scouts and us, the color guard, readied behind her. Miss Marsha, one of our college-aged counselors—the one who unapologetically sunbathed on the grass above the flagpole—was there to support us, allowing us to do our own thing. She was not one of my favorites, this red-headed, freckled counselor—she was too ready to laugh at a kid, too quick to smirk, too obviously interested in the other counselors rather than the campers. My body was a hyper-cautious, ultra-sensitive litmus test of people's intentions. The insincerity of another would actually tighten at my chest, not unlike the tightening of a bow-hitch, the knot we had learned to tie in camp-craft class. Miss Marsha, in her madras shirt and khaki shorts, did not qualify for my A-list of counselor/goddesses.

But we didn't need Miss Marsha. We had Cauli, and, to my surprise, she whipped us into shape. Our roles were filled, poems selected to be read, flag retrieval and folding was practiced. We were good to go, ready to kick some Girl Scout butt. I was shocked to discover that authority was not necessary for Cauli's competencies to flourish. I, on the other hand, continued to hover on the other side of authority, sizing it up, gauging it, debating it, stalled by the ambivalence of my relationship to it.

But that evening, after dinner, as my anxiety grew regarding our flag ceremony, I kept my eyes on Cauli. With typical spunkiness, unfazed, she led the whole camp in, circling them around the flag pole, flag limp in the gentle blue sky. We color guard stood on the sidelines, attentive for our prompt. I was trembling a bit, deeply excited. Although I had just gone to the bathroom—the hideous outdoor johns were always a challenge for me—flag ceremony aroused instantly in me the need to either fart or pee. It was a curious response to shared expressions of patriotism that would plague me for the next decade of my life as a Girl Scout.

Cauli's booming voice beckoned us forward: "Color guard, advance." We could not have found a more appropriately commanding voice. My heart was pounding in its own rhythm of nationalistic anticipation. I wasn't too scared, strangely enough—just excited and happy. We marched in, a finely oiled group of seven children disguised as citizens of the world, left-right, left-right, as we had practiced. The scene was silent, a few soft evening birdcalls surrounding us.

Again her voice boomed: "Color guard, retrieve the colors." It was stirring, that voice, as it floated across our waterfront and almost echoed across our sweet little Lake Ely. The retriever of the flag, a girl more ready and brave than I, dramatically saluted, stepped forward, and began the slow winding of the ancient rope, releasing the colors down. Our job was to stay attentive and to gracefully and skillfully catch the flag. Never could a flag touch the earth! This was the potential catastrophe that existed in every flag ceremony. We would disgrace ourselves, Forest, the Camp, and the entire United States of America if we allowed it to happen. The flag would have to be burned, and with it, our Girl Scout esteem. But tonight we were safe. The flag lingered close to the ground, and we moved forward, retrieving it, perhaps not so gracefully, but effectively.

We folded the flag studiously, my contribution in the fourth person slot good enough to pass. I felt like I was faking it, but faking successfully, another life pattern emerging. With Cauli's booming "Color guard, retreat" demanding our exit, I marched, left-right, left-right with my fellow Foresters, feeling a proud smirk covering my face, a fart growing in my belly, ownership emerging in my quieted mind, and my Girl Scout pride exploding in my heart. As I marched past Cauli, I found myself offering her a spontaneous, full-spirited smile. She gave me an unabashedly happy, toothy grin back.

It was done. Our fate was sealed. We were friends.

I'd never really had a friend before. It was a strange and different experience, to have somebody to go down to the Dining Hall with, to sit with at meals, to be next to at campfires. She was funny, always making me laugh with her earnest, dry perceptions of the moment. And she always encouraged me along with her, forward, into life. Hers weren't formal invitations, like, "Come eat dinner with me." Her invitations were assumed, silent, and simply in place. Looking outside my bunk one afternoon before dinner, I saw her standing there. She caught my eye, and nodded toward the Dining Hall. She was waiting for me. Someone was waiting…for me.

It was clear to me and to all, without words, that I was her sidekick. She drew me into the center of life—without the magnetic warmth and humor generated in her tiny, little-girl body, I would have stood cold and alone on the outside. How different my life might have been without her beckoning.

Our relationship blossomed in the rarified air of Camp Archbald. Our two weeks were filled with rainy day hikes, learning the J-stroke in the canoe, counselors' entertainment on the final night of camp, practicing the fine art of chopping wood, fire building, s'mores—those marshmallow, chocolate, and graham cracker delights—melted over the open fire, cooking out in the unit, and so much more new and remarkable fun. Cauliflower was next to me for most of it.

As the camp session drew to a close, the question arose in me—what would happen when we went home? Who was this Girl Scout person? Could she be transformed and transitioned into my non-camp world?

I learned more about her as the ending of camp hovered. Her name was Gladys. She was Jewish—this was good, relatable, right—but she went to the other grade school, James Madison on Quincy Avenue. She also went to the cool temple, Temple Israel. She was very smart, got really good grades—much better than mine—and her parents were from Poland. She lived on North Webster Avenue, not in the Hill Section like us, but in another fairly upscale part of town.

That last day of camp was a sad one for me—the ending to this paradise of a place, the return back to the normalcy of disconnection. I wrote my mother a post card earlier in the week, telling her I was starving for "good food," that the camp food "tasted crummy." She wrote me back saying she would bring up a corn beef sandwich for me to eat—my favorite of the moment!—from Shookey's, the best delicatessen, to prevent death by starvation on the fifty-five minute ride home. Corned beef with Russian dressing on rye bread! Although I was looking forward to the sandwich, my mouth almost watering at the thought of it, nevertheless, my heart was heavy. I was leaving my new friend.

Standing in the parking lot that night after dinner, watching the parent cars stream down the hill into camp, with resulting frenzy and hysteria from the awaiting campers, I stood quietly shoulder to shoulder with Cauliflower. She turned to me, gave me one of her little particular smirks, and handed me an intricately folded sheet of lined paper. I unfolded it, piece by piece, to uncover its gem: her phone number. It said, "Gladys—347-3504."

"Call me. Okay?"

I nodded, sniffing back my tears. Phones were really hard for me. In this moment, it seemed impossible to not always and forever have her three bunks down on the left, by the big screen door.

But call her I did, gulping down my "HelloisGladyshome?" Sometimes she answered, and that was easier. But sometimes her mother or father would answer, their accents strange and thick, and that was scarier and harder. Sometimes I hung up, overwhelmed with shameful speechlessness. But I would call back, attempting to gauge her father's work hours, her mother's movements. I always called back.

And remarkably, we were effortlessly and successfully transplanted. From the Mariner's Path around Lake Ely to the sidewalks of Scranton, Pennsylvania. From the dining hall of Camp Archbald to the Jewish Community Center. From the arts and crafts cottage to the Strand movie theater. Like a healthy, robust plant, we picked ourselves up, replanted ourselves into our city lives, dropped our roots, nourished ourselves with phone calls and laughter and loneliness and love, and thrived.

The first time I went to Gladys's house on North Webster Avenue, I felt timid and quiet, making my way slowly through the darkened, hushed living room with thick plastic on the furniture into the kitchen, obviously the center of the home. Gladys's mother stood at the sink, washing dishes, with an apron secured around her. With her back to me, I saw that she was short, sturdy, and planted on the earth, the sink and the dishes her universe. She did not turn around of her own accord. Gladys said, "Ma, this is Nan," and as she did, her mother slowly pivoted, gradually, time-warped, making her way toward me. She was worth waiting for. Her face was beautiful, sad, and different, dark hair busy around her head, escaped strands haloing her forehead. She nodded at me, eyes distant, wiping a wisp of hair absently away from her brow, and said, "Hello," with an accent that was new to my ears. As she turned back toward her sink, my eyes rested on the tattooed numbers on her forearm.

For all of the times in my life that I visited Gladys's house, I only remember her mother, Hannah, in the kitchen, washing dishes, cooking, wiping, cleaning. I only remember her attending to, doing for others. She related to me in brief comments, in nods, always her tasks being foremost in the moment, always her gaze elsewhere. In spite of her emotional remoteness, she was simply there—the house, I imagined, would have collapsed without her consistent, muted presence.

Her father, Sol, on the other hand, was a dynamo of energy and movement. He was short, lean, and European-faced, with a broad forehead and a prominent, wide nose gracing it. He consistently wore work pants, short-sleeved shirts with a pen protector, and numerous pens in his shirt pocket, and he always had a Fedora on his head, no matter the season. He both terrified and fascinated me. He jabbered constantly, a counterpoint to his wife's silence. He advised, mentored, taught, and instructed, inhabiting the entire forefront of the moment, as his wife held the neutral, silent backdrop. He was a survivor in every sense of the word—he would continue to exist no matter what circumstances Northeastern Pennsylvania or the universe could possibly throw at him. As he gestured and pointed, the tattoo on his forearm chillingly hinted of horrors unimaginable. His voice had a certain tone to it—one of stubborn insistence, adamant whining. Most of the time, I didn't know what he was talking about. I just sat, awed and humbled in his presence, wanting to embrace him while willing the time with him to end. Gladys fielded his intensity, both meeting it and challenging it, while holding up the agony of her mother's depression. She, my friend Cauliflower, as the oldest child, was the bridge to the dominant culture for these dear, misplaced people. She was the one to interpret our culture for them—from Girl Scouts to SATs, from the mother-daughter banquet to required dues for our high school sorority. She, my friend Gladys, was busy.

I did my child's best to get to know them, to listen, to practice not being afraid of the shadows that lingered behind their eyes, of the families lost to them, the world stolen from their hearts. I grew to love both of her parents dearly as the years unfolded. In their differences lurked the doorway to my own broken heart, locked inside its own perceived uniqueness.

It was not accidental that Gladys and I found each other, and hung closely to our friendship. My passivity, her action; my broken-hearted shyness, her brazen approach to the moment; the differences inside of me I tried so wildly to hide and the actuality of the differences of her family—we were a balancing act of love and support for the other, without mentioning a word of it to each other or to ourselves.

We developed, my friend and I, a Saturday ritual. Since we didn't see each other during the week, attending different schools and temples, we would meet on Saturday afternoon in downtown Scranton. I would take the city bus, waiting on Mulberry Street and Colfax Avenue, impatiently tapping my foot, searching down the hill for a bus chugging up the grey street. Gladys would take her neighborhood bus, and we would meet outside the Globe Store, Scranton's largest department store.

We would religiously have lunch in the restaurant in the back of the Globe Store, the CharlMont. This was not a kids' place, nor a teenage hangout—it was frequented by old women shoppers grateful to sit and relieve their achy feet. But we both found solace there, fascinated by the mirrored walls, the white frame chairs in the French style, with plastic seats that stuck to your legs in the warmer dining days, the polite waitresses with downcast eyes, wearing their frilly aprons and little white, starched caps. And every Saturday, no matter the season, no matter the year, no matter the developmental stage that life was dragging me through, I would order the identical meal: a roast beef sandwich on a poppy seed bun, with mashed potatoes and a dollop of gravy. The consistency of it was so healing, so calming, so wonderful for my heart. In my sea of turmoil and challenge, the CharlMont held me fast. We talked and laughed over our meal, but hurried, hurried to our matinee, the main feature of our trip. The meal was the lovely jewelry box. But the matinee—that was the gem, the gift inside the day.

We had two theaters to choose from in downtown Scranton— the Strand or the Comerford. And every Saturday afternoon, no matter the season, no matter the year, throughout our childhood, into our teen years, until we graduated from high school and left town, every Saturday we saw a movie. We struggled with our choice during the week, over the phone scanning the movie ads, calling on the heavens for divine intervention—anything that would help us make the best decision. Genre made no difference; we were open to all. After our lunch we hurried toward our selection, never people to compromise a nanosecond of our coming attractions. Being a moment late for a movie never was nor will be an option in my life.

Walking from the daylight of reality into a darkened movie theater, sliding into the world of creation, leaving behind the turmoil of childhood, the grief of adolescence, squirming down into the upholstered seats, opening my heart to the thrill of the previews reflecting what might be, the opening credits guaranteeing what was to come...the life I struggled with faded as the world view of the movie swept over me, taking me away. Sitting with Gladys at my side, a constant anchor, year after year of movies swept through my world. We saw, to name a ridiculous few, and in no chronological or preferential order:

Hush, Hush, Sweet Charlotte
The Birds
Bullet
Little Big Horn
The Spiral Staircase
The Nun's Story
Breakfast at Tiffany's
The Thomas Crown Affair
Spartacus
Splendor in the Grass
The Sound of Music
Etc.

Each and every movie offered me escape from what was, and possibility for what might be. Each and every Saturday brought me Gladys's support and sisterhood in this pursuit.

Our friendship flourished in many other realms, from camp to high school, from the Jewish Community Center's activities to our ineffective dating records. From our college experience, brief roommate-ing in grad school, our weddings, divorce (mine), birth of children (hers), death of our parents (all), we have had each other's love. But through all of these stages, the qualities I noticed on that soft summer day in 1956, with Cauliflower madly leading songs, have continued to touch me and make me whole.

"This place was my solace. Camp was the miracle of my life, the place I came alive." Middle row, center.

6

~

Banished!

Summer, 1965

"Over here, Nan," hooted Terri into the wind, arms waving semaphore-like above her head. She stood on the lawn by the flagpole where a gaggle of my unit sat, awaiting me.

I happily trudged down the path from the Lodge, clutching the hand-sewn, felt mailbag carefully. Mail for our unit, Samoset, the oldest scouts in camp, the counselors-in-training—or CITs, as we were called—was close to my heart.

I smiled into the breeze, and, as if time stood still, I fully and bodily sank into the lusciousness of the moment.

The cap of the blue sky shimmered with a brilliance that whispered of early fall. The warm sun was diluted by a delicious, soft breeze, creating a balance of warmth and chill on my bare arms that completely riveted me, calling me present. It was the final weekend of my two-summers-long counselor-in-training program at my beloved Girl Scout Camp Archbald. Actually, this summer was the climax of the ten summers I had spent here at camp, loving this spot of earth, memorizing its trails, breathing in its smells, mastering its skills, and flourishing in its rigor, love, and encouragement. This weekend was our zenith: we would be receiving our reviews from our CIT training days, days filled with testing of fire building, song leading, camp-craft, pup tent pitching, waterfront skills, and practice teaching with the younger units. After receiving our scores, we would be initiated into that rarified world of counselor-hood, which held profound power and meaning to us all. Next summer we would return to camp to become, like our heroes before us, the cool, the loving, the competent, the all-knowing counselors, just like the ones that raised us up and loved us through the years, to this very moment. We would become their wonderfulness, and carry on their tradition of compassionate, loving regard for all.

It was a heady moment, as we stood on the threshold of this profound initiation.

I picked up my pace, scraping my dirty Keds on the dusty path, hurrying toward my friends who sat sprawled out in a wobbly horde. I smiled at their collective sprawl, and began handing out mail, tossing the beloved envelopes toward each recipient with a flourish and a flick of hand:

"Margie Regean, for you," with a flick and flip of my wrist.

"Terri Z., and you, too," tossing a cream-colored envelope in her direction.

"Miss Gladys Roth, ah-haaa," I cried, and started sprinting around the sprawling unit, holding Gladys's coveted letter above my head as she chased after me with pretend feverishness. Guffaws and chuckles followed us, only to be interrupted by our call to lunch by the camp bell. Our mock struggle released as Gladys lunged at the letter, tripping me in the process. As we tumbled to the ground, laughing, the rest of the mail was hastily and effectively distributed. We got up, dusted off our bottoms, and wandered as a loose group toward the dining hall.

Walking down the hill, I mused, considering my awe and love for this place. *More than a camp*, I thought, kicking at the familiar dust. This place was my solace, its culture of girl-centered experiential outdoor education exactly what my broken child's heart needed. I lived from summer to summer, counting months, weeks, and days until my return to this hallowed earth. Here remarkable things happened: I counted, I knew how, I shined, I was fully loved and wholly accepted for who I was. Camp was the miracle of my life, the place I came alive.

We tramped up the rickety and so-familiar steps to the south side of the dining hall, the door squeaking behind us, and found our seats at the three perpetually sticky tables designated to Samoset. Once seated, counselors filed in, randomly selecting tables to head. It was the cosmic lottery, and from my young-girlhood, I always hoped upon hope for the good counselor, the cool one, the funny one, the one I had a monogamous crush on. Miss Rosie, a round and affable young woman from a younger unit, came to our table. We nodded our collective approval, and prepared to sing grace together.

Our two counselors, Ginny and Scarlett, were noticeably and unusually absent from lunch. I whispered to Gladys, "I wonder where Ginny and Scarlett are?"

She shrugged and whispered back, "Maybe they're still processing the testing results."

The grace leader, a senior scout, stood at the front of the dining room and held up her hand as silence spread throughout the room. She led us in one of my favorites, "God Has Created a New Day:"

> God has created a new day
> Silver and green and gold.
> Live that the sunset might find us
> Worthy His gift to hold.

Voices floated together with that Girl Scout magic of harmony and perfection, the music filling every niche of that open, knotty pine space around us. I loved the mealtime graces—although my Jewish sensibilities tried to restrain my heart, there was often a flooding of feeling and warmth that filled me when I participated in them. It would be years before I began to consider the power and gift of the underlying faith the Girl Scouts offered me during those early years—my first touch of tender conviction that I was not alone.

Once the song was completed and the benches scraped back, we all sat for our lunch of baloney sandwiches on white bread, chunks of government surplus Velveeta cheese, salad of iceberg lettuce with minuscule slivers of a carrot-like substance randomly tossed in, cole slaw of a strange and yellowed color, sweeter-than-sweet lemonade, milk, and ancient Girl Scout cookies, stale and soggy, amazingly damp to the bite. Yet food never tasted so good as it did in this fresh air of aliveness and connection.

We jabbered through the meal, mouths stuffed with white bread, full of ourselves, as our trials and tribulations of CIT testing almost lay behind us. Miss Rosie was funny and sweet, allowing our headiness some airtime. I was feeling both mellow and excited. Nobody ever failed the program. Sometimes girls had to repeat certain phases of training during special mid-year camping sessions. But that was rare, almost unknown. And, frankly, I knew my own competencies. I knew myself to be a star in our tiny galaxy of scouts—I was a strong swimmer, a white cap, the highest designation. My canoeing skills were accurate and reliable. I could build a dynamite and effective teepee fire formation quickly, find my way around a campsite, and my practice teaching with the younger campers, despite my terror, went well. I was known and loved for my abilities—the complete dichotomy of my life in the city, where I was hesitant, withdrawn, and plagued with self-doubt.

I led a double life. I was blessed with this camp, and my progression through it was just about to take another leap. I would be a staff member next summer, the summer after high school graduation. With my friends we would take our place amongst the green-Bermuda-shorts, green-high-socks, and white-scout-shirt crowd, the uniform we coveted for all those years finally ours. We could go to the staff house, where massive amounts of cigarettes were consumed, have nights out, and go to the Schnitzelbunk, a popular bar in New York state where the drinking age at eighteen accommodated us well. We could be, we would be, for others what those cool and wondrous counselor/goddesses were for us.

I saw my world stretch out before me. Despite the terrors of the next, my senior year—SAT testing, college applications, and leaving home—my launch into college would come after next summer, the first as a member of the Archbald staff, the perfect and inevitable launching pad into life. This was very cool—it was everything I always wanted.

We rowdily finished this, one of our final meals as campers. Gladys and I walked down the steps to wander back to the unit for rest hour, that mandatory after-lunch time when no activity could be scheduled, due to the brilliance and insight of the Girl Scouts, who knew that we girls, no matter the age, needed our down time.

And then, the strangest of things, one so out-of-sync with normalcy, began unfolding. We saw Ginny and Scarlett walking toward us. Something was amiss, I could feel immediately. There was almost a chill in the air as they approached. Ginny, dark and compact, wore her typical straw cowboy hat slouched down, bumping into her huge sunglasses. Although I couldn't see her eyes or even her face through the mask of it all, I felt her walk hesitant, out of rhythm. She was one buoyant twenty-four-year-old, who was working on a Masters in Divinity. But she was not bouncing right now.

And Scarlett, round and ruddy, looked straight ahead, through us and past us. This was really strange for someone as gregarious and contact-ful as Scarlett. I wondered if Gladys felt it, too. There was no time to check in with her. Our counselors were headed right for us, marching directly into the path of our amble. We four stopped abruptly under the old oak, its branches like palms opened, outstretched to gather the glory of the sky. I could only think of the showdown in the movie, *Gunfight at the O.K. Corral*. There was a moment of long, unusual silence during which I could hear my heart's song, its rhythm rapping. We stared at each other in a deep and unusual hush of silence.

Scarlett, the senior staff member, a physical education teacher at a junior college, coughed, and broke the silence. "Nan, we need to talk to you alone."

My blood seemed to chill, my bones heavied, that lovely afternoon warmth banished. I had never seen a look like this on Scarlett's face. Like a mask she stared at me, but not really. She seemed to be steadying herself, a balance point existing somewhere behind me. And Ginny was completely unreadable, unapproachable, hidden behind hat and glasses. These were two women I knew really well, who knew me really well back. But not in this moment. In this moment, there was no access. In this moment there was no knowing. Gladys fussed at my side.

"Oh," was all I could muster. My voice croaked out, pathetic and tiny.

"Let's go up to Schoonover Hall," Scarlett said, all business, and turned, formally pivoting on her heel, to head up the small hill. Ginny, as if in a trance, followed her. I felt the blood drain from my face, my hands get cold and tight. Like in slow motion, my breath sounding louder and louder in my own ears, I turned on legs that were not my own. My eyes met Gladys's. I couldn't look, couldn't bear to attempt to unlock her moment, my own being such a flattened, devastated blank page. I walked away from my sidekick, my perpetual Girl Scout buddy, and traipsed up the hill, alone now, my stomach dropping further with each vacant step. I was being pulled toward my destiny.

I walked behind them, this in itself a strange and unusual experience. They were my heroes, my mentors. Never did I feel anything but kinship and support from them, in an equal, open way. But behind them I trudged, steps heavy, thoughts vacant, air diminishing, legs heavier and thicker with every step. When I made it up the rise, either ninety seconds or a thousand hours later, they appeared poised, almost stilted, sitting on benches in Schoonover, waiting for me. The echo in the open troop house magnified my footsteps as well as my labored breathing—or so it seemed. I shuffled over to them and almost plopped myself down, so little control did I have of my basic muscle function.

I couldn't breathe

Scarlett coughed. "This is hard, Nan, but we're here to tell you about some decisions that have been made about your CIT testing."

My lungs, already starved for oxygen, for energy, constricted even more, balloons depleted, squeezed of fuel. My tongue, its thickness almost choking me, forbade verbal response.

She continued. "Decisions have been made...decisions about attitude, about maturity levels..."

Ginny squirmed, silent and petulant.

"Decisions about...the Lodge, Miss Anna, the administration..." Scarlett faltered, choked a bit on the last syllable, rebalancing herself, eyes steadied on the floor beneath me.

"Decisions about...it has been decided that...your skills and attitude are not up to par to justify your CIT graduation tonight." She sat back on the bench with a sigh.

In slow motion, I watched myself as I slid down a rabbit hole, a dark, soft, endless rabbit hole, losing my footing and grounding in this moment, skimming down the shoot, slithering and sliding away from reality. Scarlett's words floated toward me from a distance, from a galaxy lifetimes away from me. I heard virtually nothing but my own pounding heart, and the sound of my body dropping, slithering away.

I awoke briefly from this nightmare to feel Ginny's hand on my knee. Her glasses were off, her hat tossed aside, her face passionate and twisted:

"Miss Anna. This is Miss Anna's decision. As the camp director, she questions your maturity level and your capacity to contain your actions. We challenged her to no avail." Darkness washed over her face and she spit out, "This is not even about you."

What? It certainly felt as if it were about me. This was about me more than any other moment in my seventeen years had been about me.

Scarlett glared at Ginny and came forward again, bending forward toward me. "There are ways....we have some ideas.... we can work with..."

And I lost it again—my footing in reality, my ability to process this severing, this execution of my heart's dream. I felt the rabbit hole beckoning me, urging me downward. Tearless, thoughtless, hopeless, heartless, dreamless, I sat there and allowed my life to end.

The meeting ended, the day passed into night, my pain slipped and slid and claimed every bone, every cell, every molecule of my being. This trauma, this severing was a physical thing, living, alive, inhabiting my body. There was no sleep, no celebration for the others who passed the training, no celebration campfire. Only my individual grief and our collective disbelief filled the unit. We were, as a group, my friends and I, silent, disorientated, and seething. I, however, was many, many moons away from seething. My grief stunned me, rammed me into silence. The plug on my life energy was pulled. I had no future.

Darkness settled over Samoset that evening with a silent, deep vengeance.

I lay on my cot in the cathedral of my tent, my other tent mates finally resting, with sleep eluding me. No sleep for me tonight. I thought perhaps I never again would be given the gift of sleep. The grace we sang at lunch so long ago kept haunting me, racing, running, flowing through my brain—*Live that the sunset might find us—worthy His gift to hold.* The sunset had come and blotted out what was holy, what was rightfully mine. The gift was no longer mine, no longer mine to hold.

I was not worthy.

Not worthy.

Not worthy.

The night was long and endless. I both wanted to sleep to escape the pain, yet didn't want to miss one nanosecond of this, my last night in my beloved Archbald.

Dawn did arrive, soft grey filtered light tiptoeing into the tent, birds harkening to a new day. A day of forever leavings.

This new day was a slow-motioned continuation of the nightmare, the nightmare that refused to end. Trying to understand that which was not comprehensible, trying to process that which was not integrable was exhausting and impossible. I was stunned into stillness, my friends around me, orbits of caring and disbelief.

This was Friday, the last day of camp, the end of summer. But it was void of victorious initiation into the next phase of my life. There was no next phase. My life had literally ended.

Memory melts, words float soundlessly; people's movements, jerky and disconnected. I remember my mother's car floating down the hill. I see myself running toward it, flinging open the door, and throwing myself into the seat, frightening her, frightening myself at my urgent, passionate neediness. I couldn't tell her, couldn't say it, had no words. Scarlett intervened while I sat in the car. I watched them talk, Mom and Scarlett. Scarlett's energy seemed to return as she took control, gestured, waved, moved her soundless hands around. My mother seemed planted, rooted, with each new piece of information, pushed down into the earth. Their conversation humiliated me, shamed me. I averted my eyes. I wanted to go away, to banish this nightmare from my psyche, yet I never wanted to leave, knowing I could not return to this hallowed earth of mine.

I refused my mother's suggestion of talking to Miss Anna. It was not an option. I stayed in the car. Somehow our car was magically packed up with my duffel of dirty laundry, muddy boots, soggy sleeping bag, dented footlocker. Our only option was to leave, to drive up that precious, perfect hill, and leave my camp, leave my life, leave my hope behind us. Somehow we navigated our way out of there, toward deeper heartbreak and cavernous loneliness.

Fall and senior year and the city unfolded with a grainy, flat emptiness. My mother eventually did have that talk with Scout House, and managed a compromise—if I worked with a Girl Scout troop that winter and spring, to prove my maturity, they would consider retesting me. Still I could not return to my beloved Archbald that next summer. My mother and father, not fighters, submitted to the authority of Anna Johns, 4 feet 10 inches, 230 pounds of Girl Scout convention, as I had done, as we all had done, for all those summers that she lorded over the camp. Her word was the law. It was 1965, decades before a sense of child advocacy was born, decades before a parent would threaten an institution with a legal confrontation, a challenge to their tradition and decision. At least, *my* Jewish, lower middle-class parents couldn't do this. They defended me, but their life energy turned toward me, not toward the institution that betrayed us. Although I didn't know it for decades, I wanted more, so much more from them.

Although I despised working with the seventh graders in the troop as an aide that year, I dutifully showed up every Tuesday afternoon and ineffectually and halfheartedly supported them. The activities, the badges, the community work bored me to tears, tears which were plentiful. It was never scouting in the city that touched me. It was summer—outdoors—experiential activities that were mine for the loving. My confidence was banished, my heart severed from my body, my future bleak and empty without Archbald as my shiny star of destination.

The long, endless year unwound. College applications came and went. I was rejected by my first-choice school, the all-girls school that I half-hoped would become a camp, another camp into which my life might fit. I settled for my second choice, the school where my sister was going to be a senior. It was near the ocean. That was the only draw, the only solace.

After high school graduation, my friends all went back as staff members to Archbald that summer. I found a private camp in the Poconos, and got a job in its hot, humid kitchen, a pathetic Plan M. No flag ceremonies for me—no canoeing or jay-stroking or teepee campfires. Just loss and loneliness and endless racks of dirty dishes that the privileged campers from Long Island tossed into bucket after bucket after bucket. Bucket after bucket for me to carry, to empty into the dishwasher, and to scrub clean, only to be dirtied again.

Only to be dirtied again.

Throughout our lives, Gladys and my camp friends have attempted to dissect, to understand the decision of that summer, the decision that changed my life. Some thought it was the Girl Scout council's homophobic response to my budding self. Others believed my light was too bright, too uncontainable and uncontrollable for them. Still others believed that Miss Anna's secret relationship with Jane Ann Burns, a staff member who moved into the Lodge that summer to be "closer" to her, was the backdrop to this drama. My freedom of self somehow threatened their cover. We will literally never know. This mystery will outlive me.

Anna died several years after that summer. Her reign finally ended, only death releasing her council-wide control. My miraculous return to Camp was years down the road.

For the time being, however, I sat, between high school and college, emptied and alone, without my tribe, without my past, without my hope, and without my future.

7

Ticket To Ride
1966

I could have been the only person in the history of my college to go through the registration process backwards. It is an accomplishment that I have worn with dubious distinction, one which held great shame in the moment of its achievement.

The amount of terror churning in my body during my first college registration process practically blinded me to the signs indicating direction and flow of the system—big, red cardboard arrows pointing to this window or that, to this process or that, this alphabetized segment of the incoming class or that one. Wearing my new freshman beanie and my tan London Fog trench coat, hoping to strike a cool yet subtle freshman figure, I wandered from station to station, hardly hearing the directions given me. By the time I reached what I thought was the conclusion of the process, the upperclassman working there, puzzling at my paperwork, exclaimed with a sucking of breath, "You paid and you didn't register for any classes," with an astonished disbelief that echoed loudly around us for all to hear. You could have fooled me. I might not have noticed that I hadn't registered for specific classes by Thanksgiving-time, so thick was my trepidation at this, the next organic stage of my life.

The Great Hall, once Woodrow Wilson's estate, echoed with the steps of my Weejun loafers as I frantically retraced my steps, going against the flow of oncoming, calm-looking registering students, heading back toward the course offerings station. I shakily circled in my choices on the cardboard card with a trembling number 2 pencil, settling for whatever classes were still available, despite the teacher and course preferences I had figured out with my sister, L., a senior at this school. Since an afternoon had passed since these courses had been available, many of my preferences were closed out. The significance of this error felt wrenching, another nail in the coffin of my minuscule self-esteem. I was internally shaky, and deeply cold despite the September afternoon. My parents waited for me back at L.'s house, anticipating my call, ready to pick me up, to share a final meal, and for us to bid each other adieu, launching me into this next moment of my natural development.

Our two-day freshman orientation would begin the next day, then a "free" weekend, and, on Monday, classes would launch. My ambivalence was so thick—I had waited breathlessly to leave the obvious failure of my high school years, filled with academic mediocrity and social ineptitude. But now that I was facing the unknowns of college, I felt frozen and unready, like a Thanksgiving turkey not cooked enough to come out of the oven. I was simply uncooked, inexperienced, terrified of speaking, and unclear about how to act. Most of the time, I felt that I could hardly breathe.

Registration finally complete, our final family meal concluded, we three stood outside the cinder-block dorm. This was the moment. My parents hugged me with cautious, great concern, trying hard to not be too demonstrative, yet clearly expressing their care. My father, always the softie, had a few tears in his eyes. Noticing them, I made a conscious decision: I refused to engage with his feelings—they were always a slippery slope carrying me away from my own world. This was the great moment of my individuation. I held my breath as I turned away, walking back toward the dorm and toward this brave new world of my freshman year, 1966.

Initially, things didn't go that well. My roommate completely broke the stereotype of who and what I imagined my freshman roommate might be. I saw her as the potential cool friend, the popular one ready to take me in. She would be Jewish and blonde, completely tolerant of my idiosyncratic ways, amused by my dry sense of humor, and the key to the unlocking of my social terrors. Absolutely none of this formula manifested. Her name was Janelle. She was Italian, swarthy, from northern New Jersey, a business/accounting major (this was a major turnoff for me), had a boyfriend at home, left every weekend to be with him, and was completely uninterested in socializing with me or with anyone. It was ironic. Finally I had a roommate, like in the movies. But no, she would not be the one with whom I would share my heart and go on double dates. No, we would not be reading each other our diaries. She kept her side of the bleak, cramped cinder-block room sparse and tidy, poring diligently over her accounting books. I put up my little college banner on my side of the wall, and on my desk, a picture of my parent's dog, Nick the Yorkshire terrier, who replaced me during my parents' empty nest terrors. My small picture of Peter, Paul, and Mary I kept out of sight. That was only for me.

I was thrown to the winds of fate, alone.

Orientation weekend unfurled painfully, with meetings and a guided tour and the Greek fraternities and sororities presenting their "houses" to the incoming class. I bonded with a chunky girl named Sue, another life pattern emerging: find a safe and non-confrontational person, perhaps even less well-off than I was, and hang there, finding solace in their less-coolness.

Classes were a blur of confusion, blending into each other that next week. Freshman English took place in a packed lecture hall with the professor pacing frenetically, waving his hands like a drunken traffic cop. I was both captivated and annoyed by his constant churning. Physical Science was taught by the greenest looking man I had ever seen. His skin was jaundiced a green-yellow, his palms pale and sickly—all in all a strange-looking man. The History of Western Civilization boggled my mind in its vastness— *all* of Western Civilization, like, the entire thing? The textbook outweighed my old bowling ball. And there was my disturbing encounter with the limitations of "women's basketball" in physical ed class. I stretched my mind to listen, to pay attention. I found that if I sat right up front, under the professors' noses, I would be able to focus my attention more sharply. I would rush in at the beginning of a class to grab those un-coveted front-row seats. Like a tuning fork I was tight and on hyper-alert, on guard to emit a pitch to respond to any oral demands that might be placed on me.

It wasn't fun yet. I muddled through, making my way.

First semester was complicated. My head swam. Getting used to Janelle, my un-roommate, eating in the carbohydrate-heavy cafeteria with the noise and stimulation of many different groups of students, attempting to attend to my class work—this was not the escape I had so hoped for during high school. As I forced myself to pay attention in class, to take notes, to review them, I found that studying and worrying seemed to collapse into one collective activity. I was so busy worrying about having to talk in class and taking tests that my capacity to focus was stretched, thin and brittle.

I was exhausted and yet, of course, I continued on, the train of life taking me forward, in spite of myself, in my pursuit of higher education.

One Saturday night in early November, with our first holiday break hovering on the horizon, a somewhat cool girl in my dorm named Alex invited me to come over to her room after dinner. She was short and round, but cool, and could always be seen wearing her standard outfit/costume of wide-legged bellbottoms, low brown leather boots, paisley shirts with wide, pointed collars, and an endless and interchangeable selection of shiny, big-buckled leather belts. I liked the style, my first introduction to the hippie look, new to my world of pleated skirts and circle pins.

Not wanting to go to another horrid, noisy, and confrontational fraternity party, I quickly accepted. Grateful for the invite yet cautious, I knocked on her door tentatively. She answered with a "Ho!", which I imagined meant, "Come on in." I pulled at the heavy, industrial door with all my strength. It opened and another world emerged to greet me.

Alex was sitting on the floor with Iona, her roommate and friend from home. They were cool, both wearing wide-legged bellbottomed jeans, fringed tops, and no shoes. The light in the room was off, with some strange backlighting filling the space softly, differently. I guardedly poked my head into the door.

"Hi," I said, immediately embarrassed by my obviously superficial greeting. I should have thought of something better to say.

"Hey," they collectively snickered, making me uncomfortable until they both wildly waved me in with a sincere friendliness.

"Come on in, come on in," Alex called loudly, continuing to swing her waving arm through the air. They both giggled.

I slid down on the floor, leaning against the opposite bed, facing them, and perused the room. It looked nothing like *my* dorm room, with its tidy orange ribbed bedspread and organized freshman chaos.

Their desks were piled haphazardly with books, ashtrays, incense holders, pictures in a variety of frames, album covers scattered about, and loose-leaf paper abounding in wild, untamed piles. Indian-print bedspreads, with stenciled pictures of elephants and Indian goddesses, covered the beds, with bunches of multi-colored throw pillows tossed randomly about. The air smelled heavy and rich. There was a huge poster on one wall that said, "*What If We Gave a War and Nobody Came?*" The colors of the poster seemed alive and fluid.

Something was going on here that was not happening in my sterile room down the hall. I swung my attention back to them.

"Hey," Alex said again, as if greeting me anew.

I had no clue what to say, so I just nodded.

"Wanna smoke a joint?" she asked, jumping right to the point.

A joint? *Like, marijuana?* I wondered. Did I want to? I had no idea. Probably, I imagined. I wasn't sure.

"Sure," I said. And with that single word, my life changed.

Alex rolled a towel under the dorm door crack with a precision and knowing that was impressive. Here was a girl who knew how to roll a towel. I felt a bit nervous, but excited, too. Iona lit the tiny, rolled cigarette with a Bic lighter. It instantly smelled divine to me. She took a giant inhale, choked a bit, and passed the joint to Alex. Alex similarly repeated the process, holding the smoke in, face reddening, breath breaking up. Iona cracked up and they both started laughing. Alex handed the joint to me.

I looked at it. *Whatever*, I thought to myself. I took it.

I had smoked cigarettes a bit in high school, going out between classes for a smoke break in the alley next to Central, our school, in order to be cool. I had smoked Newports, and then Marlboros, a habit that did not take root. *Nevertheless*, I told myself, *I know how to smoke.*

I really didn't know how.

The joint was light in my fingers and wet from my companions' full-hearted, full-lipped participation. I brought it to my lips, inhaled, and the world, as I knew it, was erased. I was filled with warmth and light. Ginger ale had strangely and instantly entered my blood stream. My head tingled, my throat burned, and I was, from that first toke, in love. I wanted more. From the first toke, I simply wanted more.

We passed the joint for several rounds and finished it with more snickering and coughing and shared, giggled conspiracy. The knot in my chest that always existed, that tuning fork waiting to explode with instant pitch, seemed to soften, to release. I felt giddy and happy, open and a part of what was happening. I felt a part of these cool people.

"Hey." It was Alex, talking from above the ocean's surface somewhere. "Wanna hear *Sound of Silence?*"

Gladys had given me the new Simon and Garfunkel album for my birthday, so I knew it and loved its poetic coolness. My hostess put the album on the record player in the corner, and familiar yet so unfamiliar sounds flowed over me:

Hello darkness, my old friend.
I've come to talk with you again
Because a vision softly creeping,
Left its seeds while I was sleeping.
And the vision that was planted in my brain
Still remains
Within the sound of silence.

This was astounding! It was as if I were hearing music for the first time in my life. The words, which I knew well, touched down into my belly, tugging at feelings, meanings, and remarkable connections. *A vision softly creeping!* A vision was creeping inside of me, too, right in this very moment. *Planted in my brain?* Inside my brain, right in this moment, there was a vision being planted. Me, too! This was amazing, this marijuana thing.

I looked around the room. The poster, with its cool anti-war message, was vibrating, dancing to the sounds of silence! This was freaky, but I loved it. I loved it like I'd never loved anything before in my entire life.

I loved this feeling of freaky, this feeling of difference. The reality in which I lived was so constricting, so frightening. This was a different world, a new world, a different stop on the locomotive. I had changed train tracks and been deposited at a completely new station. I loved the feeling of connectedness to Alex and Iona, who appeared to be in their own world tripping out, but a parallel world to mine. It would take years for me to realize that this was an artificial connection, but, for now, I felt such a part of it. I loved the black light, as they had earlier explained to me, and how it softened the war poster, urging the letters to move and dance and flow. I loved not being afraid. I loved pretending that I was okay.

I loved this part of college, where silence had a sound.

Although I could have stayed forever, the night did end, the pot ran out, the music stopped, the energy sizzled. It was obviously time to stand up, a feat calling for great focus and powers of concentration. Stand I did, and, thanking Alex profusely, but in low and hopefully cool tones, I left the smoke-filled, freedom-filled room. As I wandered my way back down the dorm corridor, I realized the hallway looked so much better. I hoped and imagined that I looked better, too. Opening the door to my empty room, Janelle being in North Jersey with her faceless fellow, I threw myself recklessly on my bed, snickering with my new insights into life.

A vision *was* planted in my brain.

College had quickly improved.

As the days and weeks of my first semester unfolded, I spent as much time with Alex and her posse as was possible. The other aspects of my world—studying and managing the stress it caused me—took a back burner, and seemed to hold me less hostage. Going to fraternity parties because I was supposed to go also got easier. I discovered the strategy of relying on the beer keg, always flowing freely and fully available. It helped.

Another aspect of my life began to unfold second semester— sorority. My sister, L., had great friends in the "good" sorority, Delta Phi Epsilon. I was strongly encouraged to "pledge" this sorority, for sisterhood, for access to good Jewish boys, for the unfolding of my place on campus. Again, the train moved me forward, regardless of any preference or discernment on my part.

I went to my first D Phi E "tea," a Sunday afternoon gathering at the Student Union, with cautious interest. Some of the sisters were strikingly poised and lovely, with perfect hair-dos in flips and pageboys and well-applied mascara. Others were less formal, more real-feeling to me. They talked about their sorority, their functions, their service to the community—*who could possibly care about those things?*—all pretty uninteresting, I thought. Yet something drew me. Here was a place to be. Maybe this was who I really was. Maybe this would be my new camp. I moved forward, expressing my interest in the sorority.

I did receive a coveted "bid" to pledge, only because, I am certain, of my sister's deep relationship with Maxine, the president. Pledging gave me a focus, took me away from Alex and her evening parties, as it took me away from my studying anxieties. We had things to do, the eight of us "pledge sisters"; housework in the sorority house, traditions to memorize, parties

"We took pictures in the college rose garden before and after the bland ceremony."

"Graduation, like most of my college experience, was simply anti-climatic."

to go to, older "sisters" to please. I had to prove myself as a good Delta Phi Epsilon potential sister, whoever that might be. It was slightly fun, but not really. Most importantly, it was a place to be. It gave me somebody to be. And it gave me other people— other people to be with.

My pull to Alex and the pot subgroup was strong, and I managed to keep that alive, too. Two very distinct worlds emerged— counter culture vs. sorority. I wanted both. What was real? Who was I? What was my tribe?

I really didn't know, and I surely couldn't have articulated the question. I just went along, tooting down the track, seeing where life might deposit me.

8

·❧

Wha? She Doin Wha?
1970

On my application, I had selected Latin America as my first choice. With my tiny, pathetic comprehension of Spanish garnered from high school and college classes, it seemed the only logical choice. But more importantly: Latin America was the only region I could fathom. My relationship to the world was fairly limited. Gravely pondering this decision, I literally couldn't imagine another region of the world in which I might serve. I felt a flash of shame over my limitedness as I sent in my application. Four years of college hadn't opened my sights any more—it had just barely shown me what I didn't know.

So on that mild April afternoon, standing on the porch of our sorority house on Broadway Avenue next to Hoffman's squat, brick funeral home, the envelope from the Peace Corps rested heavily in my hands. Here was the envelope, the moment I had awaited since first hearing JFK talk on television about the Peace Corps in 1964. I instantly knew I wanted to be a part of it back then, as I lay in my parents' bed on that rainy afternoon, thankfully missing my high school classes due to intense menstrual cramps. Heating pad, television set, no school—it all opened me up to the possibilities. Watching that thirty-minute documentary, high above me on the grainy black and white television screen showing a village in Africa with a volunteer offering support in planting crops, I knew this "service to the world," as the President called it, was a way out for me. Or a potential way in.

Perhaps there I'd fit in.

In that village, in that barrio, perhaps even I'd fit in.

Almost four years of college had afforded me tiny glimpses of community—my sorority had become my home, literally and figuratively. I had found ways to live my pothead tendencies and still be a good D Phi E sister. The anti-war moratorium had been launched that fall—I solemnly stopped going to classes for a brief time, to honor the protest against the war in Vietnam. But I guiltily kept writing my paper for my Emily Dickinson course, and hypocritically felt I couldn't miss my student teaching seminar. I had one foot on the dock, one foot in the boat—nice Jewish girl, trying to do it all by the book, and stoned hippie, demanding that society be legitimized. Neither felt complete or authentic. And the boat was leaving the dock without me, as the dock itself began to fade from sight. Graduation was seven weeks away.

What was next for me?

What if I didn't get accepted? What would I do? Student teaching had opened the doors of possibility slightly, but I couldn't imagine just getting a job, just plugging in to the dominant culture like that. That felt deadly to me.

My fingers played at the envelope. It was thick. What was the folklore about thick envelopes—were they more prone to acceptance letters? Unable to hold the unknown any longer, I ripped at the envelope. The folds of paper opened to me. *Miss Futuronsky. You are accepted to enter Peace Corps training on June 15, 1970...*my heart flipped. I scanned the rest of it wildly, hands shaking. *Your assignment will be the Philippine Islands.*

Where was that?

I hopped around the porch jubilantly, and went inside to share my good fortune with anyone who would listen. I had a destination, a focus, a place to serve. The rest of the day exploded into what might be.

Telling my parents was a less jubilant experience. They, of course, had known of my application and my desire to go and serve. They were quiet about it, as was their tendency, their general parenting perspective being that of benevolent denial.

That night I called home after my dad had closed the store so I could tell them both the news at once. It also gave me the day to celebrate without their inevitable, less-than-enthusiastic response.

"Hi, Mom, it's me. Guess what?" I tried to be mature and contained as I spoke into the telephone.

"Is everything okay?" My mom's voice rose with typical concern. "Sidney, it's Nan—pick up the other phone."

"Hey, hello. What's happening, Poncho?" my father weighed in, using one of his pet names for me.

"Yes, everything is fine. Guess what?" There was nowhere to go but to dive in.

"I got accepted!" I offered, hopefully baiting their enthusiasm.

"To that teaching job in Matawan?" my father interjected, his voice high with hope. I had applied to a few high schools around the Jersey shore.

"No, to the Peace Corps!"

Dead silence. It was a long, empty moment, with the three of us accessing our verbal territory, moving around each other with stealth-like, strategic quiet.

A prolonged stillness prevailed, both during the call and afterward. My traditional Jewish parents, just praying I would find the right guy and settle down, were stumped by my choice to journey across the world, to live in a filthy, unsanitary village, to eat nameless food, and to serve an invisible and thankless cause.

The rest of my extended family was blasé about my choice, not surprised that I might be heading down an out-of-the-box route. When we told my Grandmother Katie, my father's eighty-nine-year-old, half-deaf mother, that I was going to serve in the Peace Corps in the Philippines, she wrinkled up her nose, frowned, and thought carefully and deeply about this tidbit of information. Then she said in her broken English, her Eastern-European accent always thickening her tongue:

"Wha? She doin wha?"

Somehow she said it all.

I stuck to my guns over the next few weeks, committed to my youthful dream of making the world a better place. My parents were stymied, their anxiety growing. The Philippine Islands? That didn't sound safe. New Jersey, the location of my college, wasn't safe to them, let alone these islands thousands of miles away, mere uncivilized and un-Jewish dots in the South China Sea. Yet it was my choice, of course. My choice to get out, my choice to serve, my choice to try again to reinvent myself.

I was both terrified and pumped.

Graduation, like most of my college experience, was anti-climatic. My parents were quietly proud, dressed in their special clothes to honor the occasion. I was relieved to be done with my course work, of course, yet strangely empty. The blank slate was quickly descending. We took pictures in the college rose garden before and after the bland ceremony. The weather was forgiving, the humidity low, a gift from the gods of long, public ceremonies. In typical Futuronsky family fashion, we celebrated with food, and went out afterward to the Old Orchard Inn—

quite a fancy eatery. My sister L., her husband, Rog, and their tiny new baby, the miraculous addition to our family, made our party complete. Marcy, my baby niece, sat strapped into her baby holder in the center of the table, next to the carrot and celery strips, quite the perfect and never-to-be-forgotten centerpiece. She was the highlight of my graduation day for me.

I had moved my belongings out of the sorority house and had a few long and unfortunate weeks at home with my folks before I would reconnoiter with my new Peace Corps group in Philadelphia to kick off our two-month training process. The time was tense and boring—Gladys wasn't home and Scranton held little allure for me. My parents' anxiety accelerated as the day of my departure approached.

My strategy was to ignore their apprehension, denial being a strongly developed muscle in our family system. I focused on gathering the appropriate clothing and items as dictated by my Peace Corps communications, such as:

- Good walking shoes
- Bug repellent
- Waterproof gear
- Sunscreen
- Sun hat
- Prescription medication

It doesn't sound too different from preparing for Girl Scout camp, I thought positively. As I gathered supplies, I kept to myself, circumventing my father's angst. My mother was a worrier, of course, but my father, with his tender heart, big love, and lack of boundaries, was a complete marshmallow of caring. His feelings were bigger than America, and could overcome the most strident, hardhearted of persons. I had known and adored this guy for almost twenty-two years. I knew I had to keep my emotional distance if I was going to pull this off. I knew he wouldn't, couldn't prevent me from going. But I couldn't risk feeling the territory that his emotional world would take me into—his fear would be the doorway to mine. I had to keep that door tightly shut to keep moving forward.

My parents insisted on taking me to Philadelphia. I tried lobbying for a simple bus ride, but they refused. No negotiation was possible here. The day before we were to leave, June 14, my father got sick. This was not an unusual occurrence. My father was sick regularly, and any physical ailment typical for another person became a big deal for him. He was just that way: he got sick. The night before my departure, he began running a fever. This put me over the top emotionally. All I wanted to do was get myself out of there. Nothing was emotional quicksand for me quite like my dad's unending illnesses. Still, there existed no option of taking a bus to Philadelphia. My parents would not allow it to be that simple. It was their parental obligation to hand me off to the United States government in person. Nothing short of that would suffice.

I went to bed that night with anger seething in my belly as I lay there, worrying about him. It always managed to be about him! Here I was, on the threshold of my childhood dream, about to be released from the culture that had controlled me and restricted me, and seemingly my only option was to worry about my father. Although I couldn't articulate this issue, I surely knew in my belly that something was fishy on Arthur Avenue. This was not okay.

The day dawned, and with it, so spiked my father's fever and hypochondriac tendencies.

"His temperature is 102 degrees," Nurse Tillie, alias my mother, reported grimly in the hushed hallway outside their bedroom, thermometer in hand.

I felt crazy with anxiety and manic with anger. This was my day, damn it. How did he manage to wrestle it from me?

Needless to say, Sidney rallied "enough" to drive me, along with my pale mother in the reluctant role of navigator, the 104 miles to the Lantham Hotel on 17th Street in downtown Philly. Navigation got tricky when we got off the highway, the unfamiliar city streets blending into each other senselessly and without any obvious numerical order. But we managed to make our way, the dysfunctional family unit that we were, forging forward.

I sat in the backseat amidst my "supplies" and attempted to still my pounding heart. My world was flooded with feelings. I was frightened about my father's illness, as I had been trained from childhood to be; terrified to launch myself into a strange group of people; eager to eject myself from this insane family; furious at him for taking this day away from me; and wildly eager to help other people. It was an exhausting 104 miles, as were all of the 21+ years that led up to it. I was tired, as my dad navigated his Buick into the parking lot of the hotel.

"Okay," I said, popping out of the car, ready and never ready for their goodbyes. It wasn't that easy. They wanted—needed—insisted on—coming in with me, to "meet the coordinator," to help me settle, and so on. So, come in they did. They stood sheepishly around the fringes of the hubbub in the lobby, cluttered with tables with Peace Corps administrators checking in eager volunteers, my peers assessing each other from afar. Oh, I wanted them gone, and I never wanted them to leave—my father looking sweaty and pale, my mother's focus following his every gesture. Just my luck he would keel over right there, and die at the table with the volunteer roster on it. That would hold a certain irony.

But no, no deaths occurred. Perhaps the only death was that of some aspect of my childhood. After schlepping in my luggage, which carried supplies for me for the next two years of my life, and after meeting my orientation roommates, to my embarrassment and dismay, they embraced me one final time, each one of them, father and mother, both weak with concern. I could not meet their concern, their energy. I pushed it away from me, as if I were wearing a Colgate invisible shield from the old commercial, repelling those nasty germs. They turned, shoulders sagging, looking old and tired, and trudged away. I could not bear to look. It felt terrible to part from them like this. But I had no other option.

Into the orientation I slid. Meetings and appointments, doctors' exams and lectures, it was a whirlwind of activity. A traumatic highlight of it was my first gynecological exam, delivered by a grizzled army doctor who needed a shave and was wearing a wrinkled khaki uniform—it wasn't good. After four days of administrative busyness, we got onto two yellow school buses and wound our way north to Saxons' River, Vermont, where we would spend our ten-week training session.

We sixty-three eager volunteers continued to assess each other, cliques emerging organically and rapidly.

The days were full, with language training taking up the mornings, cross-cultural training the afternoons, cautious pot smoking occupying the evenings. I found a small niche of people with whom I was slightly comfortable. A girl named Dina emerged as a buddy, being the only other single woman in our specific language group, which was Cebuano. From Fort Worth, Texas, she was blonde, innocent, and very touched, unlike me, that my parents had escorted me to Philadelphia. She was amazed to hear that I was Jewish. I was her first. We took a picture to document the first-Jewish-contact moment.

Time blurred by that summer, with anticipation and eagerness everyone's fuel. My assignment was given: I would be going to Butuan City, on the island of Mindanao, to work in the Butuan Central School District as a teacher of English as a Second Language, and as a teacher-trainer. I wouldn't be planting crops with the locals—I had yet to plant a crop in my life. But teaching—teaching was good. I was trained as a teacher, right? I had some TESL training during our summer in Vermont. Surely my eager readiness was enough.

It seemed forever, but the training did end. We prepared to fly from JFK to Guam, from Guam to Tokyo where we would spend the night, and then, finally, the destination: Manila. The trip was a journey in patience and discomfort. It was a time-warped series of days, collapsed into themselves. Finally landing in Manila, the relentless heat, the piercing brightness, and the pungent smells physically slammed into me. I slept for a day and a half in our shared blackened hotel room, awaking into befuddled confusion. I had no idea where I was for several long, heart-pounding moments.

Dina and I journeyed together down to the island of Mindanao, where we would meet our host families for our in-country training, and eventually make our way to Butuan City, our destination. She would be in an outlying school district—I would be in "town." Dina would be my closest neighbor in my Peace Corps family, a very good thing. Her kindness and sincere naïveté were comforting to me. With her, it was okay to be afraid. Her demureness transformed my fear into a humorous bravado. We were a good set, a good balancing pair of neuroses.

In the whirlwind of those first confusing days, I eventually found some precarious balance. Food, with new and greasy ingredients and outrageous flavors, began to settle a bit more.

Although a few weeks in the country made me a little more used to the merciless sun, the ogling men never lessened their hold on my heart. They were inevitable, everywhere, of every class, and fully demoralizing to me. They frightened me in their sheer delight at my presumed promiscuity. Their verbal abuse was appalling to my sensibilities and so triggering. Nothing had prepared me for their constant onslaught of, "Hey, babeee—you want some, babeee?" as they grabbed their crotches.

Landing in Butuan with Dina at my side, the plane circling down into the grassy runway, which looked pretty runway-less to me, my heart was momentarily hopeful. Here was home, here was possibility. Here was my tribe, my clan. My potential contribution bubbled in my heart.

My host family embraced me excitedly at the tiny, cinder-block terminal, squeezing me with delight. I was a score for them, a feather in their bonnet. Bidding Dina a cautious farewell, we climbed into their tiny car and headed to their home in a "suburb" of the city. It took me long weeks to realize their solid, upper-middle class station, the father being a customs official, proud of and talkative about the bribes he received. They had two children, an unusually small number: Clara, a nine-year-old spindle-legged girl who avoided me totally, and Boy-Boy, a five-year-old demon of a boy-child, who seemed to control the entire household with his tantrums and demands. A series of live-in relatives/helpers confused the issue—I was unable to tell them apart. They giggled behind their hands at my entry into any room.

But it was my school assignment that captivated me, that interested me, that held hope for me. Here I would work and offer myself, my contribution a support to the community.

My first day at school, my new uniform wrapped tightly around me, was auspicious. I took the jeepney, a tiny public transportation jeep packed with people squashing the seats, into town. Dina and I had practiced our commutes and had them down. I smiled at the hordes who shared the jeep's bench with me, and squeezed my arms around my legs. Hopefully nobody was looking up my dress.

I wandered into the school complex in awe—my own place, my own opportunity to give back the opportunities that had been so freely given me. The administrative staff, expecting me, had the children lined up to sing me a welcome song. The children were adorable, fascinated with me, following me everywhere, giggling every time I turned around to smile at them. It was heady, satisfying.

I met the principle, a prim, tiny woman named Mrs. Villanueva—we called her "Mum," a term of respect. And I met Mrs. Conte, the superintendent of the entire district. She was older, grey hair pulled in a bun, bigger than the rest but still not as bulky as I was. She was a bit more serious, and held herself with an aloof air. We called her "Mum," too.

The first few days were energizing, hopeful, and fun. The kids followed me around, shrieking with delight at my presence and attention. The next week, I had a conversation with Mrs. Conte that forebodingly foreshadowed my Peace Corps experience:

"Oh," she said, animated and excited, "you are the best, the best Peace Corpse we have ever had." As usual, she used the somewhat infuriating word "corpse", rather than corps. They had had many over the seventeen years that Peace Corps was in country. I had been there a mere eight days.

"My goodness, Mum," I said, flattered that my brilliance was already obvious. "But let me teach, let me help. Let me show you what I can offer."

"No," she said happily. "No, you are the best. You are very

white, you smile, and you speak our language," which at that time meant my few feeble attempts at Hello, Goodbye, and, Where's the milk?

I repeated my urging, my offering of teaching, of contributing. She shooed me away with a flick of her hand.

"No, you are the best Peace Corpse."

In that moment, I had no way of knowing how accurate her assessment of their need of me might be. In the weeks to come, I was expected to perform at school and district functions, wearing native costumes and singing folk songs. It both humiliated and terrified me—I managed to get out of their demands, to their dismay. Dina, always the good citizen, was able to meet those expectations, singing and dancing. Her blonde hair and pale skin put her at the top of the charts. I could not. I dropped in favor. I got tan quickly and easily in the blistering sun, to their dismay. My teaching colleagues always tried to give me their sun umbrellas.

"No, no, it's fine," I would patiently educate. "In our country we want to be dark like you."

Blank stares met me.

I tried to focus on my contribution at school. But alas, their need of me was more ceremonial than practical. I slowly began to realize that I had nothing much to teach them or their children.

My heart sank.

During my second month there, I found myself wandering around the school one day between classes. The children were outside playing, their voices and shouts shrill and undistinguishable to me. The dust was thick in my nose, this extended, never-ending dry season clinging tightly to my skin. Exploring unused rooms, I opened this door, then the other, trying to make this place my own. The classroom walls were open at the top, leaving room for the hope of air to circulate. The roof was tin and when the rains finally did bless us, it hammered away, pounded away, making shouting the only teaching option. I was on reconnaissance that day, discovering my place, owning my tribe. My teacher's uniform of shiny pea green, made by the seamstress with several bolts of material rather than the one that it took to sew a "normal" teacher's uniform—my relative largeness amazed her—felt tight and rubbed under my arms. I felt cranky and so endlessly, deeply, infinitely hot, hot from inside out. I was never not hot, from the middle of the dark night to the bright peak of day. I lived hot, slept hot, walked hot, ate hot—uncomfortable, sweaty, sticky, hot.

I put my hand on the metal knob of a small door and flung it open, effortlessly and with startling smoothness. And there before me, Mrs. Conte hunkered, the deputy superintendent of the entire school system in which I worked, crouched over a large dented tin can, rear end bared to the winds, knickers around her ankles, whale-like, with a golden stream of endless urine releasing from her.

I froze, unable to move—at all. Somehow I became mesmerized, hypnotized by the flow, the infinite current of yellow coming from her. Her eyes met mine, accusingly, her wrinkled brown forehead furrowed. Unfortunately her eyes did not prompt me into action, but only kept me locked more solidly into the moment. I released her stare, my eyes darting back to the fountain of fluid flowing out of her. Somehow her urine had become my solace, an addictive balm to the pain of this situation.

I stared and stared, fascinated.

The only words, the only thoughts that existed in my entire being were those of my Grandmother Katie, who lived some 17,000 miles away from the sound of Mrs. Conte's endless pee. Her words repeated over and over again inside of me, sing-song-like:

Wha? She doin wha?

Wha? She doin wha?

It was a moment that never ended.

Eventually, with great struggle, I tore my eyes away, willing my feet to move toward the door. I leapt back into the corridor, covered with sweat, her pee still echoing in that damn can.

Wha? She doin wha?

This rhythmic refrain giddily picked up speed, careening around my brain. I felt the deepest, loudest laugh of my twenty-two years building in my belly. I ate it down, swallowed it down, willed it down. This was not the moment for laughter, I thought soberly. Actually, it wasn't funny at all, I realized. The laughter dissolved into the churning heat of my always-nauseous belly, trying to extricate itself of today's strange lunch.

Where was I?

Where was I? Where authority was stripped of its illusion of dignity and control, where authority bared its butt, hung it out there for all to see? Where was I—where my greatest contribution might be my ability to dress up in native folk costume, and butcher the singing of national songs, for all to laugh and applaud? And where was I—where my white skin was a respected mark of distinction and a privilege to be protected and honored?

Nothing in my PCV training or in my twenty-two years might have prepared me for the rush of despair that washed over me. Leaning against the flimsy banister, I felt faint with anguish. I could have fainted, slumped to my knees and remained there, in the dust, in the infernal heat, forever. But I didn't. I gathered myself, headed to the other wing of the school to prepare my

"I had disappointed them.
My darkening skin betrayed their hopes for me,
hopes in my whiteness."

lesson—to teach little brown children to speak a language that bought them a smidgen of power and privilege in an unfair and inequitable culture. Shakily I picked up the stub of chalk in my classroom and turned toward the pitted, blank blackboard.

I held the chalk for a long moment, unable to think of anything to write.

The days flowed disappointingly into themselves, weeks churning forward. The sky finally opened. The heavens, not unlike Mrs. Conte's endless urine on that bright-hot morning, gushed endlessly into the earth. Dust spontaneously evaporated, metamorphosing into mud as I had never known mud to be—black and gooey and all-powerful, claiming shoes and ankles and feet back into itself. My skin, practically charred from the sun, became a brown-black barrier that separated me from my now reticent, embarrassed Philippine colleagues. I had disappointed them. My darkening skin betrayed their hopes for me, hopes in my whiteness. Their need was for me to maintain and sustain their belief system. Ironically that was the one thing I could not do.

Yet I continued trying. Teaching, managing the obnoxious men, the impossible climate, the hordes of children who followed me everywhere. But my spirit was crushed beneath the uselessness of it all. Day after day I continued to teach, standing at the blackboard before class, chalk in hand.

I had nothing to write.

I had nothing to say.

The only thing inside my head was the nonsense rhyme that lived in me, sing-songy and all powerful:

Wha? She doin wha?

I didn't know the answer.

9

Hey, That's No Way
1971

Into this void of my broken heart flowed Honey. Honey, my love. Honey, my lover. Honey, deliverer of the first real kiss.

I loved her deep and warm, soft brown body both supple and strong all around me. She came into my bed night after night, and we fell together, our arms made for one another, our legs linked in the dance of our united passion. Her long, jet-black hair tickled and tantalized me as we rolled and explored our quest for sensation. She was all I ever imagined, all I ever wanted—a strong, soft woman's body, available, offering herself to me.

We never once spoke of our loving.

Honey was a delicious rich coffee-brown, minimized by her family and her culture for being too dark but oh, so perfect in my arms. Her body was compact, strangely solid despite her petite frame. We had met at a party that my Peace Corps friends and I had attended, and I was instantly drawn to her powerful yet soft presence—jovial, commanding, the life of the party. She was an anomaly, born and raised in a small barrio outside the city in which I was living and teaching, but attending a large university in Manila as an accounting major, subsidized by a rich and darkly controlling aunt. This was remarkable for a young woman of her status. She was cultured and westernized in ways that made her trips back home to the barrio uncomfortable and odd. She had more in common with us Peace Corps volunteers than she did with her parents, her siblings, or her surroundings. Her sister, Susanne, was the queen of the family because of her light-skinned, western beauty, and scorned Honey's western traits. My friend was, like me, a fish out of water. Her education was making it near impossible for her to return to and relax into the home of her birth. Despite her passionate love for it, it no longer fit her.

I, too, had exiled myself from my home, from the culture of my birth, because I could not find a fit for myself there. I was committed to serving the world, my lofty hopes a smokescreen, covering up the personal suffering that drove me 17,000 miles away. My Peace Corps experience had turned out quite differently than I had imagined. There wasn't much to serve in the Butuan Public School District. The teachers, initially open and interested in me and my teaching ideas, shied away from me as my skin darkened, as my enthusiasm waned. My assignment felt like a façade—they wanted a white teacher, my twenty-two-year-old mind told me, as a showcase, to parade around at their meetings. I could not bear perpetuating this imperialistic perception. This was true—they did adore the status of having a white teacher on their staff. Yet I was too young, my perspective too narrow to see beneath this initial layer of cultural incompatibility to the next possible point of connection.

And once Honey entered into my life, the lens of my awareness drastically shifted. Honey—her family, our trips to the barrio, our courtship silently intensifying—was all-consuming to me. My disappointing school assignment took an uncharacteristic backseat. When my living assignment became untenable because of the host family's idiosyncratic tendencies (the father barricading the house nightly at sunset, my host mother's great jealousy toward my friendship with her husband), it seemed obvious and natural for Honey and I to find an "apartment" together in town. She would work at her cousin's car rental company for the summer, I would continue at school, and our unspoken relationship would have an opportunity to grow in the dank, humid intensity of the Philippine heat.

We climbed up the stairs that day to view the available apartment, which bore no resemblance to any apartment I had known in my life. The windows were open, screen-less; the three rooms tasted of mold and mildew. The kitchen, an open space with a tiny refrigerator and a filthy two-burner stove, sent shudders through me. Evidence of rats was everywhere.

"We'll set traps," Honey offered brightly from behind me, my stomach churning. No problem—this was not unusual in her world. In mine, this was beyond horrifying. Mice, maybe. Rats? Never.

We caught seven, as large as average-sized cats. They horrified me, alive or dead. Simply the thought of them sent shivers through my fully Americanized body. A worker from Honey's father's bus company came to remove them, nailed in their traps. Their blood smeared the floor in the kitchen, gagging me. We set up house with Linda, a distant relative and "helper" living with us and doing the work of shopping, cooking, and cleaning. We would never be expected to do those things. Linda scrubbed the remains of blood out of the ancient tile, working to rid the place of mold. It didn't quite happen—the taste of mold was always on my tongue, its smell infiltrating my nostrils.

It was a most unusual Peace Corps housing arrangement. It was a most unusual housing arrangement for a Philippine woman, too. We were most unusual, our interest in each other growing, accelerating, as the rest of the world, the hot, humid, intense world of Butuan City, faded from my sight.

Our passion grew in that apartment that summer, our evenings filled with the sounds of our inexperienced yet earnest love-making. I was secretly terrified and obsessed with Linda's potential discovery of us, but never shared that with Honey. Our time together, our love-making, was unspoken. In the light of day, we never mentioned it to each other. We were chaste, roommates, friends. But in the evenings, our bodies wordlessly opened to the other.

The heat of summer accelerated, ratcheting up the inevitable dust which clung to my clothes, my hair, its fine particles lacing my books, Honey's guitar, our sheets—everything. I felt covered by the grains of inescapable earth, a shower hardly a moment's reprieve before the crumbs of finely layered grime found me again. My patience was thinning, the heat eating away at my limited tolerance. The weather was maddening, the sun unending, the humidity pressing against me with a life of its own.

Circumstances in my school were deteriorating, going from bad to worse, and then to even more shockingly bad. My teaching colleagues, appalled by my living situation, which so violated their status quo, began blatantly ignoring me. Or so it seemed through my defensive, vulnerable eyes. I had fallen from grace, from white savior to copper-skinned miscreant. It was a humiliating, embarrassing role, so unfamiliar to me, the good Jewish girl eager to please. I pretended to not care, drawing further away. Not attending school was easy—I was shockingly not missed. My classes were covered, without incident. I imagined the school administrators were happy to have me—their embarrassment—gone. I was filled with shame, ultimately conflicted about my love and passion for Honey. With nobody to confide in, my world seemed to spin out of control. I had to work—I couldn't just freeload off the Peace Corps. Yet I couldn't imagine going back there, to that school that mirrored my failure so powerfully. I would have to face the music, talk to the Peace Corps representative, get another assignment. Yet that would probably mean leaving here, leaving her. That was not an option.

Honey's arms held me tightly at night. Yet, in the heat of the dazzlingly bright day, I was alone, humiliated, and so ashamed. Even Dina, my confidante, my friend, was not a safe place for confiding this, the love, the shame of my life. Life around me and inside of me was swirling out of control.

It came to me when I was walking home from the store one day. A herd of children scampered behind me, laughing, snickering, running close, pulling away, palms extended, begging-always-begging for money, sticking as close to me as the mighty dust—or so it seemed. Their once adorable games that used to both thrill and amuse me now ground into my being and deeply annoyed me. Inside my head, I screamed and cursed at them, willing them away from me, willing some personal space around me. I bit at the insides of my cheeks violently, forcing the eruption to implode rather than explode. The inside of my mouth hurt. I put my finger inside—I was bleeding from my own willful implosion. That's when the thought came to me:

I must get out of here.

The thought was shocking. Leave? Never. How could I leave Honey? I could not. She was the love of my life. She was all I had.

But once the thought was released, like a bird out of the cage, it flew, it flitted, it hovered all around me, constantly. I woke into it, walked with it, its whisper haunting me.

Must get out of here.

Must get out of here.

Days passed, rainless days of heat and dust, pain and silence. The more passionate the nights, the more silent and empty the days clung to me. Eventually, after a few weeks, as we sat at our humble kitchen table covered with a sticky red-and-white-checked plastic table cloth, drinking our coffee from our chipped Raggedy Andy and Annie mugs, Honey looked at me, cocked her head to the side as was her habit, and said:

"So. What *are* you going to do?"

I was taken aback, her obvious yet shocking question startling me. I had no answer, none, at all. I looked at her. What was I going to do?

Must get out of here.

Must get out of here.

Remarkably and uncharacteristically, I started to cry, big, gulping tears, hiccupping tears, wordless tears. She came over and wrapped her arms around me, rocking me a bit.

"Shhh. Shhh. I've been thinking. I have an idea."

I continued sobbing into her armpit, thoughtless, hopeless.

She continued. "Let's leave here. You go first. I'll come over to the States and meet you." Her voice was soft, promising, alluring. Her words brought me up into stillness, abruptly halting the tears.

"Really?" I was amazed. There was no picture into which this suggestion might fit, but my heart grasped at it anyway. Was this even a possibility? We could be together, away from the insanity, the hypocrisy, the intensity of this island? We looked at each other for a long, quiet moment.

Maybe it was possible.

Over the coming days, we hatched a plan. I would terminate from the Peace Corps through the official channels. We would go to Manila together—she would escort me to the airport, send me off. Then she would secure her visa, wrap up business, and come over.

Logical or illogical? Real or absurd? I had no way of gauging. I just knew that it got me out of the pain I was in. But to leave her? Unthinkable. For how long? Honey imagined a few months would be all it might take to secure her visa and fly over to the States to meet me.

We moved forward with the plan. There seemed no other option. I wrote my official termination letter to Bob Smith, the Peace Corps representative for our region. I didn't even go back to school. There was no reason. Whatever items remained in my locker could stay there. Whatever relationships I had built were already destroyed.

Honey spoke to her family. They always knew she would leave and come to the States; they just didn't realize it would be quite yet. They were hesitant, her dear father loving as usual, her tyrannical mother skeptical and questioning. My family, of course, was elated. Although they were unaware of the details of my struggles, they knew it was a challenging world in which I lived.

We got our tickets on Philippine Air for our trip to Manila and continued dismantling our apartment. Dina, my only other PCV friend, was broken-hearted we'd be leaving. However, she was attempting to create another assignment for herself up the Agusan River in a more primitive setting that would free her from her own struggles with Philippine hypocrisy. So my leaving was timely. Dina, too, would be gone from Butuan shortly.

I was ripped with conflicting emotions. To be gone from this place, the pain of it, the heat and devastation and disappointment of it, was like removing 2,000 pounds off my chest. I would be gone! Yet, in the next breath, the realization of leaving Honey swept over me. Gone from Honey? How would I survive? How would I sleep? Eat? Would my heart continue to beat? I really didn't know.

We took the hour-long flight to Manila on a steamy Saturday afternoon. The tiny, un-runway of the Butuan International Airport, as it so proudly called itself, faded behind me. I closed my eyes, only to find relief and profound sadness vying for my attention.

Manila, as usual, was a physical onslaught of never-ending sounds and putrid smells that walloped me as we stepped off the air-conditioned plane. With Honey to guide me, it was certainly easier. She took the lead commandingly, as always, arranging our luggage, getting transportation, her ability to function always smoothly supreme. She got us into a cab to go to her aunt's house where we would be staying for a few days before my flight on Monday afternoon.

I hadn't quite realized the status of her aunt. As we drove through the elite section of Manila where she lived, I became more uncomfortable. The houses were flamboyant mansions, huge and gated, with armed guards standing in front. Each was set mysteriously back behind the gates, with elaborate gardening and hedges, and intricate driveways leading to their entrances. The taxi wove its way past the guard, who approved our entrance at Honey's nod, and we made our way inside the property.

I felt terrified, wholly out of place. As horrid as the squalor of my little Butuan neighborhood was, it was mine. I was used to it. This bizarre reversal of culture shock rocked me physically, emotionally, and energetically. I felt disorientated, almost dizzy, as the cab came to a stop. How strange that I wouldn't be more relaxed in the western-like opulence that surrounded me. To the contrary. It was bewildering.

Where was I?

The driver dealt with our luggage as Honey and I made our way inside the thick mahogany door, which had been silently opened by a maid wearing a neat grey uniform covered by a white smock apron, with a white starched cap on her head. Her downcast eyes did not meet ours.

Honey's aunt, her mother's sister, had made a fortune in logging the many forests of her native Mindanao. She and her passive, alcoholic husband had lived in Manila for many years. She was a powerful, formidable woman. As she entered the tall, open foyer, her high heels clicking against the slate flooring, she seemed to take up the entire space. Her eyes met mine. Her face darkened and I deeply knew: she did not like me. She never did, and she never would.

Honey addressed her in Tagalog, with respect, kissing her on the cheek, and then introducing her to me. She met me, this matriarch, in one of my life's lowest moments. All I had understood about myself had disintegrated, and the worst awaited me: leaving my love. I was overweight, bloated from the heat and stress, wearing clothes that didn't fit, exhausted, and emotionally spent. I couldn't fake a mature social interaction. I stammered a hello in my feeble Tagalog. Her face clouded even more with veiled suspicion. She obviously was not delighted with me as her precious niece's friend, let alone suitor.

The weekend was a haze of undigested grief that lived in my belly, squirming and churning, burning and alive. I could not stop humming the Leonard Cohen song that I so loved before I left home—it seemed to sing my life moment. It haunted me in its perfection:

I loved you in the morning,
Our kisses deep and warm,
Your hair upon the pillow
Like a sleepy golden storm.

Yes, many loved before us,
I know that we are not new.
In city and in forest
They smiled like me and you.

But now it's come to distances
And both of us must try.
Your eyes are soft with sorrow,
Hey, that's no way to say goodbye.
Grief for what was to come choked me.
It would come to distances.

The air conditioning in the house was blasting, the thick curtains drawn to keep the sun away from the precious upholstery. I hated that house, its stiltedness, and her aunt, with her narrow, frowning eyes, judging me, berating me in silence. I hated myself for my failure, for my loving, for my leaving. We ate large, elaborate traditional meals at a huge table with her aunt and strange, silent uncle. Honey and I pretended that everything was normal. We didn't talk about our plans. We didn't talk. Talking was not our strength.

We walked around the neighborhood, Honey proudly showing off the wealth. Yet the estates depressed me as they lay against the artificial, manicured backdrop of that contrived expression of riches. The contrast to Butuan was startling, nauseating to me. Our nights in the king-sized bed were quiet. I was wildly paranoid about her aunt down the hall and began pulling back from her. I couldn't live without her touch. And now I couldn't live with it, so intense was its reverberation of loss.

The weekend somehow passed. My pain blurred into numbness. I was the walking dead, just following my footsteps from moment to moment.

As much as I willed it away, Monday dawned over the rarified air of the wealthy suburbs. The day was shapeless, one moment, one event melting into the next. Somehow I found myself in yet another taxi, my luggage, so innocently and eagerly gathered twelve months ago, now haphazardly tossed behind me, seemingly my only remnants of this year in the tropics.

Despite all my attempts to silence him, the disembodied voice of Leonard Cohen whispered along with the wheels of the taxi:

I'm not looking for another as I wander in my time.
Walk me to the corner, our steps will always rhyme.

You know my love goes with you as your love stays with me.
It's just the way it changes, like the shoreline and the sea.
But let's not talk of love or chains and things we can't untie.

Your eyes are soft with sorrow,
Hey, that's no way to say goodbye.

The tune endlessly haunted me, the words whispering their truth, as the taxi screeched into the airport parking area.

The airport vibrated with its typical chaotic noise and movement. Honey busily arranged my luggage and checked me in to the airline. I stood to the side, a bystander to my own life, strangely witnessing this monumental yet banal life transition. I hovered, Honey busy, almost cheerful.

Time clicked forward, heavy, consistent.

Finally, of course, the moment I had dreaded came, disguised as an ordinary boarding announcement for my flight to JFK. I turned awkwardly toward her. Her bright smile confused me and I looked away. She pulled my shoulders straight, looked me in the eye, and smiled again. I was lost to my own pain, anesthetized by the moment. She pulled me close with a squeeze of my shoulders and then pushed me away. Losing my balance in the turning, I walked quickly away, down the ramp, toward the plane, and away, forever away, from Honey.

10

Plan B
1971–72

The ascent of the airplane climbing its way out of Manila, while cutting me loose from that country of heat and pain and failure, dropped me into an excruciating, breath-robbing grief. Relief had not a moment to settle—I had to fight for breath, almost gasping at the fist of pain that clogged my chest. Had I actually left Honey, the person for whom I'd prayed my entire life? It was inconceivable. What would I do now?

The tug between release—I would not have to face my Peace Corps failure nor the unbearable difficulties that country presented me in every moment—and the contrasting anguish over abandoning my first love swept over me in a blurred exhaustion. I strained to peer down toward the disappearing earth, both painful and precious earth that I would never walk on again. Clouds surrounded the plane. There was no visibility, only the blur of my tears, tears that I tried to choke back and hide from my seat mate, a middle-aged, razor-thin Philippine businessman in a shiny suit who scrutinized his in-flight magazine hungrily.

I had absolutely no idea where life would take me now. I was leaving every single thing that I loved, as well as everything I hated. There was nothing left, no direction, no indication of next steps. I groaned silently and sank back into my seat, pulling the blue faux-velour airplane blanket over me. I napped and secretly wept and felt sorry for myself, sick at heart, over the next twenty hours of flight.

My first conscious thought upon stepping off the airplane and descending into the entire universe of the JFK airport was: *This place is spotless!* Gone was the Philippine scramble, the Third World smell and feel of constant, erratic upheaval and movement. Here was the illusion of organization and cleanliness, things I had lived without for over a year. It felt strangely unreal, almost unnatural.

My sister's daughter, Marcy, now a tot strapped in a tiny stroller wearing striped engineer overalls and a matching cap, was the first thing I saw when I walked out from customs. She was no longer a baby, but a tiny person disguised as a train engineer. Where had her babyhood gone? Where had I been during that year? Helping mankind, serving the healing of the planet? Living in dust and mud and the spoils of my own disillusionment?

My family swept around me in an emotional, wordless cloud of concerned reunion. Not much was said, but much was communicated. Somehow my luggage was gathered. How strange! The same luggage that Honey navigated not twenty-four hours ago was now being commandeered by my father, Sidney Futuronsky. The constant objects handled by two radically different people in two entirely different universes? It didn't seem plausible.

Nothing seemed plausible.

Memory melts, time fades.

I awoke in my bed on Arthur Avenue sometime mid-afternoon, the familiar green, white, and purple bedspread covering me. Despite the Pennsylvania heat, I was chilled. A week had passed since I landed, but I had not landed yet. I was content to stay right there, tucked beneath that shield of plaid, nursing the largest hemorrhoid in the history of Pennsylvania. Obviously my body had something to say about the shift of water, food, temperature, air, and general environment. If I lay very still, if I breathed very carefully and cautiously, Ms. Hemorrhoid would remain placid and civil. If I breathed unconsciously, or moved slightly, flaming eruption as I had never known it in those regions would take place. My life energy was dedicated to stillness, to placate Her.

My mother was worried, so Dr. Eisner came to take a look. His shiny bald head, so familiar, looked bumpier to me, more wrinkled, almost prune-like. I lay on my back in stillness, contemplating his baldness. He sat heavily on the bed, causing havoc below for me. I winced and twitched my annoyance.

"Roll over," he offhandedly requested.

Roll over? What are you, friggin' crazy? How would I ever do that, without seismic activity, without fiery volcanic eruptions of pain? I looked up at him, this face of a man I had known forever, through camp checkups, tetanus shots, and stomach flues. Obviously my demeanor communicated my lack of willingness. He reached out a large paw of a flabby hand, pushed at my shoulder, and, to my disbelief, flipped me onto my stomach. Pain seared through me. He peeked down my pajamas and separated a cheek for a firsthand look.

"Yep," he said, in his folksy way. "Sure is a heck of a hemorrhoid."

Medicine was prescribed. It didn't help. Only time helped, as each day, my rear end seemed to land more, to adjust more, to release more, to acclimate more to 207 Arthur Avenue. No rats here. No spiders, no hordes of children clamoring for my attention and money. No warm woman's body to hold mine. Only my body, alone, betrayed by my own failure. Betrayed and alone.

Days peeled by—I was "adjusting," now lying on the couch watching Lucy and Desi on television, taking my time, transitioning. This was an advancement, an improvement. Out of bed, into the den. The healing powers of daytime television floated over me.

More time passed.

I was out of the house, deemed ready for "the talk," it seemed. I sat in my father's car, midday, in front of the Everhart Museum, three blocks from my childhood home. The sun was bright, reflecting off the windshield. My father sat facing me, twisted toward me from behind the wheel. I was stunned simply by the fact that it was daytime and he was not in the store. I had never sat with him anywhere during daytime hours but the grocery store he owned. He looked at me, his face twisted, too, with an unspoken pleading.

The words began.

"We read your letters. All you talked about was her."

I could feel the blood drain from my face, my hands grow stiff.

"We could tell. We could tell. You can't do this. You can't be with her."

Were my ears deceiving me? Was this really happening? I sat speechless, motionless, thoughtless.

"We read between the lines. You can't do this. You can't be with her. This is wrong and bad. You are a nice girl. You will be miserable. We won't let you." His voice was unfamiliar, disembodied, coming from above, from below, from anywhere but from the lips and the heart of this good, kind man.

I was stunned.

"Your mother and I forbid it. We forbid it."

My mother and father forbid it? They who had never forbidden anything in my life, now forbade "this"? My permissive Jewish parents who feared all authority, even their own, were forbidding something? And what was "this," anyway, this nameless, wordless, unspoken thing that sat in the car with us, throwing a dirty, dark shadow over our lives?

I squirmed and stammered something.

Completely uncharacteristically, he continued. "No. Stop it now. You cannot see her or talk to her. It cannot happen." He began to cry, his trump card. As always, I could not withstand the assault of his feelings.

And the words, God forgive me, tumbled out of my mouth: "No. No. I didn't do it. It wasn't that. We didn't do that. No. Nothing. Nothing happened. Nothing ever happened." My voice was unfamiliar to my ears, hollow and tinny.

I continued to plead my case, without logic or meaning to myself or him. My life was being threatened. My only protection—my "no"—I overused. A left jab, "No," a right jab, "No, really no." I deflected. I deflected because my life depended on it. I denied with all of my strength.

The scene fades. The light leaves the day. Silence fills Arthur Avenue.

More time passed. A plan emerged. I would go to L.'s in New Jersey and look for a teaching job. This was real. This was concrete. This was possible. I received a call about an interview.

I stood alone in my mother's kitchen. The clean linoleum, the organized cabinets, the washer and dryer, the spotless green Formica table that came out of the wall—none of it shocked me any longer. I was used to it. It was my birthright, these things, this cleanliness, this order. I was walking and talking. My father and I pretended our conversation had never happened. Never again in my life did we mention it. He would die many, many years later without our whispering a word about it. And I would support our collective silence.

As I opened the washer to put in a load of not-hardly-soiled clothes, unnoticing and ungrateful for this convenience, the thought grabbed at me:

I am back. I am here. I know what I have to do. I can make it look right.

And in that moment, I knew I would call Paul. Paul, my college boyfriend. Paul, Jewish and round and faux hippie—a talkative, harmless, annoying guy who "loved" me. I felt nothing around him, his sexual attempts benign. Our interests in film and writing, the counterculture, and marijuana—that connection seemed enough.

I picked up the phone and dialed his number.

He answered.

Time passed.

Inside my head, I rewrote history. I told myself Honey couldn't get her visa. *She's delayed,* I reasoned with myself. *She'll never come.* This story, at one time contrived, hardened into truth inside of me. By the time she did arrive that next year, Paul and I were married, living in our cute little Matawan apartment with the shiny black Parsons table, the red vinyl chairs, his mother's old black-and-white striped couch, and a matching chair. I spent many a night on that couch, escaping the lovelessness of my marriage bed.

Honey sat across from us. I did not recognize her in this setting, the shiny black Parsons table holding her dark, copper hands, which flitted and moved like tiny bird wings, fluttering and alive. Her hands relayed her only indication of emotion. Her face was blank, that familiar, crooked, half-smile of self-deprecation on her lips. Her eyes spoke nothing. Her attitude was neutral, unreadable. I remained contained, gave away nothing, felt nothing. I went through my unwritten script of platitudes, as if I were visiting a friend. Paul, like a beached whale plopped on the shoreline, sat next to me, hoarding the spoils of our unspoken war of the hearts.

My heart, defeated, surrendered to the numbing reality of the moment.

11

⤳

Suburbia, U.S.A.
1972–74

It looked good, and that was all that mattered. The apartment was "adorable," as my sister deemed it. I was on the right track now, I was certain. This was exactly what I was supposed to be doing. Married. Teaching. A grown-up citizen of suburbia. Paying taxes. Grading papers. Offering Simon and Garfunkel lyrics to my senior English poetry class for study. Watching Ingmar Bergman movies on weekends in an appropriately stoned-out state. Attending to my family from afar. And miserable. Completely frigging miserable. Not that I could articulate that to anyone, let alone to myself.

Miserable.

Paul nattered. He chattered. He talked, he lectured, he rambled, he instructed. Whatever one talked about—a specific Shakespeare sonnet, the lyrics to Bob Dylan's newest album, or a scene in one of Robert Altman's movies—he knew. He knew all about It. And the quieter I got, the noisier he got. The more I pulled away, retreating to my inner world, the more he clamored on.

I learned to listen less without showing it, to turn down his volume inside my head without actually exiting the room. And the less I listened, the less attention I paid to him, the more he nattered. We were dancing in a crazy, endless circle, getting further away from each other, and from ourselves.

It wasn't pretty. I almost knew how miserable I was, but I kept peddling quickly, keeping myself from noticing the obvious. I attempted to hide the truth from everyone around me, presenting myself/ourselves as life's perfect couple. I hid the truth so well from everyone else that I lost touch with it myself.

Despite the loveliness of our bedroom set—a blond, heavy wood with a Spanish flair—our bed was a cool and lonely place. As much as he, my husband, scrambled and attempted, there was always a reason for lack of physical contact. The reasons that I generated, that life itself seemed to generate, were reality-based. I had my period, had a cold, didn't come to bed until late, had to wake up early, was too stoned, wasn't stoned enough. He needed to shave, shouldn't have shaved, and so on. These reasons, tiny lies, took a foothold in my world and morphed into a greater reality. Their small fabrications wove into the larger fabric of our lives, digging trenches that seemed non-reversible. I didn't actually realize that we were not lovers. I just steeled myself against relationship with him, on all levels, and continued along, holding my breath.

I didn't have friends. My Peace Corps friends were still abroad, my sorority sisters scattered throughout New Jersey working. My only remaining college friend was Jane Hinan, smiley, happy Jane, a sorority sister who was doing some graduate work at a Jersey university. She would come up on weeknights that Paul had school. We would get completely high, go to Burger King, pull ourselves together for the ultimate stoned challenge of ordering and eating enormous amounts of food, come home, smoke more pot, and crash on the black-and-white striped couch, watching brainless television. Never in a thousand years would it have occurred to me to share my loneliness, my doubts, or my disappointment with her.

Teaching was the vibrant, throbbing heart of my world. I taught junior and senior English at an excellent high school, Monmouth Regional HS, fifteen minutes south of our apartment, a straight shot on the New Jersey Parkway. Every morning I went the *opposite* direction of the traffic, that incessant stream of endlessly crawling creeping vehicles that headed north every day. I taught college prep classes to reasonably attentive middle-class students, and was in both professional and personal bliss there. The students provided me with the perfect forum for my dance: I'm-a-member-of-the-establishment-I-have-the-power-and-the-roll-book-but-not-really-I-am-just-like-you-one-of-the-people. I was of the establishment but separate from it, better than it, more advanced, compassionate, humane, and present than the system. I—as a teacher—was dedicated to being cool. And to being liked. It almost worked.

We read *Siddhartha* in my senior World Lit class and analyzed the lyrics of "I Am a Rock" in my Contemporary Poetry class:

A winter's day
In a deep and dark December;
I am alone,
Gazing from my window to the streets below
On a freshly fallen silent shroud of snow.
I am a rock,
I am an island.
I've built walls,
A fortress deep and mighty,
That none may penetrate.
I have no need of friendship; friendship causes pain.
Its laughter and its loving I disdain.
I am a rock,
I am an island.

Don't talk of love,
But I've heard the words before;
It's sleeping in my memory.
I won't disturb the slumber of feelings that have died.
If I never loved I never would have cried.
I am a rock,
I am an island.

I have my books
And my poetry to protect me;
I am shielded in my armor,
Hiding in my room, safe within my womb.
I touch no one and no one touches me.
I am a rock,
I am an island.

And a rock feels no pain;
And an island never cries.

My students were reticent, reluctant to talk about their understanding of the meaning of those lines. I prodded and pried out their responses fearlessly, certain of the poem's value in their developing years. Most kids were polite enough. Some, like Hal, the tall, lean guy with straggly long hair in my sixth period class, were less contained—he rolled his eyes and readily showed his obvious boredom. Hal would interlace his fingers, extend his palms away from himself, and crack his knuckles in the most significant of moments in our discussion. I chalked it up to his developmental challenges. In truth, he frightened me.

I was fairly certain that I was a cool teacher. I tried hard, really hard. My department chairman, a rumpled and messy tweedy guy named Martin Sharp, who perpetually needed a haircut, seemed to tolerate my forays into youth relevancy and validation of counter-culture values. He sat quietly during his first observation of me that year, tucked and folded into a desk in the back of the room, looking strangely uncomfortable, as I worked the class, explaining how Siddhartha's journey into understanding was not mind-based, but rather experiential.

"Does this mean we don't have to study?" half-joked Charlie, a square boy/man and popular fullback for the football team with a bright red crew cut, who was wider than his chair.

"No, no, not at all," I stammered, wondering what the answer was. "No, of course you have to study, for goodness sake." I offered a mature, professional chuckle. Such a good member of the faculty was I, promoting proper study habits. "But more is needed. More. Is needed." I didn't really understand what I was talking about, but it sounded like the right answer. My written evaluation from Mr. Sharp was good enough. *Keep focusing on academic objectives*, he had written under "comments." He'd broadly checked the "acceptable" square.

Acceptable. He should only know. The kids love me, I thought.

And that was my life.

Five days a week I worked at teaching, bringing meaning and value to the lives of privileged kids whom I believed needed meaning and value. Most weeknights, I smoked a lot of pot to bring meaning and value into *my* life. Weekends were movies, theater, and errands, while smoking more pot to bring even more meaning and even more value into my life. Keeping my husband at bay, keeping my demons at bay, keeping myself moving fast, I found a committed and loving partner in marijuana's warm streams of soft smoke.

One bright Saturday winter morning, sun reflecting off the blanket of snow that covered our parking lot, I found myself gloriously alone in the bedroom. Paul was out for the morning, doing some errands and visiting his widowed father, Joe. I knew I had a few hours of sacred silence, a weekend gift. Wildly wiping down the beautiful bureau of blond wood, making concentric circles with a rag doused in furniture polish, I felt a little hungover from the amount of pot I had smoked yesterday. *Triggered by the Pledge smell,* I thought. I put down the rag to reach for the Excedrin, my always-handy, daily best friend, when my eyes gravitated to the round pink plastic container on my matching blond wood night table. There sat the dispenser of birth control pills that I took faithfully.

I stopped in my tracks, awareness seeping into me. Like a lightning bolt, the thought penetrated my denial: *I am not having sex with this man, yet I take these stupid pills!* In that painful moment of awareness, I was fully conscious of the absurdity, the pain, the emptiness of that contradiction. My body went cold. I collapsed on the side of the bed, head in hands, and cried. I thought of Honey, warm, soft Honey, so many miles away. I allowed myself three sobs, giving myself a mere moment's memory, and then, tore myself away. *Too dangerous, can't go there.* I sucked in my breath, made the bed, put the insight on the back burner of my consciousness, moved out of the bedroom, and started frenetically cleaning the bathroom tile. I continued along my journey of denial.

Jane and I continued our forays to Burger King; Paul and I, our journey into foreign films. The status quo of my life was tightly contained. Somehow the long winter passed. Spring brought ease in temperatures, flowers blooming outside in the carefully tended beds that the apartment complex maintenance men anonymously cultivated, and shattering news at school.

There was a handwritten note in my cubby mailbox in the

general office: *See Mr. Sharp today during your prep period.* The note, in his broad script, initialed *RS* with his particular flair, didn't sit well in my hand or my belly. Heavy-hearted, I trudged through the long day. What might he want? It just felt—ominous. Whenever he wanted to see me in the past months, he would just poke his head in my classroom. But not this time. Why?

Finally fifth period, my prep period, arrived.

I knocked on his door and opened it. His was a tiny, closet-like office packed with books—big books, little books, textbooks and non, they lined the walls, the desk, and sat in defining piles on the floor. This was a book man. He looked up absently, peeking over his bifocals. He was reading: a book.

"Oh. Sit down." He seemed neither happy nor surprised to see me.

I had to move a pile of books from the second chair to make a place for myself, repositioning them on the floor next to me. My pile wasn't very straight or neat.

He coughed into his hand and brushed his fingers through his hair, seemingly uncomfortable.

"Um, Nan," he said, eyes looking around the room. "I've got some unfortunate news."

He went on to explain, in a roundabout fashion, that there was a reduction of history courses being offered next school year. Staff from that department would have to be cut. One of the history teachers had a dual certification in English. He would come and legally take my spot in the English department. Since I had least seniority, I would be out a job.

I died. I sat there, and I died. I died several deaths during his rambling. I was officially and completely dead by the time he completed his long-winded, non-emotional, impersonal explanation.

He coughed again into his hand, examined his knuckles, mumbled an apology, and muttered, "I truly appreciate your whole-hearted attitude toward teaching. Keep it up." He dismissed me with a wave.

"Thanks," I said, as I stood to go. He fumbled with his chair, leaning uncomfortably toward me to extend his dry, warm hand. We shook, like the adults that we were.

I walked down the hallway I so adored, dead. I was shocked, broken-hearted, and, by seventh period, righteously furious. *Surely this can't be okay. These students need me.* I felt shaky, as if my world would end. I called Paul, my sister, the teacher's union, my father—anyone I could think of—gathering righteous fuel for my crusade of injustice.

Right or wrong, the school week passed regardless.

The board of education was holding its monthly meeting on the last Thursday of the month at 7 p.m. in the administration annex, and my name and changing status would have to be read into the notes of the meeting. Some of my favorite (me to them, them to me) students decided to come to that meeting, to speak their protest. I was terrified and excited, secretly hoping for a sit-in of sorts. As the chairman of the board offhandedly began to read my name into the minutes, Juanita Barnes, a strong young black woman from my fourth period class, a favorite of mine, stood up and called for discussion. She was instantly hushed up and seamlessly escorted out of the room, sit-in quickly aborted. My fate was sealed.

I was bereft, broken, my heart snapped in half. To silently proclaim my protest, I wore my T-shirt to school with the great Bob Dylan lyrics on it: *Clowns to the left of me, jokers to the right, here I am stuck in the middle with you.* I don't think anybody noticed. June arrived. No matter how much I moped, the final day of school came, heralded in by celebrating suburban birds outside my bedroom window, whistling and chirping up a storm. Numbly I dressed, walked to the car, made my final pilgrimage south on the Parkway, and attended the final staff meetings of the final day. It was so uneventful, yet so profound. A few of my colleagues mumbled their concern, grateful, I am certain, that it was not them facing unemployment. At noon I collected my final paycheck from Mrs. Jacobs, the blonde, buxom school secretary, without fanfare, wandered back to my car, and drove out of the parking lot, stunned and alone.

No more *Siddhartha*. No more "I Am a Rock." No more.

Despite the injustice of it all, despite the fact that I was a "favorite" of the students—I was relevant, I was hip, I was young —it still happened! It was shocking. I had mistakenly believed that, because it was a bad decision, it wouldn't really happen. But it happened. I was laid off. Not unlike my banishment from Archbald Camp, it felt senseless and tragic to me, a physical loss, deeper than the issue itself. It meant I had to face my life.

I wove my car, Fred the yellow Rambler American, onto the north ramp of the New Jersey Parkway, blinking away the tears, flowing into the steady, always steady stream of traffic. Heading up toward exit 120, my exit, I thought of Siddhartha—still traveling, still journeying, still looking, still searching. Just like him, that which was the dearest to me was yanked away yet again. Renunciation, force-fed. What had I said that day in class about Siddhartha? *Not just the mind*, I had said to that kid— that kid I would never see again—*but experience*. Experience must be part of the learning. I had no clue what that meant as I reached for the joint in the car's ashtray.

Held in the grip of suburbia, I continued driving north… like Siddhartha, aimless and wandering.

12

~⁓

Women Only
1 9 7 3 – 7 4

The flyer, scripted in lavender and pink, proudly proclaimed, "WOMEN-ONLY DANCE ON SATURDAY EVENING. LIBERATE YOURSELF." It was sponsored by the Lesbian Feminist Liberation, a consciousness-raising and political action group whose Sunday afternoon general meetings I had been attending for a few weeks. I wasn't sure about this word "liberation," which they seemed to use so often. I wasn't sure about their meetings, either—I had trouble following both their agenda and their philosophy. But I was surely happy, albeit terrified, to have a place to go to explore this new realm. After leaving Paul the month before, I knew the time had arrived to explore myself more fully.

I had never seen a lesbian before, let alone been in a room filled with them, until that first Sunday three weeks earlier. I had successfully made my way into Union Square in New York City to LFL, as they called themselves, traversing many miles, attitudes, and worlds. I had actually walked into that large, hollow auditorium that echoed loudly with our assorted footsteps. All sorts of women were there, some whom I might imagine seeing at the New Jersey mall where I would stonily window shop, dazed by marijuana—my recreation-of-choice as a suburban housewife. Then there were the more radical women with male-looking crewcuts—they frightened me. The women wore: skirts, dungarees, overalls, baggy flannel, tight leather pants. Everybody was there, under the banner of "lesbian." It was beyond eye-opening. I found an empty folding chair, sat down, attempted to steady my nerves, and tried to follow their discussion. It was about a writer named Germaine Greer and her theory about females and eunuchs. I wasn't sure what eunuchs had to do with it, but I was in a room full of lesbians. That's all that mattered to me.

And here I was, three weeks later, driving to a "women's only dance." Considering that, only one month before, I'd been sleeping in a big empty bed with my husband snoring next to me, life, which had been stalled for so long, seemed to speed me forward in its wake.

This would be my first women's dance. I had no idea what to expect. Peggy, the quiet, wispy young blonde who had befriended me at the meetings, invited me to stay over in her loft on Bleeker Street after the dance so I wouldn't have to drive back to New Jersey. I had a little overnight bag stashed behind Ruby's back seat—Ruby, the red Volkswagen I'd gotten custody of after separating from Paul.

I would be meeting Peggy at the dance, which was held at P.S. 118 on West 9th Street. I was improving at my drives through New York as my confidence steadily increased. I also reasoned that, with an out-of-state license plate, parking regulations seemed not to apply to me, which freed me up considerably. This was a perspective that returned many months—and many tickets—later to haunt me. But for now, I parked wherever dear Ruby wanted to park. I found a relatively legal spot on the corner of Sixth Avenue and 9th Street, fairly close to the dance. Maneuvering Ruby into the tight spot, I noticed my trembling hands. This was big. A women's only dance.

Dances from my past were traumatic, of course. Bar mitzvah

parties for all the Jewish boys my age were my horrid rites of passage into social heartbreak. Awkwardly and alone I stood on the side of the dance floor, watching the pretty and popular girls jitterbugging, their petticoats swirling. I was both devastated and shame-filled. I hated going to those parties but, of course, had no choice. The unquestionable locomotive of my life took me there. And college frat parties offered me strategies for coping —drugs, alcohol, and bonding with somewhat creepy guys as cover—but were still profoundly uncomfortable. And now, this phenomenon called "women's only." I had no idea what to expect. It was a brave, or not-so-brave new world for me.

I lit a joint as I walked across 9th Street. I figured it would calm me down and open my heart. Nobody seemed to notice or care. After a few weeks of traveling into New York, I was becoming an expert at city pot smoking, keeping my eyes open and crossing streets to be people-free in order to indulge. It gave me a feeling of heady freedom. The few blocks to the school went quickly as the heat of the joint filled me with sensation and courage (I hoped). It finished itself quickly, and I saved the roach for later, stashing it into the coin pocket of my dungarees. My outfit had been carefully planned out—faded blue jeans, worn Adidas sneakers, and a grey corduroy shirt. It was the best I could muster, my "look" eluding me. My pea coat kept me warm against the early November damp.

I was officially stoned, I noticed, as I crossed the big intersection on Sixth Avenue. My legs felt a little wobbly, my mouth was parched. I was acutely aware of sensations of prickly heat dancing around my hairline. I felt carried down the street mindlessly, an invisible locomotive of destiny larger than myself delivering me at the doorstep of P.S. 118. I hadn't thought much about free will. It surely didn't feel like I had much of it.

Somehow I managed to navigate the clumps of diverse-looking women standing outside the brick public school, which was adorned with the enlarged flyer in purples and pinks that I had already seen, now announcing the dance. I stumbled into the card table serving as an admissions table, tripping on my own feet. Hot-faced with shame, I paid my $5, nodded at the unfamiliar women, avoided their friendly welcome, and, with blinders on, walked into this new genre, this new thing, this new world called "women only."

Yes, it was only women. And lots of them. Some were gyrating expressively and wildly on the dance floor of the gym to Diana Ross and the Supremes, which was blasting from the sound system. And yes, as I so suspected, they were dancing with other women, which was startling both visually and emotionally. Some actually appeared to be dancing alone, another woman-only phenomenon. Others were standing by the refreshments table talking. Even more *women* were standing in little bundles and mounds throughout the gym. A cavern of social anxiety dropped open in my belly, probably aided by the pot. *Where should I stand? What should I do with my coat? My hands? What am I doing here?* I thought of my husband-less apartment in Matawan, N.J., standing empty in this moment. Oh, to be home, alone, stoned and watching some really good public television nature show. Or something.

Or something.

Camille waved to me. She was a large, pudgy woman I had met at the meetings. Her jolly, attentive kindness made her a safe place for my anxiety. She was talking to Peggy, my rail-thin hostess for the post-dance evening. I wandered over to them, attempting to look casual and cool to hide my trembling knees and shaky nerves. They were a welcoming circle of good cheer.

Camille helped me deal with my coat, hanging it on a skinny wire hanger dangling from a precarious coat rack in the hall. I stuffed my hands into my pockets, seemingly the best response to their complete inactivity and uselessness. Peggy and Camille introduced me to a few women in their circle, names I couldn't retain, faces that didn't interest me. *No sparks here,* I thought. Someone handed me a paper Dixie cup. I took a sip—sweet and strong. Spiked Hawaiian Punch, swimming in vodka. I took another, longer gulp, which seemed to intensify the dancing sensation around my brow.

"Wanna dance?" Camille casually suggested. *Dance? Oh my God. Like, move? Out there? In front of everybody? With* her?

"No." My answer was a flat, level, emotionless closed door. Camille shifted her body away from me, looking at the dance floor. It was obvious to everyone but me that she was hurt by my curt response. I was oblivious, too self-obsessed to notice. I hung with these easy, non-threatening women, the un-cool crowd for a while. I eventually got bored and drunk. Both elements allowed me to move away and find my own spot, to create my own relationship to the event.

I hunkered against the gym wall under the basketball net, and settled in. I had finished my first cup of punch, and then my second. I was sipping happily away at my third. I was feeling quite relaxed by now, and felt myself swaying with good humor and the music. Then I saw her.

She was standing across the gym, talking intensely with another woman. She was African-American, quite beautifully dark. She wore a blue head wrap of some sort, jeans, Frye square-toed blond boots, and a black bow-necked sweater. Someone had described her to me last Sunday as "political." Her name was Julie—she had spoken on one of the panels I had heard and not listened to. She was intently proving her point, using her finger to accentuate the thought, jabbing it in the air. I thought the gesture was quite endearing. I was smitten. She was mine, I imagined. *She's destined for you, and you, for her*, the pot and vodka whispered at me.

Of course I was too chicken shit to do anything about this profound insight besides ogle and imagine and fantasize—the story of my life. I continued to suck on the Hawaiian "punch." And punch it did have. The marijuana and vodka conspired together to loosen my suburban inhibitions. I remember dancing crazily with a woman wearing feathers—feathers in her plumed hat, feathers in her boa, feathers around her neck, feathers everywhere. I remember doing the limbo with another woman with the most amazing biceps I had ever seen—although it was a cool November night, her chartreuse tank top showed them off notably. Things might have gotten a tad out of control, but the matriarchy supported me. Loyal and kind Camille and her posse of uncool people came to the rescue. As I was being assisted/dragged toward the exit in my drunken haze, I saw Julie across the gym floor. My heart said goodnight to her. *Goodnight, my love.*

My rescuers hoisted me quite dramatically out of the gym and into someone's van, to transport me down to Peggy's apartment. Ruby spent the night where she was, along with my overnight bag, and I spent the night where *I* was—vomiting on the floor of Peggy's bathroom, memorizing the patterns of oblong tiling, the cool of the toilet against my blazingly hot forehead acting as a calming, sobering force.

I had a great time. "Women only" was a success. It worked for me.

I recovered from the evening, snatched a few hours' sleep on the bathroom floor, had brunch with my kind hostess the next midday, retrieved Ruby the Car, and returned to suburbia. The next few weeks found me tracing the route from Matawan, N.J. to Greenwich Village, from suburbia to the City, to liberate myself and to pursue Julie. Adrenaline, that wacky aphrodisiac, drove me hard.

Julie was for me. We eventually made our way toward each other over the next few Sundays. She lived in the Upper East Side with her mother and two dogs and was a political "activist," the specifics of her life kept quietly mysterious. We gravitated toward each other's arms as December came upon us. Our first tentative hug was standing in the hallway outside the LFL meeting. The second and longer one was in Ruby the Car, gear shift rudely between us. The third hug, the one that simultaneously led to hugs four through twenty-two, were in Peggy's apartment.

There was chemistry.

She was dark and soft, a richer and deeper brown/black than Honey. Her skin was so supple—so softly delicious that it obliterated all memory of the revolting nights with Paul, the man with the hairiest back in America, snoring next to me. I became fascinated by her softness. My worldly intent was to trace the outline of her skin with my fingers, my toes, the insides of my arms, my tongue. I was smitten.

Within the realm of the smitten, life moved quickly, lightning-fast. Once the door to change opened, hurricane winds blew me forward. I gave the cute little suburban apartment back to Paul, who was bunking on his father's couch. I found a loft on Christopher Street for rent in the Village Voice, and went to see it that next weekend. Climbing up two flights of intense, twisted hallway with strangely irregular steps, I found myself thinking, "This is not suburbia."

The space was one medium-sized room, windows facing

onto the crazy wonderfulness of Christopher Street, the gay Mecca of gay Greenwich Village. One entire side of the room was a brick wall that had been painted an unfortunate and ghastly yellow. A huge loft bed dominated the space. It was "furnished" as the ad promised, which meant a single, itchy, squeaky tweed couch framing the window. The kitchen was tiny—who cared? who needed to cook in New York City?—the shower was a rickety, plastic-like thing; the toilet, passable. No telephone was needed, I concluded, since there was a payphone right outside my door.

I looked out the window. It overlooked the Ramrod, one of Greenwich Village's most notable men's bars, and certainly one with a distinctive name. The Duchess, the Village's only women's bar, was three quarters of a block away on Sheridan Square. The Path train, which would take me to Newark if I chose to not drive Ruby to the noisy, chaotic junior high school where I now taught, was a block in the other direction. Newark, my place of employment, was only a twenty-minute drive—no matter how unimportant that presently ranked as a priority in my life.

It was auspicious, all factors conspiring to transport me from suburban housewife to city-dweller, from miserable heterosexual to someone who would comfortably (or uncomfortably) attend a "women's only" event. The signs were all good. I took the apartment—Janice, one of my co-teachers from Webster Junior High School in the North Ward of Newark, and her boyfriend helped move me in, using their station wagon to haul my stuff. I left behind me all the fancy marriage booty—the china, the crystal goblets, the sterling silver set, the matching bed sheet sets, the soft, fluffy towels, the bedroom set with the beautiful blond wood, all. I took a few suitcases of clothes, two pots, and a frying pan. I was lightening up the load.

With the Christopher Street apartment in place, my courtship with Julie could be officially launched. We spent late nights in coffee shops with others, debating the fate of the matriarchy—really just a cover for our overt flirting. We attended events in the community together. Gradually she began sleeping over at my loft, bringing one load of clothes down from the Upper East Side, then another. Over time, without our discussing it, she moved in. Without conscious choice, I found myself embroiled in a relationship. I was taken, partnered. I was—in love? Maybe "in lust" was more accurate. But I was surely in commitment. Once dedicated to something, good or bad, right or wrong, I was there.

And there I was, with Julie. She was a mystery—try as I did, I knew very little about her. I didn't understand why she didn't work, and didn't know how to consciously retrieve that information. I couldn't figure out how she had money. I didn't know why she always wore her head wrap, even in bed, never seeming to change it. I didn't understand her educational background, what was real or fabricated about her history or, rather, her her-story. I tiptoed around issues because she was black. I was committed to being sensitive, politically correct, conscious, and non-racist. But as a result of my hyper-sensitivity to race, I was essentially out of authentic relationship with her. Much would have to transpire before I realized that.

Secretly I was elated that she was black. Her blackness, our biracial connection, was politically chic, an unconscious yet delicious nose-thumbing at the establishment from which I had separated. It mattered even more to me that we make our relationship work, because we were a biracial lesbian couple. Things could be overlooked in the bigger picture of healing our political wounds. Or something like that.

So she moved in and we never mentioned it. She didn't speak of her past or how she used her present time. And I didn't ask. I trudged to work each day, exhausted from the glory of early love—late nights spent in essential political discussions, stoned lovemaking, coffee house explorations. That lifestyle, combined with seven hours a day spent with rowdy junior high school hooligans, was showing its effects. I was beginning to fray, my adrenaline drying up, squeezing to a stop.

My family was in the dark. I was committed to giving them as little information as possible about my new New York life from the phone booth outside my window, shouting above the hilarity and gaiety of the Ramrod Club. I was individuating, breaking free, finding myself, and all the while pushing away those who loved me more dearly than anyone on planet earth. It was my version of being twenty-four years old.

Mixed with the combustion of Webster Junior High School, I was a powder keg, waiting for a match—a tired lesbian feminist, just out of the closet and needing sleep and stability. The explosion was around the corner, on Webster Avenue, in the North Ward of Newark, N.J.

13

❧

Webster Junior Whatever
1 9 7 4 – 7 6

If experience has to be part of learning, then Webster Junior High School was the PhD of my teaching career. After losing my job in my tidy suburban high school, I spent a few despondent weeks depressively job searching. I was stricken silent and still with loss. In the middle of that miserable, muggy New Jersey summer, I interviewed for and accepted a job in Newark, N.J. It was certainly public knowledge that Newark's school system, along with the rest of its social services, was deficient. I knew that, but I was relieved and elated to have a professional next step in place—I was needed in Newark! Once again, meaning in life could come to me through my professional contribution— saving the world was possible.

On September 3rd, the day after Labor Day, dressed in my rayon shirtwaist professional-looking dress, smart flats, and matching bag, I stepped starry-eyed into Webster Junior High School to offer my academic and social contribution. The cognitive thought, *Newark's school system has a reputation for being deficient*, went from my brain to my cellular being in no time flat.

It was an ancient fortress of a school built in 1910, plopped down in the North Ward of Newark, which was, at that moment in the city's geographic history, the murky boundary between Italian, Hispanic, and black neighborhoods. The floors were over-polished to a slippery shine, making effective runways for sliding young students who would run down the substantial length of a hallway and skid the last twenty feet, regardless of any human or non-human obstacle blocking their progression. There were 684 students that year, in grades seven, eight, and nine—an unfortunate and menacing age combination. Many of the seventh graders were young and tender; the ninth graders, especially the ones held back a year or two, old and sophisticated in the ways of the street. The age range felt as if it jumped species rather than just two or three years. Racially, the school's population was about 50/50, black students gradually beginning to outnumber the Hispanics. This biracial tension injected an edge of constant, palpable strain into the air.

The first time I met the principal, Mr. Deluca, the Italian holdover from the old Newark days of white school administrators, he was walking toward me, a well-dressed, smiley man, nodding happily in my direction. He extended his sweaty hand in welcome. We exchanged pleasantries, and as he turned to continue along his welcoming way, I noticed that smack in the middle of his back, in the center of his well-fitted navy suit, was a hand-written paper sign that declared: "Fagot." It was a misspelled omen of two powerful syllables. We didn't see him much around and about the school. He chose to spend his time inside his first floor office, focusing on the "administrative aspects" of Webster Junior High.

The vice-principal, the man in charge of school discipline, was Mr. Cartier, the smallest, frailest looking man I had ever seen. He had a thick southern accent, his black dialect hampered by a strange speech impediment. His voice unfortunately came out in Michael Jacksonean wisps of breathy sound—not an effective disciplinary tool. On the school's P.A. system, his announcements were impossible to decipher, comical forays into absurdity. That first day I deeply understood the core truth of Webster Junior High School: the balance of power was precarious—the captive audience, the students, were almost in charge.

I took on my classes with a cautious gusto that warm September day, waiting for the bell to ring, the school opening its doors for students. I was hopeful. I was assigned to Room 391 for the first two periods, and would then skip from room to room throughout the rest of my schedule. *Okay, I can deal with that, no biggie,* I thought. I tentatively wrote on the cracked blackboard of Room 391, with its creaking floor, overcrowded desks, and peeling paint, "The journey of a thousand miles begins with a single step." My plan was to teach from that evocative quote by Confucius.

The bell rang ominously, and students tumbled into the building, like cattle at feeding time. One could almost feel the old building shake with their galloping entrance. I found myself holding my breath. In several long seconds, the door to Room 391 was thrust open, and in poured a species of human beings with whom I was not acquainted in the slightest—twelve- and thirteen-year-old black and Hispanic students, from wiry to bloated, from short to gangly, from really young to ancient-looking teenagers, from fair to pitch black in complexion, from hyper to near comatose. They streamed in, slower ones being pushed out of the way, vying for seats in the back, oblivious to me and my presence in all possible ways.

There was a lot going on, much interaction between them that was quick and unintelligible to my ear. I could superficially tell that the black kids stayed together, as did the Hispanic ones. I tried to get their attention:

"Hello. Welcome. Can I have your attention, please?"

I might as well have been speaking a foreign language. Perhaps

I was. I tried again, getting uncomfortable with the rowdiness and length of their disregard of me and the classroom they were in.

"Hello. Hey. Stop that. Come on. Listen. You in the back? Guy with the red shirt? Stop hitting him. Stop that. Hello. Let's take roll. Hey."

Nothing. No response. Some of the quieter kids looked up at me with big eyes, as if to say, *Good luck with that.* I continued:

"Yo. Hey. Stop. Okay. Class. HAS. BEGUN. NOW. STOP."

There were snickers and a quieting, a simmering of noise. I had an opening.

"My name is Mrs. Bostic."

They broke out into hysterical laughter. I had lost my tiny edge. Beginning again, I shouted:

"SHUT. UP. RIGHT. NOW. BECAUSE. YOU. HAVE. TO. LISTEN. TO. ME."

Oh, my God. Did I really just scream at them? And within the first five minutes of the first day of school? My liberal heart was swimming with guilt. I was sweating profusely now, a long stream of moisture leaking down my spine.

Trying again, I shouted, "Okay, this is seventh grade English class. My name is Mrs. Bostic." More unbridled hysteria. Why did I even bother saying it—my name that was obviously unbearably funny to them? "This year we are going to study..."—some antics in the back, that same skinny black boy, punching the kid in front of him in the bicep—"Stop that." Maybe ignoring worked. "We will study reading, writing, and..." What the hell would we study? For certain, for dead friggin' certain, we would not be studying Siddhartha. Siddhartha had yet to make his way to Webster Avenue.

And so on it went during that endless first period. Time passed, with my begging for their attention, attempting to control their bickering and general chaos. We got through half of the roll in that fifty-minute class period. I was dismayed, dizzied with the energy and confusion in the room, stunned by how much of my energy it took to attempt to monitor them. Finally, the God-sent, the grace-sent, the miraculous: the bell rang. They sprang to their feet with more gusto than I could ever have imagined, and pounded their way out the door.

Period one. Day one. Year one. Webster Junior High School.

Webster Junior Whatever.

And essentially, it went downhill from there.

The first day, I met some teachers on my break period in the teachers' lounge, a depressing pea green room with a chipped metal table, a tiny refrigerator, a few battered chairs, and a window with bars on the outside. There was Janice, a wonderful African-American woman, there for too many years. She eyed my dress from behind her diet soda, smiled, and said, "Honey, they put mirrors in their shoe laces, to be able to look up dresses at your panties. I wouldn't wear a dress if I were you." That ended my foray into the mature shirtwaist collection. Carol, a hardened bleach blonde—a closet alcoholic, I would later learn, who was a few years away from retirement and tougher than the kids—was committed to keeping standards strong. James/Janie, a transitioning transgendered male to female, was charming and warm, a remarkable survivor in that environment of constant pandemonium and potential onslaught. They welcomed me, like survivors in a lifeboat pulling me in; they put me at ease, gave me caffeine, and sent me back out into the wild.

The absurdity of the days passed into weeks, months. I gained a slight semblance of effortful order, as some of the more terrorizing of students disappeared. We slogged our way through remedial workbooks, emphasizing capital letters, sentence structure, and basic punctuation. These kids certainly lacked the wonder and fascination that the students in the Philippines had always shown toward me. The kids in Mindanao would sit, stand on their heads—they'd have followed me to the ends of the earth if I'd asked them to. The Newark kids, in this age grouping and in this school, were in general untamed and unreachable; either they were wild and impossible to control, or subdued, tired, and disconnected. Either way, they didn't give one flip about me and what I was trying to teach them.

We trudged on with basic skills.

During the lunch periods, the sound of drums from the schoolyard penetrated the building. The Hispanic kids beat out their rhythms, claiming their space.

Where was mine?

I was bored out of my mind, but, since my marriage had ended, my unsuccessful heterosexual life closed, more important things held my attention. For the first time in my life, my professional expression took a back seat to the evolving and unfolding drama of my personal life.

The impossible had happened and continued to unfold—I was now spending endless evenings with Julie and our immediate gang. Flirting, politicizing, pot smoking, love making—all these things crept into the wee hours of the night, disrupting my suburbia sleep schedule. By the spring of that first school year, I would drive to Webster exhausted, making the twelve-mile drive out through the Holland Tunnel bleary-eyed. I began a pattern of going to the nurse's office during my free period at school, claiming any discomfort—headache, stomach ache, whatever ache—and lying down on the sticky leatherette couch, sleeping deeply until the next bell would awaken me. Keeping awake in class became the survival issue, these catnaps my saving grace.

Time peeled away. Julie's mysterious presence captivated me. We morphed seamlessly into a couple, attending all the politically correct events in our community—women only dances, rallies for justice, the ubiquitous lesbian potluck. Life was heady. I had a girlfriend. My family was pushed into a corner somewhere in my world. And my professional life was, in the words of Paul Simon, "slip slidin' away."

Unbelievably, the seasons melted into one another. I survived my first year at Webster, living through unending chaos and deadening boredom, but buoyed up by consistent paychecks that bankrolled my alternative lifestyle. I was a lesbian feminist, a radical, yet still I participated in the oppression of other people. Still I needed the paycheck, and secretly pretended that my presence made a difference there.

I spent a hot and giddily exciting summer in the City—the street fairs hopping, the pedestrians throbbing through the Village—living off my Webster paychecks. There was much to do, to explore, to enjoy in the women's community. The days were hot and sticky, the nights filled with excitement. I explored New York, myself, my newfound community. Too quickly, it ended, and, too quickly, another fall arrived. Another first day at Webster greeted me. For this one, however, I was wiser in the ways of the school. No shirtwaist, no evocative quote on the board. I met the kids strongly, put out my guidelines, and prepared to tough it out.

Some days worked better than others. On a good day, I got through my five teaching classes without incident. On a harder day, stronger confrontation met me. Daily I struggled with mind-deadening boredom and exhaustion. Try as I might, I couldn't even pretend that I was contributing anything. I was simply showing up, passing out workbooks, keeping everybody somewhat subdued, and slogging, slogging through.

Slip slidin' away.
You know the nearer your destination
The more you're slip slidin' away.

That second year, I had a double-period class, English 7-Remedial. It was actually a redundant title; English 7 at Webster already was remedial. This was remedial, squared. This extended class was to give these hard-pressed students not fifty, but a hundred minutes to dive into basics. This class unfortunately was directly after lunch, a disadvantage for the students and myself. It was beyond deadly. It was a 100-minute block of time that was unmovable, intolerable. From 12:30 to 2:10 p.m. daily, I descended into an adolescent cesspool of hormones, social issues, and post-sugar-filled lunch physiology. We were set up to fail.

The greatest challenge out of the twenty students was a tiny little boy named John Tisdale. He was wormy, squirmy, unable to sit still for a moment. He was jet black, had huge eyes, long skinny arms, wore ripped little short sleeved tee-shirts no matter the season, and had a lisp that threatened the vice principal's for first place. He wasn't a bad kid, he just couldn't stop. He couldn't stop: Moving. Talking. Shimmering. Whispering. Shaking his head. Mumbling to himself. He just couldn't stop. And for some strange reason, God forgive me, I needed him to stop. He had to stop. My job was to make him stop. And it didn't work. It only wired him up more.

I was tired and hung over from late nights and too much pot, numbed out from lunch, facing this double period, confused about Julie—who was she? What was our life together about? Facing this block of time with these twenty kids felt like life's most hellish punishment. Walking into Room 391 and facing them each day felt like a firing squad to my heart. I dreaded the time in body, mind, and spirit. There was nowhere inside of me that could have relaxed with these kids, with John, with this time. It felt like cinder blocks were strapped onto me. I was going down.

We tried turning off the lights, meditating, taking naps, having intentions, doing check-ins with each other, drawing our feelings, positively identifying success—every possible trick in the book of teacher-on-the-edge. Nothing shifted me or them. I felt doomed and deadened. And I am certain—by the age of twelve, they already knew they were failures. I was unable to change this for them.

One late winter afternoon, the light beginning to shift toward springtime, I grudgingly opened the door to Room 391. Julie and I had had a fight the night before—more like a battle of silence. We weren't talking to each other, all because of some misunderstanding about grocery shopping. I was exhausted. The room clattered and clanked, the heat in the ancient pipes grumbling its way free. I eyed the class cautiously. Everybody was in their place, a good thing, a positive start.

"Princess, please pass out the workbooks," I said stoically to Princess Jones, a chubby, adorable, slow-as-molasses girl in pink tights and matching jumper. Her round, cherubim face was ageless and ancient. As Princess begrudgingly handed out the tattered workbooks to her placid classmates, John, my John, my famous button-pusher John Tisdale, began humming. Humming was not a bad thing, not an evil thing, but with John, humming led to singing, which led to shouting, which led to screaming, which led to running around the room, which led to throwing things. Which led to teacher exhaustion. I had to nip it in the bud.

"John. Tisdale. Please. Stop. Humming." I recognized how ridiculous my voice sounded, how whiney and absurd a request it carried.

No response. John continued to hum, playing cars with his pencil and eraser, imitating the sound of engines revving up.

I was revving up.

"John. John. Tisdale. Stop. Stop. Right. Now. Stop. Humming." My request was absurd even to my own ears. If only I could have ignored him, continued along with the class. But I could not; I was stretched too taut, the container of my heart too constricted.

John ignored me with his usual placidness, increasing his game, becoming a bit more vocal than before. His cars now sounded like trucks.

"John. Put down your pencil. Now. John."

Why did I care if this poor, tattered little boy played with his pencil? Why couldn't I move along? I couldn't. Tragically, I had no capacity to be flexible, to allow him to be who he was.

And the rest is history—I accelerated, he accelerated. I demanded, he got louder; his trucks becoming locomotives; his locomotives becoming jet planes. He got louder, I got angrier. I got angrier, he got more manic. We danced around each other, this little boy and I, until finally, without even knowing it, I was chasing this child down the third floor hallway, around the corner, and down the back stairwell. I really didn't even realize it until I saw him, crouched on the floor in the stairwell, his arms shielding his face, looking up at me with terrified, wide eyes—a face that I will never forget. In that moment, I came soaring back into myself and realized, in that instant, that it was time to leave Webster Junior Whatever. Paycheck or no paycheck, retirement from urban teaching had arrived.

"Nan? Are you okay out here?" My friend Debbie who taught in the room down the hall had heard the ruckus. She peeked her head into the stairwell, looking at me with the strangest of expressions. I looked at her, I looked at John huddling on the

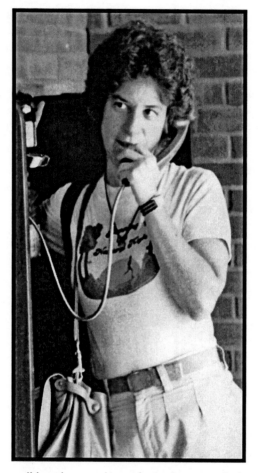

"I might as well have been speaking a foreign language. Perhaps I was…"
Taking a break at Webster Junior High.

floor and, finally, I was able to look at myself.

I gave notice that Friday in a cryptic letter to the Newark Board of Education. After several brief discussions, Julie and I decided we would leave the City and move up to the Catskills, where we had once visited. To cease my participation in this institution of oppression, to leave the City that subjugated so many and was good to so few—those were my political contributions to the planet.

Packing up my things beneath the loft bed on Christopher Street, sitting in the glow of the pasty yellow brick wall, I had a queasy feeling in my stomach. Was I excited? Or was I simply liberated? Was I awake for the first time? Or was I preparing for a very painful sleep?

I had no clue.

14

≈

The Country Life
1976

The tidy yellow farmhouse sat nestled into the palm of a grassy little hill. The pastures surrounding it were dotted with black and white cows serenely munching, and a working silo stood picturesquely to the house's left—a far cry from Christopher Street's erotic bedlam. The scene was perfect, this bucolic image of a sleepy Catskill farm: our new home. Little did I know that, come summer, that beautiful silo would emit the most god-awful of rotten smells that would stick to my hair, my clothes, my tongue, my nose hair, unmercifully following me everywhere. But, yet again, the externals looked good. Reality fooled me since it looked so right.

Julie and I had escaped the tyranny of middle class America. I had renounced my participation in Newark's racist, oppressive school system. Now I would live close to the land with my black woman lover, separated from the inevitable inequities of this classist, racist society. I was convinced that I was eligible for unemployment. Since I quit my job, I wasn't officially qualified. Yet I knew righteously that I deserved it, and that seemed leverage enough. I had some savings and a deep, virtuous belief in our motives. Julie would continue to live off her disability checks, a source of income that baffled me, since I wasn't exactly sure what she was disabled from. I hadn't the language to ask—

somehow it was a forbidden subject, like several others that were emerging in our lives. The longer we were together, the more things emerged that we just didn't talk about.

Like my family. She made it perfectly clear, without saying much, that I had a choice—my family or her. Of course I would pick her, my lover, knowing that I could keep my family in my life, at bay, pushed to the sides of my days. I was protecting her from my parents' inherent racism, I rationalized, from their classist beliefs and sanitized lifestyle, where things were more important than essence. It was a political choice—and I understood, as the woman's movement had taught me, that the personal was political. My political reasonings were shrouded in the cloudy denial of dysfunction. I couldn't see what I couldn't see.

We moved into the house in late fall, bringing with us Butchie, Julie's dear mutt of a dog from Brooklyn. He took to the Catskills' round little hills with ease and grace, liberated from the concrete of Brooklyn. At twenty-seven, I, like Butchie, was liberated, retired from the harshness of the city and from the black hole of inner city teaching. I saw this as my well-earned retirement.

The days were crisp that fall and filled with preparation. There was much to do for the quickly approaching winter: wood to gather for the fireplace, a contract to create with the oil company for backup heat, a neighbor to recruit to plow our driveway, the deep silence of the surrounding hills to adapt to, the little Catskills towns to explore. I began my unemployment paperwork with great focused diligence. We explored auctions on weekends. Julie became fascinated with hand-carved farm tools, her collection of them annoyingly taking over our mudroom.

The flow of my days was ease-filled—no more seventh periods from hell. I would wake, smoke a joint on the front porch to make the most of the new dawn, barely stretch, eat a breakfast of granola and soy milk, walk in the woods, pretend to write, and watch the cows. There certainly was an afternoon joint, and several evening ones, too, to maximize the experience. My Hawaiian bud, arriving monthly from my friend on Big Island and delivered by our friendly rural route mailman into the little mailbox on the road, was being put to good use.

Julie was always right next to me. We were a fused unit. She didn't smoke pot, but acquiesced to my usage. This part of my life was non-negotiable. I compromised everything else, but my drugs were not negotiable.

We had one car—Ruby the Volkswagen. Together Julie and I traveled the dirt roads of the Catskills that threaded the main road, Route 28. I drove; she navigated. I never left her side, nor did she, mine.

She was stocky and solid-bodied. Quiet and introspective, she hesitated thoughtfully before she spoke. When she talked, she tended to cover her mouth with her hand, which I found endearing. I later discovered that she did this to cover some dental imperfections. I never noticed her missing side teeth. Literally, I never noticed. After our relationship had crashed, one of our only two friends said to me, "And what was up with her teeth?" I was startled. Teeth? Strangely, I had never noticed any missing teeth. I could only see what I could see.

She was deep and brought a strong sense of political and social justice to any conversation. She was a perfectionist—whatever she became interested in, she immersed herself in fully. When fly fishing became her passion that first spring, she researched, talked to experts in the sporting goods store, and gathered extensive data. She purchased high-end equipment and practiced the art, taking Butchie and me to the many idyllic streams and running brooks between our little hills. I sat on the bank, bored and stoned, wanting to go. To go where? I didn't know.

I get ahead of myself.

That first winter embraced us in her gloriously snowy arms. Snow banks towered over our little dirt road, Dry Brook Road, and Ruby, her snow tires ominously rumbling, courageously made her way up and down from the little hamlet of Arkville. The nearest supermarket, an A&P, was in Margaretville about fourteen miles away, our regular pilgrimage. We built fires (Julie), did jigsaw puzzles (Julie), marched in the snow (I was urged to go). We watched the seasons unfold.

Yet all was not right in paradise, I unconsciously knew. In order to keep in touch with people, I had to create an elaborate secret phone code with the few people left in my life. To call me, one had to dial our number, let the phone ring the proper amount of time, and then hang up. Then I would call back. One ring indicated Karen, my friend from The Duchess, the women's bar in New York. Two rings was Carol, my New York painter friend. Three indicated Debbie, my friend from school.

Inbound calls upset Julie. Somehow she was threatened by them, even though the amount of people in my life was quickly diminishing. My parents didn't call. We had an arrangement—I would call them weekly from a phone booth in town, with Julie waiting silently and impatiently in Ruby, engine running. I allowed this to be because it was the price I had to pay for paradise, for my political statement to be lived, for my life's vision to be realized. *It's a small price*, I thought, in the hazy netherworld of my introspection, *for all this freedom.*

Freedom began to make me anxious. Although the spring-time was a glorious explosion of life and color, sounds and smells, hydrangeas exploding like luscious snowballs all around our house, I was uneasy. To my dismay, my unemployment claim was rejected. I was furious with the bureaucratic system that denied me my rightful due. I became obsessed with righting this injustice, and turned to a nearby liberal representative in state government to support my "case."

As time unfolded, Julie's responses to me changed. Although we were inseparable, we seemed to float in that togetherness, each in our own, separate world. The passion that exploded between us on Christopher Street in our coming together had cooled, but we remained welded together in spite of its diminishment. I didn't care. It was too hard, too much of a bother, to keep attempting to approach her intimately. My own world of fantasy settled in around me.

One soft summer morning, the gentle light in the day seemed to caress Julie's cheek as she sat at our fabulous oak table, purchased at auction for $87, as she patiently tied her fishing lures. My morning marijuana buzz hovered around me, supporting my dispassionate observation of her. I felt something so strongly— what was it? Was it love? Lust? Neither, I thought. It was a determined, stubborn, bound loyalty that fused us as one. We were a couple that the dominant culture couldn't accept. Damn it. We deserved our lives. We would make it work, no matter what.

She organized the perfect garden, buying all the right tools, sorting through all the right seed catalogues that clogged our table for many months. Every row of seed had its purpose, its place, its function. Like tiny soldiers, they stood at attention, growing toward the sky—the corn, the cukes, the leafy lettuce, and later in the season, the mutant pumpkins. I couldn't stand weeding, was essentially bored by the process. I smoked my pot, watched her work, and did the minimum I could offer.

Summer was intense—the smells coming from the silo appalled me. Amidst whatever was fermenting beneath its black plastic covering lurked a creature with a life of its own. I woke to its taste, walked in its stink, swam in its heaviness. There was no escape. It drove me mad. Try as I might, there was no exit.

My parents, their silent, unspoken concern heavy between their words on the payphone, were circumspect, quietly urging me to come home, to look for work. I shook off their attempts, lost in this perfect world of increasing imperfection.

The first rupture in my denial took place one cool fall evening, that first year. Julie and I had a minor disagreement— the only places we squabbled were the tiny, mundane corners of our lives. I wanted to go to town to call my parents—she didn't. Something happened inside of me; something simply broke. Sitting on our futon couch in the living room, I got up, started screaming senselessly, wordlessly, and went running out of the room. She caught up with me in the kitchen, stood in front of the door to prevent my exit, and turned toward the corner. There she wrapped her arms around my massive begonia plant, barely lifted it off its table, and smashed in onto the floor. I completely lost it, and pushed my way, howling, out of the house. I watched myself, an impartial observer, observing myself on my knees, my hands cupping my ears, eyes squeezed shut, trying to will away the moment. It was a particular, odd moment to notice:

Oh, look at me. I'm screaming. I'm crying. Look at me. I'm out of control completely. Oh, here is Julie now, running behind me, eyes wide, whites of her eyes expanded, opened bigger, it seemed, than might be humanly possible. Oh, look. Here is Julie now. She is grabbing onto my jacket, ripping, tearing destroying my favorite Air Force jacket with the orange lining, my pride and joy, with the cool epilates, ripping away at my sleeve, tearing at my sleeve, separating it from my jacket. Here is Julie, startled, stopping. Here

I am, sleeve disconnected, hanging loose and flapping about. Here I am, now silent, exhausted, alive again.

We stopped, stunned, looked at each other, flooding back into the present moment. It was as if we finally connected to ourselves and to each other for the first time in oh, so long. We fell into each other's arms, crying. We made our way up toward our bedroom. Our lovemaking had a drive and passion so long absent for us.

But this wake-up call did not change our behavior. Our individual isolation grew, our ability to reach out to each other or anybody else trickled to a stop. We lived on Dry Brook Road alone, an island of separation and loneliness. Her freak-outs triggered my freak-outs—mine, hers. Each was followed by reconciliation in bed.

Whenever I got upset, she would run outside and take the distributor cap off of Ruby's engine, stalling any attempts I might make to get to town, to walk the aisles of the A&P as if it were a haven, a refuge of connection. It enraged me, infuriated me. I could not contain my anger at this. I did not. Her behavior escalated the craziness, my senses blurred with fury. I felt so violated.

Our only escapes were monthly forays into New York City for Julie's allergy treatments. We would stay at her mother's exclusive Upper East Side apartment. Once inside the fancy lobby and carried to the twelfth floor in its elaborate elevator, the apartment door opened to the taste and smell of putrid dog pee. The apartment was clogged with clutter, filth, and turmoil, turmoil that obliterated chairs, that covered the sofa, that smothered choices for sitting or sleeping. The pee and poop of two ancient dogs eviscerated the fancy parquet floor squares, popping them free from the floor. I hated being there, yet had no language, no escape, no choice in my participation in the craziness, in the destruction that existed inside these women's lives. I fully participated, and, in the name of loving, agreed silently to destroy my own life.

Another season passed. My unemployment finally came through in the dead of winter, amidst its silent, pristine stillness. The checks came regularly now, delivered, along with my drugs, by our no-longer-friendly rural route postman. The locals couldn't figure us out, ostracizing us now, literally turning their backs to us at auctions, at the stores in town. *It doesn't matter*, I mumbled under my breath. *Fuck them.*

Yet their response to us was understandable, since we couldn't figure ourselves out. And it did matter. It mattered so very much. To be that alone, without community, without friends, without family, without work, without feedback and fun and others, deeply damaged me. I was a full participant in the destruction of myself, of Julie, of our possibilities together. I found refuge only in the billows of marijuana smoke that constantly surrounded me, its smokescreen cutting me off from reality.

Our violent outbursts increased. Either one of us might trigger the other. We switched roles in the dance of this craziness.

In the middle of our second year, our second winter heavy around us, my mood dropped to an even lower level. I trudged to the barn one sub-zero morning to start Ruby the Car who lived there, my breath heavy in the frozen air. I found myself muttering to myself, slogging through knee-high snow. Out of the frozen air a thought sliced through my denial, filling me up: *I must get out. I must. Get out. Of here.* It stopped me cold in my tracks. I felt both instantly ashamed of the thought and excited at its possibility. A seed was planted. Once in my consciousness, it grew, it spun, it blossomed. I could not stop imagining, plotting, scheming an escape. But, there was no way. There was no exit.

How could I possibly leave her? Both the logistical and emotional aspects of this were impossible. I felt as if I were in a prison of my own making, a successful, all-encompassing prison.

Weeks passed as I fretted February away. Muddy March, my second Catskills mud season, was grey, dreary, and damp, and it brought out the worst in me. My mood was foul, our physical struggles escalating. My exit plan remained feeble and un-formed. I felt hopeless.

We were going on our monthly journey to New York City for Julie's allergy shots. I had the idea of enrolling the help of our only friends: Carol, the painter, and Karen, the long-time waitress from The Duchess. We usually visited them in the Village during the evening of our stay. But how could I tell them? How could I elicit their support? Julie was always there, in the room, sitting next to me. I hatched a plan. While visiting at Carol's studio apartment on MacDougal Street, if Julie went to the bathroom or into the other room, I would give Carol a note asking for help. I shivered with possibility.

The ride down the New York Thruway was long, Ruby clicking her way toward the metropolis that had once held so much promise. Butchie the dog sat in the back seat, looking out the window at the grey morning. We were quiet. I went over and over the possible words of the note I would write, deliberating:

Carol. Don't say anything. Will call later. Need to leave Julie. Help me?

I felt terrified, my heart cold with deceit. We made our way to the Upper East Side, deposited Butchie and parked Ruby. I sat in the waiting room of the doctor's office while Julie got her shots.

Don't say anything. Will call later. Need to leave Julie. Help me?

Did it make sense? They couldn't really help, but telling them became essential to my heart. I wrote the note on a piece of small lined notebook paper in my bag. Once written, I folded it into eight squares, and shoved it down into the coin pocket of my jeans. I felt as if I were committing a crime. What if she ever saw it? What would happen to me? If I stayed? If I left? It was all unthinkable. Julie walked out of the doctor's examining room. I jumped up, jittery and guilty. She didn't seem to notice.

We had dinner with Julie's kind and dysfunctional mother, Edna, at a Japanese restaurant. The two of them chattered away about Julie's plans for a garden. My chopsticks felt heavy in my hand. What was I thinking? I felt miles away from the too-warm restaurant filled with yuppies and with us—whatever we were. We were a lie. This I now knew. We were a lie that would never end.

Sitting in Carol's little apartment that evening, idle chatter again surrounding me, I felt as if I were shivering with dread. Would I really go through with it? Carol's little Zebra Finch, Freddie, was singing away in his cage, oblivious, as they all were, to my deceit-filled suffering.

I must get out. I must. Get out. Of here.

And then, the unthinkable happened, the miraculous happened: Julie went to the bathroom. I dug into my pocket, my fingers struggling for the note. Finding it, I yanked it up and out, leapt up, and ran toward Carol, who was standing by the bird cage. I thrust the note into her hand breathlessly and quickly sat back down. I looked at her as she unfolded the complicated little note. Disbelief spread over her face. She looked up at me, eyes wide, and nodded wildly. We heard a toilet flush, a door slam, and Julie came back into the room. Carol and I were silent.

Later that evening we were back in Edna's apartment, preparing to sleep on a mattress on the floor that had been cleared of folded towels, old newspapers, shoes, and empty plastic shopping bags. I excused myself, saying I was going to use the phone.

This was code for *calling my family*. Julie squinted her disapproval, yet I headed toward the door, took the elevator to the lobby shakily, and rushed into the street. The payphone on the corner was empty, a gift and an omen. My hands shaking, I dialed Carol's number. The ringing haunted me. *Hurry up. Hurry up,* I willed.

"Hello?" Her voice was a question mark.

"Carol? It's me," I managed.

"Yes, yes, tell me, what?" she urged.

I started to cry. Between sobs, headlines dribbled out:

"...have to leave her...not good...fighting...bad...bad fighting...feel sick...all the time...can't get out..."

Karen was on the other line. Their validation, their quiet caring, their commitment to helping me was startling. The craziness I was feeling softened beneath their caring. They were not surprised! That amazed me. They imagined such things were happening. How could that be? They were committed to helping me, to figuring it out. Once I was back in Arkville, I would call Carol under the guise of calling my parents. I shakily hung up the phone.

Oh, my God. Somebody else knew. And. They would help.

Driving back upstate to Arkville that next day, I felt wrapped in treachery, a liar and a fraud. I couldn't look at Julie, for fear that she would know. I kept my eyes on the road and my breath under control. I was no longer alone. A plan was being hatched.

Over the next few weeks, my payphone calls, Julie waiting in the car, were coded, single-word exchanges with Carol. Her warmth and kindness brought tears to my eyes. She and Karen were committed, she kept repeating, to helping me figure it out. *Don't worry,* she said. *It will be okay.*

Over the calls, a plan emerged. It, my great escape, would take place during our next monthly New York City trip. I would drive down, business as usual. Once in the City, I would pretend to call my parents. I'd return to Edna's apartment aghast, and say that my grandmother was dying and I had to go to Scranton immediately. Julie would never consider coming with me, into the heart of enemy territory. Once I left, I would make my way back to Arkville, pack my car with whatever I could, and simply leave the rest. I would then go to my parents' house, and the next day I would call Julie and read a script that Carol, Karen, and I had concocted. Then, finally, I would be free.

It was tricky and it was huge. Could I do it? The month unraveled slowly, my planning taking up my every thought. Could I do it? I thought through each stage, each aspect of the escape, all the variables and possible obstacles. It was exhausting, frightening, and confusing. There was no going back. Maybe, just maybe...

The time finally arrived for our monthly trip to New York. I felt as if I lived in two bodies. One sat numbly next to Julie in the car, the other continued to rehearse every detail of this plan obsessively and constantly. Driving down the Thruway, Paul Simon's new song kept following us on the radio:

The problem is all inside your head, she said to me.
The answer is easy if you take it logically.
I'd like to help you in your struggle to be free.
There must be fifty ways to leave your lover.

Just slip out the back, Jack.
Make a new plan, Stan.
You don't need to be coy, Roy.
Just get yourself free.

Hop on the bus, Gus.
You don't need to discuss much.

Just drop off the key, Lee.
And get yourself free.

Art was imitating life. The song was haunting and threatened my cover. I was dizzy with worry and fear. Nevertheless, all the events unfolded as usual, as Carol and I had planned. Julie uneventfully went to the doctor. We had our usual dinner with her mother, who inquired about my silence. I told them I had a headache. Headache? I had a life ache. We moseyed back to the apartment, window shopping. The speed inside of me was breakneck. I tried to breathe. Back at the apartment, I looked around. I couldn't think about it. I had to just move the memorized plan forward. I prepared to go out to use the phone, as I usually did. Julie looked at me quizzically as I headed to the door.

I had practiced this moment dozens of times in my head, strategizing every single detail of this, imagining it, sensing it, living it. And now here it was, unfolding.

"Be right back," I offered.

First the door. I walked through it, despite her dissatisfaction. Then the elevator, holding my breath. Next the sprint to my payphone, calling Carol for a final check-in.

It all happened as we had planned it.

Carol's voice on the line encouraged me, urging me on. Back up to the apartment I went, entering with my guise. This was the big move, the key to the locked door.

"I have bad news." The door slammed behind me.

Julie looked up from the mattress.

"My grandmother." I started to cry, from fear, from the intensity of the lie, knowing that my Grandmother Katie was, at that very moment, probably sitting on her raggedy couch, reading *The Scranton Times* with her magnifying glass. I couldn't even think about my Grandmother Sonia as part of the lie. I had to keep her far away from my thinking, so intense was my devotion and my love for her. Oh! How I missed them both.

"I have to go."

A few legitimate tears.

"To see her before she…"

More tears.

Julie didn't disagree. I gathered my few belongings, stuffed them in my pack, hands shaking. She stood. I hugged her goodbye, taking in her familiar scent one final time. I couldn't think. I couldn't stop. I had to keep moving. I hugged Butchie the perfect dog, and said goodbye to Edna.

I walked, dead woman walking, toward the door. I opened it. It closed behind me. I walked to my death/my birth, the elevator sliding open, carrying me away. On remote control, I sprinted toward Ruby, safely ensconced on the side street, opened her door, tossed in my bag, and started sobbing. Hands shaking, I managed to get my key in the ignition. She turned over at my bidding. I navigated out of the tiny space, pulled into the stream of traffic, and headed for the West Side Highway. The escape route.

The four-hour ride upstate was a forever journey in fear and darkness. I was already shivering with exhaustion. I wasn't used to being alone, to driving alone at night. The blackness surrounding me was threatening, yet what I could see of the landscape, so familiar. The plan was working. I drank a tepid Diet Coke to keep awake and to keep moving forward. Finally, after an endless amount of time, my mind wild, I found myself driving up the driveway to our house, our sweet little pitch-black house. I unlocked the door to the mudroom, made my way over Julie's endless collection of farm tools, and turned on every light in the house, to bring me courage. I still didn't think I could do it. It was a little past midnight.

I ran to the closet, grabbed my suitcases, and started shoving clothes and books wildly and randomly into them. Not everything would fit—the canoe that I was still paying off, the chainsaw that I bought—who cared?

The problem is all inside your head, she said to me.
The answer is easy if you take it logically.
I'd like to help you in your struggle to be free.
There must be fifty ways to leave your lover.

The crazy song screamed in my ears. I worked all night, trying to be detached, non-attached, to sort through my life's possessions, to take what mattered, what would fit. To leave the rest. From sobbing, to stone-cold sober, to sobbing again, my responses shifted, making no logical sense.

Finally, near dawn, I was done. Ruby was crammed. There was no more room for another object. I stood in the mudroom, looked into the house. I had tried to tidy as best I could. I felt as if someone would come in, someone would discover me. Julie would find me. No, that was an impossibility. She didn't drive. She didn't have a car. Oh, my God, I was stranding her. *Oh, my God. Forgive me, Julie,* I whispered aloud to no one. *It's the only way I know to help us, to make us free. To make us well.* I took a breath and said goodbye to my dream of the country life.

More diet soda, as the new dawn saw me headed toward Pennsylvania. My parents eagerly awaited me—no questions would be asked, they said. The trip was long, the car moaned her way west and south.

After an endless amount of driving, there was my childhood house, standing quietly in the morning light. Beyond exhausted, I walked up to the silent front porch, put my key in the door. It clicked effortlessly open, as if I had never left it. Nobody was home. I walked in, a survivor from the war of my heart.

The house was clean, orderly, profoundly familiar. I had no tears left—if I had, they would have drenched the sanctuary that opened itself unto me.

There was a note on the refrigerator, our usual place of communication. In my mother's orderly script it said:

"Honey. We'll be back about 2:00. The zucchini soup is on the top shelf. Love."

I was home.

15

❧

This Time For Real
1976

We didn't call ourselves the Matriarchal Mischief Makers—
the 3-Ms—for nothing. This was serious business. Responding to
this oppressive, power-over hierarchy called the U.S. government
was our responsibility as radical lesbian feminist separatists.

I took my role in this Movement seriously. Since liberating
myself from my life in the country with Julie, I now understood
the downfall of our relationship as our internalization of power-
driven, patriarchal roles. That meant I was free at last to fully
commit to the Movement. My return to New York City and to
the lesbian feminist community was for real. I would commit
myself deeply and fully to the undermining of the structures and
"powers that be" to make room for womyn's ways, womyn's
process, and womyn's sensibilities. (We spelled it with the *y*, to
take the *men* out of our name.) It was inevitable. Womyn would
erode the corruption that was inherent in our culture, and bring
an end to racism, classism, homophobia, and lookism. And I
was part of that transformation.

The main post office in New York City was a pseudo-
impressive symbol of the federal government. It stood haughtily
on Eighth Avenue and 33rd Street, an imposing structure of faux
marble, imitation Greek statues, and ineffectiveness. I went there
monthly to pick up my delivery of Hawaiian bud, the purplest

of juicy marijuana leaves carefully wrapped in cinnamon sticks to avoid its detection. I was regularly appalled at the length of the lines, the slowness of the service, and the surly attitude of the public servants who attended the windows. I had no fear about receiving this illegal delivery, due to both the effectiveness of my friend in Hawaii, and the ineffectiveness of this absurd postal system, which my tax dollars unwillingly supported.

We had been planning for several months now to make our guerrilla graffiti attack on this symbol, this office of the post; to put our mark on it. At midnight, on Tuesday eve, March 19th, as coordinated after our reconnaissance of their security system, we would spray-paint the façade with the truisms of our Movement for all to behold.

Patti would drive. While we did the deed, Patti of the wild, spiky bleach blonde hair and intensely pierced ears would wait in her nondescript brown Ford Falcon, engine running—our escape vehicle traveling incognito as a regular citizen's car. The womyn doing the action, the sprayers, were a motley crew. Sue, tall, long-legged, and sharp-eyed, was a veteran of many guerrilla graffiti attacks. She was our coordinator, the mastermind who brought us together, laid out our plan, and who would guide us that evening. Meadow was another sprayer—she was young, soft face covered with soft brown curls, and lovely in her quiet, committed determination. She came from an upper class family in White Plains, renounced her academic career in an Ivy League school, and was committed to up-ending the systems that bestowed her privilege while denying it to others. I had a little crush on Meadow from afar, and found myself tongue-tied and a bit fumbling in her presence. Turtle-Dove, another veteran of 3-M evening actions, was a tiny, quick-moving pale woman, adorned with an abundance of earrings, beads, and bangle bracelets to embellish her usual outfit of denim work shirts and torn jeans. And I was the novice, the new kid on the block, a virgin to the world of guerrilla graffiti.

We met. We met and we met again. In true womyn's community fashion, we continued to meet. We met to discuss the discussions, to plan the agenda of the next meeting, to assess the effectiveness of the last meeting. We met to consider what to spray on the building, where we would write it and, of course, how we would write it. It was a true commitment just to keep up with the meetings. The meetings were long and passion-filled, always spiced with some marijuana or hash to enhance our perspective. I was the quiet member, always unsure of my particular belief or perspective. I took my cues from Sue and piggybacked on her opinions. That seemed safe, and safe I wanted to be.

I just wanted everyone to like me. However, as the day of action grew closer, I found myself less and less sure of my radical capacities. What if I couldn't do it? What if I couldn't spray paint?

My nerves had the best of me. Simply said, I was terrified. I had to do it right, to spray paint effectively, neatly yet with a radical and forceful air, to hide my fear from my colleagues, and to win their approval. Much seemed to rest on this evening.

My feelings continued to escalate. I chose to keep silent about my fear, not wanting to prove myself a weak link in our unit. But uncharacteristically, I continued to go to the meetings, my attraction to Meadow acting as an impetus. The weather was crummy, typical New York damp and cold, which seeped through my Adidas as I hiked to and from our many meetings.

Finally, the day arrived. We reconnoitered at Sue's loft on East 12th Street at 10 p.m.

I looked around Sue's loft, candles lit on bookshelves, Indian tapestries hanging on the uneven, bumpy walls. This was cool. The five of us sat on the floor sipping Chamomile tea from chipped mugs. We all wore jeans and dark sweaters, our coats and dark hats on the floor next to us, ready to don. Meadow looked pensive, chewing at her pinky finger cuticle with a detached air about her. As she absentmindedly flipped her lovely brown curls, my stomach did a flop. Sue had insisted that Turtle-Dove leave her jewelry at home. Without it, I hardly recognized her. She looked downright common in her denim, diminished without her gussied-up accoutrements. Sue was taller than a pole, standing straighter than ever. She was on fire with commitment. Patti, our driver, paced and marched the length of the tiny space and back again, ready to go. But the time was not yet.

We passed the hash pipe. I sucked hard, gaining my courage from every toke, or so I thought. Sue reiterated our intentions, our strategies. We continued to smoke the hash and reconsider and recommit to our goals—to deface the post office was to call attention to the façade of the U.S. government. Obviously its façade, like the façade of the post office, was misleading. Our calling was to shake it up, to call attention to its contradictions and lies.

We prayed, Sue leading us in an invocation of the Great Mother: *May She watch over us; May She guide us; May She support us.* We held hands and sealed our prayers with five minutes of silence.

I was sweaty, cold, and stoned. My hands slipped with moisture, which embarrassed me during the endless hand-holding. I literally thought those five minutes would never end. My colleagues appeared so calm and cool about the upcoming action, their roles in it. Not me. The hash made my right temple throb. The excitement was turning me silly—not a strong political platform upon which to stand.

Finally we were ready. We made our way out into East 12th Street. The East Village, its grimy streets and seamy grey silhouettes of buildings, was home turf for us. Here we were safe. We slipped our way toward Patti's car, practicing hiding in the shadows. Across the street, a gay man in a furry coat and leopard skin earmuffs walked a tiny black poodle dressed in a matching leopard coat. Both poodle and man looked askance at us. I giggled back at them, both man and dog, as fear and excitement built inside of me. We slid into the car. Sue shot me a look and I attempted to contain my misplaced giggles.

Patti enthusiastically gunned the engine, and the car leapt into forward movement. Sue was obviously pissed at her, too, as she settled into the shotgun front passenger seat. That was exactly the kind of clowning around that Sue warned us against. But containing that energy was challenging for me; Patti and I were giddy with excitement. Turtle-Dove, Meadow, and Sue, however, seemed serene as we coasted up First Avenue. As we practiced, we turned left on 14th Street, the wide block being our cross-street from east to west. Once we hit Eighth Avenue, which was fairly empty of traffic, we cautiously turned right, and began to creep uptown toward our target.

With each uptown block bringing us closer to our destination, my heart rate accelerated. With each green light signaling our forward movement, the flow of my sweat increased. All we had trained for was now mere minutes away. My pounding heart seemed loud in the silence of the car. Surely my colleagues could hear it! How embarrassing.

The post office loomed on the northwest corner. Patti slipped the car silently against the curb across the street, as so rehearsed. With our dark coats, our watch caps pulled over our heads, we did look, in the safety of the car, impressive. We put our hands together one last time in a baseball-team-like handshake over the back of the front seat.

"For the Mother," Sue offered.

"For the Mother," we repeated prayerfully in unison.

Each of us grabbing our two cans of spray paint, we opened the doors and sprinted across the street. There it was, the giant, massive post office, a blank slate available as a billboard for our political maxims.

My area to cover was the west wall running between the four lampposts on 33rd Street. I had studied it carefully. Now it was real. I had a neon green and a neon yellow spray paint can—my choices—one in each hand. Struggling to get their tops off, I had a strong need to urinate. Immediate urination was urgently needed, its signals flooding me with sensation. Hopping up and down a bit to gain control, I was baffled. Nobody had warned me about the possibility of urgent urination as an obstacle in radical political actions. I was on my own to strategize—not a strong skill set. Finally the cap popped off of one can, then the other. Holding one in each, as we practiced, pressure building in my kidneys, I faced the wall. The moment was now.

I squeezed the nozzle of the yellow can in my right hand, and a limp stream of paint trickled down my hand. Oh, no, why was this happening? Frustrated, I shook the can more violently, and tried again. Alas, only a whisper of gas expelled itself. I viciously vibrated the can, shaking it up and down and dancing with it, which seemed to help delay the pee urges. Finally a hissing stream of pale paint expelled itself from the tiny nozzle, momentarily blinding me. Success! My vision slowly returning in my right eye, I aimed the can at the wall, and began my predetermined scripting:

JU-ST-I-CE

My "j" looked funny, more like a "u" strangely. The "I" seemed oddly illegible. *I probably shouldn't pro/con my work now,*

I thought hastily. I could feel my underwear dampen with each letter. The thought hit me: "I'm scared pee-less!" I found this thought hilarious and started laughing out loud, making both pee containment and graffiti-writing even more difficult. Willing myself into focus, I began tussling with the green can, shaking it alive, loosening up its neon particles for the Cause. They released themselves, thank goodness, with more ease than their sister yellows. I tried to trace over the already written script, but I had started too high, couldn't quite reach above the letters, and found the word at a bizarre and unsophisticated angle. I did my best, getting some paint mist into my eyes and rendered myself momentarily sightless. I squeezed my eyes together, willing back vision. *Damn, it's hard to have a strong political position in this country,* I thought with annoyance. Meanwhile, time was ticking. I moved on to the next word, back to the base color yellow:

F-O-R

Okay, that went well. Looking at the "o," however, it did seem to kind of collapse onto itself. *Keep focused,* I internally insisted. I shifted cans and attempted to trace over the letters in green. It looked terribly messy from my perspective. *Maybe it will look better from afar,* I hoped.

And the final word, ah ha! Spraying, it took shape well, I thought to myself:

A-L

I garnished the green letters with yellow, stood back to briefly admire my handiwork. Sue's whistle interrupted my admiration. *Perfect timing.* I pivoted on my heels, smashing the half-emptied cans into the two side pockets of my pea jacket. I hopped and slithered and skipped down the steps, my bottom damp yet my heart liberated and victorious. I did it!

We all dove into the car within moments of each other, the

perfectly oiled machinery of the revolution. Patti gunned the car, then reined it in to a more respectable, less obvious saunter. We trotted past the post office, legitimate citizens out for an evening's drive. Inside the car, we hooted, we hollered, we high-fived, we congratulated ourselves and each other. Stashing our paint cans into a garbage bag, we drove east across 42nd Street, its bright lights dazzling us. We stopped at a street corner, and Sue stepped out momentarily to casually throw our garbage bag into a trash container. As she closed the door, we knew we were now safe. No evidence, no problem. We were delighted with our brilliance.

"Let's go back and look," suggested Turtle-Dove. "Let's see our work, come on."

Sue, a bit like a reluctant mother, had to be coaxed. We all worked on her, urging permission out of her. Finally she threw her hands up in the air and gave a tiny smile of acquiescence. Patti swung the car back west and we traced our steps, to enjoy our victory.

The post office looked solemn and quiet, our wild graffiti not instantly noticeable in the dark. As the car crept closer, we could begin to see the dramatic messages painted boldly on the walls: Sue's "*END RACISM NOW*" was profoundly powerful. Turtle-Dove's "*FREE ENSLAVED WOMEN IN CITIES*" was startling, breathtaking. As we turned the corner to view my contribution, my heart sank. My wall looked remarkably childlike, as if some kid had wiggled and scribbled randomly on it. But most horrifying was the message I had misguidedly written:

"*JUSTICE FOR AL.*"

Oh, no. My heart sank. The car got quiet.

I, in my exuberance, had misspelled "*ALL.*"

Nobody said much as we headed home to the East Village. I had pretty thoroughly wet my pants while running back to the

"Responding to this oppressive, power-over hierarchy called the U.S. government was our responsibility as radical lesbian feminist separatists."

car. I was trying to casually sit on my hands, to protect Patti's seat from telltale stains. Sue kept her eyes trained on the front windshield, while Meadow hummed under her breath. She seemed much less interested in interacting with me now, although truthfully she really wasn't all that eager to interact with me before my political, public misspelling. Patti pulled the car into a legal spot on East 5th Street, a miracle and a find, giving the car a legitimized home until Friday at 2.

I got out of the car awkwardly, trying to keep my wet behind away from the others, tucked beneath the hem of my pea coat. We casually bid each other farewell, knowing we had a pro/con meeting scheduled for 6 p.m. the next day.

Sauntering down the block, I turned the corner and burst into a run, an inspired sprint, an embarrassed explosion of energy. *How quickly can I run away from these women—I mean,* womyn— *and from this memory?* I wondered. I picked up speed, my damp behind cool in the evening air. I ran toward my apartment on 5th Street, where my Hawaiian bud and reruns of *The Twilight Zone* awaited me. *Well, maybe graffiti guerrilla actions aren't my thing,* I thought, sprinting up the steps to my apartment two at a time.

It was so difficult to know how to be helpful.

At least there was justice for Al.

16

The Lady Bulldogs
1981

The indescribable high-pitched humming of forty sneakers pounding and sliding and scuffing the polished hallway floor enveloped me. The twenty high school girls who owned those sneakers, whose feet inhabited them in this very moment, raced all around me. I was held in their center, snuggled into the apex of their force field, their momentum carrying me forward, encapsulating me in their energy. It was 4:20 p.m.—forty more minutes were left in our workout. We were the Fitness Club of Malcolm X Shabazz High School. I was its unlikely faculty advisor.

In actuality, we were the Lady Bulldogs basketball team. However, the girls' basketball team was not legally able to begin its training until six weeks before the season began. By calling ourselves the "Fitness Club," we got a jump on training, slid sneakily around the Board of Education guidelines, and would hopefully start the season with our players in strong physical shape. This was my friend Annie's idea—she was the senior gym teacher and head coach of the Shabazz Lady Bulldogs, and my lunchtime recreational drug companion. After teaching English at the school for four years, I was flattered by her invitation to be the advisor for the club, and felt as if I'd finally made it. Basketball was big at Shabazz. Now I was in with the "in crowd." It felt as if the popular kids finally liked me.

One more lap around the fourth floor, I thought, *God help me.*
Then we would stomp down the back stairwell, reconvening in
the dank, cinder-block gym for intense, lightning-quick stretches
and a tough-love pep talk, led by Annie and her assistant, the
science teacher/jock, Mona Harris.

Exhaustion was settling in, my lungs burning, my thighs
screeching in complaint. My noontime joint—the daily lunch
break ritual of my Malcolm X days was driving around Weequahic Park with Annie and smoking primo Hawaiian weed—had
long worn off, leaving me edgy and headache-y. A band of sweat
dripped around my scalp line and down the nape of my neck.
My legs were faltering, yet I took strength and forward motion
from the gallop of girls around me.

Finally, I thought, as we swung as a pulsating unit through
the doors of the back stairwell. In a decisive crescendo of energy,
we stomped down the urine-smelling steps and gushed into the
gym where Annie and Mona awaited us. I huffed myself over to
a wall and leaned, in desperate need of support. The players, out
of breath and sweating, took their reluctant places before their
coaches. They knew their workout was not over yet. Annie was a
stickler for precise stretching, and a hard-assed disciplinarian at
that. She was truly a bulldog, and an atypical coach—her fierce
commitment to the girls' development extended into other
areas, revealing itself in her dedication to helping them into
appropriate college situations. But on the court, her goal was to
make these girls the strongest basketball players they could be.
Much would unfold in these fifteen minutes before ending.

But not for me. My afternoon commitment was done. I
would hang on the periphery of the stretching, strangely ejected
from the silent intimacy of the run, trying to listen to the pep
talk while inevitably missing its subtleties. My difficulties in

understanding their verbal exchanges would haunt me, limiting my understanding and my work throughout my fifteen years in this community—I simply missed things that were said due to the speed and the thickness of the inner city dialect. I had much secret shame about this limitation.

I hugged the gym wall, my sweat burning my eyes. I knew the pattern of this part of afternoons, how I would slowly begin to fade away from the Fitness Club/Lady Bulldogs. Slightly forlorn and alone, I would leave quietly and make my way toward Route 280, which would feed me back toward the Holland Tunnel, my daily umbilical cord to my home in New York City.

No matter how close I felt to the players and their process, ultimately I was the white woman headed toward New York. The "white stud," as they called me behind my back, their ghetto term for lesbian. I was not of their world nor was I of their city. I never visited the projects in which most of them lived. I could never fully know them or their everyday reality. They were cordial to me, quietly teasing me a bit outside the confines of the classroom, opportunities that basketball afforded us. I loved them and walked the line between subtle and shy pandering for their approval and awkwardly attempting to maintain some professional boundaries.

Gathering my gym bag stuffed with my work clothes, I left the gym, hearing Annie's high-pitched, haranguing voice echoing behind me. I opened the heavy basement door, which flung open into the desolation of Johnson Avenue, the heart of the South Ward of Newark, New Jersey. Empty lots faced the ancient fortress of a school, the façades of once-noble apartment buildings streaking the grey sky. I was still sweaty and shaky from the run. And hungry. Oh, so hungry. I walked across the empty street to the vacant lot that doubled as the faculty parking lot for the MXS staff. We each paid Mr. Barnville, a neighborhood entrepreneur with a round Santa belly, $5 a month to "keep an eye out." By that time of day, Mr. Barnville was long gone from his folding chair perch in the back corner of the lot, as were most of the staff cars.

But not my Ruby. My humble Volkswagen faithfully awaited me, unmolested. She was not a car that would ever interest any potential car thief of this or any neighborhood. Her modest and well-used façade, her dented left fender, the rust that speckled her wheel-wells all made her comical to my students, yet safe on the streets of New York and Newark. To my lesbian feminist community, divesting from the material aspects of our racist and classist society was essential. My students, however, precisely the underprivileged people who lacked empowerment, ironically desired the very things that we who were "politically aware" disdained. Upscale cars like BMWs and Mercedes, leather coats, expensive shoes, remarkably gaudy jewelry—all were symbols of status and success to many in the Shabazz community.

I painfully coexisted between these two worlds of political consciousness and the realities of the underclass. I inhabited neither fully nor well, their contradictions a slippery slope for me. My downwardly mobile lifestyle, a just-functional-enough car, a $300 walk-through railroad flat on the Lower East Side, plastic milk containers as the major unit of furniture, a hand-me-down table or two from my mom—all suited me and filled me with justifiable righteousness. I was not "of the system." I was working within it, working behind enemy lines to help spark change, and, of course, to offer myself both an identity and a means of support. It wouldn't be until much later that I would see the impact of my drug addiction, my low self-esteem, and my fuzzy spending patterns as contributors to my marginal lifestyle.

Once snuggled inside Ruby, I took a minute to pull my pea coat around me, smoothing it beneath the seat belt, and cranked Ruby into life. She groaned her way into reverse, then forward we went, bumping down onto the emptiness of Johnson Avenue. Darkness was just settling over the neighborhood, pressing down on the shapes of its scattered buildings and numerous vacant lots with a blanket of grey filtered darkness, tinged with yellow from the street lights. It was an eerie and lonely moment.

I reached into my glove compartment and rooted around, left hand on the wheel, tactilely searching for my ride-home joint, another daily ritual. I found it, its paper-towel wrapper taped around its thick form. I swung onto the highway, leaving the Lady Bulldogs behind me, and entered the far right lane of Route 280, my funnel to the Holland Tunnel. I unwrapped the joint, found my yellow plastic Bic lighter, and took a breath. *Ah, good*, I thought. *God made marijuana*. I lit the joint and inhaled deeply, inviting the warm, familiar smoke to enter me, to fill me, to take me away. To take me away from the Lady Bulldogs, from Malcolm X, the community that was mine and not mine. To take me away from this moment of early evening, of damp darkness. To take me away from the contradictions and the unanswered/unasked questions of my life. To take me.

I smiled, feeling the drug creeping into my face and my fingers first, filling me up with its warm, sensual feel. I relaxed a bit, navigating Ruby more aggressively into the middle lane, now that my courage was reinstated, my energy renewed, my lifelong companion of marijuana re-invoked. I fiddled with the radio dial, found WBAI, the hippie, radical, viewer-sponsored "peace and justice" radio station, and relaxed. The ride home was uneventful, my trip through the familiar Holland Tunnel without emotional incident. Home awaited, vegetarian sushi from the Japanese restaurant on First Street for dinner. A night of MASH reruns and more pot would follow. My Jewish-lesbian political action group met on Fridays and Saturdays. Tonight I could "relax." Relaxation was a term of permission that I granted myself that included a trinity of goodies: take-out food, an abundance of drugs, and television. I would sink deeply into my mattress and pass out. That was the goal, a goal that lived just outside my knowing.

The Fitness Team continued their training that year, the girls getting stronger and more fit as they began to come together as a team. The official basketball season opened, and the Fitness girls hit the court. What a transition to behold. Their ease at basketball contradicted their clomping of feet in the hallway, their struggling with verb tenses in the classroom. There was brilliance on the court.

The team leaders emerged naturally. Adrianne "Ace" Bond, a senior in her fourth Bulldog season, was a sturdy, squarely built, dark-skinned girl. Her focused aggression on the court, her strength, and her perseverance as a defensive guard bore little resemblance to the quiet, subdued girl who sat daily in my fourth period class with downcast eyes. She brought a quiet leadership and maturity to the younger, more giddy and excitable girls. Shopaine "Shoopie" Horton was another star waiting to explode into the new season. She was small, fast, and dynamic in her movements—an amazing point guard with a jump shot that startled the heart. Her smile was a million-watt burst of luminosity that lit up the gym. More volatile than Ace, Shoopie was a firecracker of energy. And the other girls, Tamara, Toinette, Cora, Charlene, Tonya, and the freshmen, Arnethea and Monessa, created a pool of talent, a goldmine of hoops' possibility. I watched from the sidelines during practices, awed. No longer needed, I would stop by to watch, finding myself invisible to the action. I would fade away through the heavy Johnson Street basement door, my exit coming earlier and earlier each passing afternoon.

The season-opening game was against Weequahic High, a Newark rival from the next neighborhood. It was held in the Shabazz gym after school, supported by pools of hooting, howling students on either side of the bleachers. I sat in the second row behind the team, the bleacher seat uncomfortable beneath me. I felt awkward and strangely out of place without my roll book, my desk, and the shelter of my teaching role. The pasty science teacher, Mr. Delvechio, and I were the only white faces. The Bulldogs won, 47 to 12. It was an emotionally satisfying victory, but a boring game. The Shabazz girls were so skillful, they regularly won the city championship. They could easily squash other Newark high schools, whose girls' basketball programs were secondary and not prioritized. The Lady Bulldogs' real test would lie in their encounters with teams outside of Newark. The suburban schools had the resources, the staff, and the commitment to create strong girls' sports programs.

Our first real game was against the suburban high school in Garfield, a middle class New Jersey town. I would accompany the team on the bus for the sixty-minute ride to this other world. The girls clamored onto the bus after eighth period, gym bags in hand, keyed up for action. They were 7 and 0. No losses, three weeks into the season. It was quite the record, garnering the attention of the sports writers in the *Star Ledger*, Newark's daily paper, and creating buzz around the city. For the girls, it was an impressive and heady moment in their young lives. Annie and Mona, on the bus first, shushed the girls as they filed into seats. I slid into an empty seat behind some of the freshman players.

The bus angled out into Johnson Avenue and ungracefully chugged forward. Looking out the window, I watched Shabazz get smaller behind us, Ruby's faded red a patch of color in the grey parking lot. We were off toward the New Jersey Parkway.

The team's excitement was high. Annie did what she could to contain them, knowing full well what was waiting for them up ahead. They settled down for the ride, their eyes sparkling with possibility. The rocking of the ancient bus nauseated me. I had a headache, as I had so often these days. All the Excedrin I gulped didn't seem to touch it. I needed to get high, but not now. I tried to relax.

We slowly plodded down the Parkway, cars streaming past us. The girls found great glee in waving to the passing cars, to Annie's displeasure. She modeled decorum, and the girls eventually settled in around her guidelines, sitting back into their seats dejectedly.

Finally, after what seemed an eternity, since I knew this road so well but not this tiptoe pace, we pulled off the exit. The bus crept its way forward. Slowly, as we pulled away from the exit ramp, a suburban neighborhood began to emerge around us. Wide, generous lawns, large houses set back, rolling sidewalks, white houses with bright green shutters, colorful mailboxes—all the normal elements of a suburban neighborhood came into sight. The girls' chattering enthusiasm quieted, their energy releasing like air hissing out of a balloon. The bus became hushed with a new and different silence. They had just landed in another world.

Gone were the abandoned buildings, the vacant lots, the souped-up Mercedes cars blasting music as they cruised the street. Gone were the landmarks of their lives, the reality of their days in the ghetto of the South Ward of Newark.

I squirmed in my seat, containing a galloping urge to make it okay for them. I wanted to jump up and yell, "No, it's not what it looks like. It's empty, this privilege, this clean, sanitized version of life. Don't feel bad." But I didn't. Of course, I didn't. And of course, they felt bad. Or so I imagined.

For the older players on the team, this was a revisit to another world. For the younger ones, it might have been their first viewing of a typical American neighborhood, one that bore no resemblance to their lives. What might that feel like, I wondered, to Arnethea and Monessa, the younger girls? Was it like landing on Mars? My headache throbbed and kicked at me behind my left eye.

And who am I in this? nagged a far-off voice. *What do I offer these girls? What do I represent? What do I believe? Where do I belong?* In that moment, I didn't have a clue.

After another eternity of silence, the bus snaked its way into a large, paved parking lot that stood next to the high school. The school was a new building, red brick, low-slung and modern, bearing no resemblance to the upright, ancient façade of Shabazz. The bus stopped with a shudder and, strangely, nobody moved. Annie stood up in the front and turned to face the girls.

"Okay," she said, clapping her hands and startling them into alertness. "Okay, we talked about this. You can do this. You are good, amazing players. Go out there and be bulldogs. Let's go."

The girls got up from their seats, reluctantly pulling their gear from the overhead racks. So much of their enthusiasm lay behind them, left somewhere north on the Parkway. One by one they exited the bus. I waited my turn, feeling shivery and frightened. Despite being a thirty-three-year-old inhabitant of this world called Middle America, I nevertheless felt shaky and afraid.

We walked down the gauntlet of tall, clean lockers, the wide, empty halls touched by the early evening light that floated in from high windows. The girls seemed to hardly look around as we headed toward the locker room designated for them. They trudged through the door halfheartedly, with Annie and her staff shooing them in. I stood outside in the hallway, trembling a bit with the discrepancy of it all.

I wandered around and found the gym. It was a huge, open-spaced facility, surrounded at the top by massive glass viewing windows. Nothing about this resembled the MXS gym, with its graffiti, its cinder blocks, its foul old-lunch-and-urine smells. I felt helpless.

Over the next hour, I wandered the manicured school grounds while the teams practiced. By 6:00, the gym bleachers had filled up and the girls from both teams were on the floor warming up. The referees, two white men in their striped shirts, looked noncommittally around while bouncing the game balls. I sat a few rows behind the Bulldogs' team bench. Two dozen Shabazz parents and fans had made their way down to support the team. I sat huddled in the middle of them, with them and apart from them.

The opposing team was on the floor in their teal blue uniforms. They were white, strong, and confident, and appeared to have a good time running through their drills. Their coach, a trim young white man in chinos and a button-down blue oxford shirt, walked the sidelines encouraging them, brushing his sandy hair from his face. Their fans filled up their side of the bleachers, outnumbering us by hundreds. They were, to a person, white. The folks on our side were black. But for me.

The teams were introduced, each Garfield girl receiving huge cheers. Our girls, splendid and slightly gaudy in their black and

Malcolm X Shabazz High School—Home of the Bulldog

"We were the Lady Bulldogs basketball team."

gold, were wildly acknowledged by us, but our voices were tiny, lost in the huge open space. The jump ball was tipped—Ace got the ball, passed to Shoopie, who dribbled down court wildly. Out of control, she tripped, and lost the ball. It was picked up by a Garfield girl who passed to a teammate near the basket. The ball sailed in. The crowd erupted. The game had begun.

It was downhill from there. The Bulldogs were sloppy, their usual ease and fluid skill nowhere to be found. Annie, in her black and gold sweats, was furious, focused, yelling at them from the sidelines. I sat frozen to the bleachers. I almost couldn't look. It was too painful to see their glorious skill inhibited, their inherent brilliance dimmed by these pale white girls. Near the ending of the first half, the Bulldogs got within a 4-point deficit, the closest they got to their rivals that day. The game ended with a final score of 52 to 38. The mighty Bulldogs had fallen.

The bus was hushed on the ride back to Newark, the Parkway dark and silent. One young thin girl—Monessa, the freshman—was sitting by herself, quietly crying. Annie marched over to her, hunkered down in the aisle, had a few strong words, and moved along. There would be no tears that night. Annie would not allow it. There was work to be done, drills to be practiced, shots to be perfected. There was no space for grief.

The bus finally pulled in front of Shabazz at almost 9:00. The girls seemed to disappear into the night as they walked away from the bus and into the thick darkness.

My ride home to New York was silent, too. No music, no radical politics on WBAI would comfort me. The sound of Ruby's wheels hummed beneath me, whispering of my questions unasked, my frustration unfelt, my responsibility unacknowledged. I tried in vain to get high. It didn't work. I looked toward the lights of Manhattan and toward that which I called my home.

17

Powerless On First
1986

The Manhattan humidity clung to me in slimy rivulets, slithering down my back in streams of clammy dampness. As I trudged up First Avenue, I imagined the heat radiating off the sidewalk could almost hold me upright. My body leaned exhaustively into this blanket of heat as I sliced my way through its sticky density. The deep rumble of buses, the lighter, higher screech of taxis, the subterranean groan of the distant subway on Second Avenue, the mixed pitch of people—all joined together in a cacophony of craziness that screamed and clamored for my attention, that ached and pulled at my head.

The light hurt my eyes and I squinted, as a dull, hung-over throb behind my left eye—always my left eye—reemerged into my awareness. "I'll do a coffee enema when I get home. That'll help," I thought, shifting the white cloth bundle of laundry onto my other shoulder. "Could this be any harder?" I groaned my wordless response to myself. Two more damned blocks to home.

It was August in Manhattan, a month when anyone with money or sense evacuated the island for points cooler, quieter, and calmer. I, on the other hand, had neither. My summer paycheck was gone. Rent, drugs, a trip to Hawaii to see Dina—whatever—had eaten it up. What was left was minimal, just enough to get me through till school opened, until my first paycheck.

To get me through.
To get me through.
Just enough to get me through.
The mantra whispered, hissed itself menacingly to me.

Getting through had become harder that summer. Well, maybe that past year. My headaches were more violent, with accompanying nausea, their pain riveting, debilitating, and fully overwhelming. The drugs and alcohol were significantly less effective. I could hardly get a buzz. It was crazily and maddeningly impossible to get stoned, the cosmic irony of ironies. Zena, my on-again, off-again lover, was even more of a pain in the ass, unwilling to be "tied down," to commit to time with me. "Damn her," I mumbled to no one under my breath.

I trudged on.

Finally, my building. Rebalancing the laundry, I reached over toward the heavy green door. Its fake brass handle was sticky and dented. It opened with a shudder and a groan. And now the real haul began. Four flights up the grimy grey hallway, each step emerging at an irregular, awkward, and challenging height. Puffing on the first landing, the smell of garbage assaulted my nose. *Keep going. Trudge on. Trudge forward.* I stumbled under the dead weight of the laundry, weeks of underwear and socks and tee-shirts, just a few hours ago scattered throughout my apartment like patches of colorful prayer flags on a desolate, grey sea. I had swept them up into my arms in a frenzy of weepy, determined activity. Under the guise of "tidying up," I had created this insane venture into clean laundry-land. Unfortunately I had forgotten about the trek *up* the steps.

It would never end, this upward forced march, this march of tears, this march of angst and agony. I faded in, faded out, faded in again, sweat and heat and hung-over pain plaguing me.

It would never end. Step after fumbling step led me forward, my legs shaking, my feet tentative.

Finally and somehow—I made it. Senselessly I found myself on the fourth floor, my apartment door confronting me. 4-F. Mable's door, 4-G, was almost touching my back in the V of the building's corner. Oh, a sigh of exhausted relief. The smell of Mabel's cooking stung at my nose. Garlic and grease floated on the hot air. The dead body of my laundry slid off my shoulder with a thud as I fumbled for keys. Keys, so many fucking damn keys. Ah, the big key, bottom slot, click click. Next key, security bolt, clack clack. Openings, clickings, clackings, so much to make happen, the door finally budged beneath the push and weight of my insistent hip. I chucked the laundry onto my kitchen floor, where it would lie barren and unattended for the next week, an uninvited visitor in the chaos of my life.

I flung myself onto my platform bed, landing with a thud, not unlike the weighted, muffled sound made by my laundry hitting the hallway. The sun streamed through my streaked window, the fake purple "curtain"—really just thin material cut to approximate size in a domesticated winter attempt at homemaking—almost intensifying the glare of the light. I closed my eyes and shuddered. Nothing to do until tonight, until my maybe-date with Zena, a date we had been bickering about and negotiating around for a week. I reached for my migraine medicine, which sat on the plastic milk carton that functioned as my night-table. I popped three in my mouth, and washed them down with the leftover dregs of a warm beer that also sat on the fake table. The beer was vile, flat, and almost nauseating. I groaned again, and rolled over, shielding my eyes from the light with the ineffective barricade of my forearm.

"Well, I don't care anyway," I mumbled. "I can get through

this day. I'll see her tonight. That will be good," I said, knowing full well that "good" was not an adjective I could accurately ascribe to my relationship with Zena. She was also in a monogamous relationship with Alexis, an absurd phenomenon that baffled all of our individual and couples' therapists. She was probably the only lesbian feminist in couples' therapy with two separate lovers, with two separate therapists, working on issues of monogamy and commitment. We divvied up weekends, holidays, and special events, attempting equal coverage, equal dating time. It was the fuel of my insanity. It drove me crazy, the rush and push and pull to get her attention, her commitment, her presence, her love. I hated her and loved her and cursed her for the struggle. Yet I needed like air in my lungs that very struggle for her love. It defined me. Its insidious insanity nourished me.

"I'm a schmuck," I grunted aloud. The sound echoed down the long, narrow walkway of my railroad apartment, a space long enough and skinny enough to be morphed in my imagination into a swimmers' lane. High and long streaked windows lined the outside walls, filling the space with unwanted afternoon light.

"What the hell. I might as well get high. What else is there to do?"

I remember finding my hash pipe. I remember holding the purple Bic plastic lighter to its hungry mouth, the flame greedily licking away at the chunk of hashish living inside. I remember laughing, the room spinning, my nausea rising, my awareness dimming. I remember nothing after that.

When I came to, the room was dark, the never-ending sounds of First Avenue still moaning inside the apartment like a coyote whining at the unresponsive, unimpressed moon. I seemed to be face down, strangely enough, my left cheek plastered against the floor. *Ouch.* I moved my face to the other side. My cheek felt brush-burned and raw.

My back hurt badly. I attempted to shift my weight, but moving was counter-intuitively impossible. I groaned again and bile rose in my throat, choking me. "What? What happened?"

I felt bad, really desperately and deeply bad. The ache in my eye was intensified, glowing with heat and electricity and energy separate from my own. It pounded and punched away mercilessly at my eye. It had its way with me, this pain. *It won,* I thought. *The pain won.* My stomach flipped at the thought. The weight of my head was dense, bowling-ball-heavy, and overwhelming. I could not even remotely imagine picking it up. Since there was nothing else to do, I started rocking my head from side to side, thumping each side with the floor of my middle "reading room." The reading room's sole furnishing was the green plastic rounded chair from my mother's Arthur Avenue porch, offered to me in a quiet, maternal way long ago, when I had first moved into this apartment. The skinny leg of the chair lurked in my peripheral vision, an anchor of steadiness.

Perhaps the rocking would take away the pain. It made as much sense as anything else in my world. From side to side I continued to rock, my head moving with its own weight, the north side of the floor higher than the south, as only the Lower East Side of New York could offer. I must have passed out again, slipping through the veil of consciousness.

Whenever I came to, I continued the rocking of my head. I faded in and out of consciousness, the rocking being the only consistent thing, the movement from north to south. The pain in me was physical and emotional and throughout my being, unending and ruthless. And then the thought that changed it all—and then the key to the doorway of freedom:

"I can't do this anymore."

I spoke it aloud to nobody. I wasn't even sure what "this" referred to. I didn't even know. Was I talking about Zena? About banging my head? About drinking and drugging? About carrying laundry? I didn't know.

"Help me." There. I said it. My truth, from the desperation and depths of my soul, was voiced, spoken aloud.

I spoke to nobody. I spoke to everybody. I spoke to nothing. I spoke to everything. I simply uttered, for the first time in my life, the voice of the excruciating agony in which I lived.

And everything around me and inside of me shape-shifted, shimmered, softened, and changed.

A quiet came over me, enveloping the room. A lightness touched me and held me close. I stopped the rocking, and started to cry, a child's cry, a baby's cry, a cry of longing, a cry of need. Something held me, something tender, something new yet deeply familiar. I staggered to my knees, and then, remarkably, to my feet, holding on to the wall. Although I was shivering from inside out, a gentle warmth safely and softly surrounded me, a clarion call beckoned me, an energetic doorway opened both before me and inside of me. And I knew it. I knew it had changed. I felt cleared out, awakened, and almost revived.

I staggered to the bed, crawled under the comforter, and curled up into a ball. I floated away. I slept soundlessly, dreamlessly, and motionlessly, the sleep of a baby, the sleep of a newborn, the sleep of an innocent. I flew away on the wings of breath. I was granted a perfect rest. I slept deeply and uninterrupted, for the first time in months

I slept for fourteen hours and awoke into a new world.

18

To Be Thankful
1986

Living without drugs and alcohol was like inhabiting a vast, empty wasteland of nothingness. My first weeks of sobriety had been profoundly strange and disorientating. I didn't want to drink or drug during them. Somehow that urge had been strangely lifted, taken from me on that hot summer night in August. I just didn't really want to be here. Not that suicide was a thought. That would take too much energy. I just didn't want to be *here*. Or anywhere. I didn't know what to do with myself. Getting high had taken up so much of my daily schedule for so long; it launched and literally book-ended so many of the activities that filled my life. I was lost, un-tethered without it. Going to AA meetings gave my day a destination, a center. I had little idea of what the people were talking about in the meetings, but going there was all that was left for me. Although I was working—school had started in early September—my time at work, like everywhere else, was a holding on, a waiting, lag time between meetings.

In school I would wait all day for the 2:32 final bell. My classes were a blur of movement and faces. I managed to contain the kids and set up the lessons, but mostly, I waited. I waited for that final bell day after day. Once it blessedly rang, I would rush out of school, steering around clumps of students, hop into Ruby for the 11-mile flight down the highway and through the Holland Tunnel, navigate the uptown blocks wildly, park on my street with its generous police station parking regulations, and sprint the two blocks to St. Mark's Place, where the daily 3:00 meeting had just begun. Panting, I would slip into my seat, trying to be inconspicuous. I didn't know why I kept going to these meetings, but there seemed no other choice. There was nothing left, nothing left to do.

I had "resigned" from my Jewish lesbian separatist political group at the end of the summer. After my first week sober, I went with dread to our usual Friday night political action group, a combination of Shabbat service and political discussion/planning session. Sitting there on the floor of that East Village tenement, the realization hit me like a weight slamming into my body—I couldn't be there if I were not stoned. It was that simple. Without being high, it was all too confusing, too intense. The rhetoric and the interactions were too much. If I were going to change my life, as the people in the meetings said, I had to change my life. Although AA people also suggested "no major changes in the first year," I somehow intuitively knew that I had to leave this family, this group that defined me, that loved me, that limited me. It seemed obvious. I told them I would not be coming back, that there was something else that needed my focus. Nobody protested very strongly. These people—the only three left in my life at the end of my drinking and drugging career—evaporated around me like an untouchable, irretrievable flimsy mist.

I was alone. There were people everywhere—during the day at work, at the meetings in the afternoons and at night. But I was alone. In my entire life I had never felt the deep level of separation that surrounded me. It was excruciating. And it was okay, too. It just was. Like a heavy cloak, I simply wore it.

They said in the meetings, "Just don't pick up. The feelings will change." They explained how the drugs and alcohol had covered up the feelings. I wasn't sure what this meant, but I continued to be driven to attend meetings.

Coming from my separatist background, the hodgepodge of people there was overwhelming. Straight women, gay men, heterosexual men, bisexual people—they were all new breeds of the species for me. I tolerated the differences somehow, surfing through my culture shock. Strangely enough, I was beginning to become interested from afar in what they were saying.

I didn't say anything to anyone in the meetings. Nobody made a fuss over me or seemed to even notice me. It was as if I, another drop of water, found a perfectly fitting place in the vast ocean of sobriety. If there had been much notice made of me, I would have bolted. Space just silently opened for me. I was barely able to terrifyingly introduce myself in the beginning of the meetings, along with other people "counting their days to ninety." My heart would hammer, my throat would tighten, my breath falter. Somehow, at the chairperson's nod, I would stutter out in one explosion, "Hi, I'm Nachama"—using my Jewish lesbian name that I'd proudly claimed years before—"I have forty-five days sober." The applause that followed my introduction was strangely about me, and not about me at all. It was an acknowledgement, a celebration of the program, they said.

Although I didn't fully get it, I just kept going.

By early November, I was relaxing a bit at the daily St. Mark's Place meetings. I recognized the cast of characters. Folks would nod to me as I entered. I felt my approach to ninety days with strange glee. My three-month celebration would be November 27th, right on Thanksgiving Day. I was on the downslide, heading toward it. I had asked Stephanie, a benign, non-threatening gay woman, if she would sponsor me. Although I didn't call her much, I saw her at meetings and we talked. She was generous with her time and spacious with her suggestions. As awful as I felt, awkward, uncomfortable, and young, it was so much better than what I felt when I was using. It was a beginning, she told me.

In early November, I began to notice a vivacious, sexy woman in the Saint Mark's Place meetings who was also counting her first ninety days. Unlike me, however, she seemed gregarious and happy. She was round-figured, wore hot, scoop-necked tight tops, long skirts that swished when she walked, and lots of silver jewelry—bracelets, rings, earrings, everything. She was fully bejeweled, in an appealing, East Village, counter-culture type of way. She had a way of flicking her head when she laughed that captivated me. And her laugh started as a low growl that erupted into sunshine. Her laughs grabbed at my belly. She was certainly not gay, this woman named El. But she was hot, and she began talking to me after the meetings. We struck up an unlikely friendship. She was probably the first straight woman to whom I related outside my family and minimal contact at work.

She teased me, calling me Knocky, short for Knockwurst. It certainly wasn't a name I would want to be called, but she said it in such a beguiling way, such a flirtatious way, that I laughed along with her. Our conversations after the meetings became longer, although without any noticeable content, stretching out into the coffee shop across the street from the meeting. I was mesmerized by her energy and flattered by her attention.

A few months before, she would have appeared to me as the enemy. I would not have spoken to her. And now, when she looked my way at the meeting, or put her hand on my knee under the table at the coffee shop, my heart leapt—as did other organs in my body.

One rainy mid-November night, sitting around our usual small table in the back corner of the coffee shop, having one of our typical talks about nothing, she leaned over toward me and casually put her tongue in my ear. She swirled it around a few times, exploring its contours. My breath stopped. As abruptly as it began, she withdrew her tongue. I was startled, embarrassed, and excited, unsure of the next step. She sat back into her chair and said whisperingly, "So, do you want to?" Her voice was throaty and deep.

I was speechless and clueless. She was heterosexual and had a clue. What was happening here?

"Um." My voice sounded young. "What? What do you mean?" I was buying time, trying to still my pounding heart and my highly activated lower regions.

She laughed another full-bodied guffaw and then looked more seriously at me.

"Come home with me." Her eyes were veiled.

Oh, my God. *But it's a school night*, I thought to myself, *and you're straight*.

"El, but, aren't you…" I stammered, "…don't you—sleep with men?" I didn't say: *But aren't you the enemy? Don't you sleep with the real enemy, men, and, by doing that, don't you contribute to the classist, racist, homophobic society that is destroying the world?* Once I thought I believed that. I had no clue what I believed in this moment. Everything was different now.

She laughed as if this were the funniest thing on earth, and snuggled closer to me. "Dear, I sleep with whomever I want to sleep with. And I want to sleep with you."

She wanted to sleep with me? It was thrilling and horrifying. The response coming out of my mouth shocked even me.

"Well, yes, of course I do." Did I? "But I can't. Not tonight."

Completely uncool.

She laughed as if *this* were now the funniest thing on earth. Then she got serious and leaned back toward me. "Well then, when?"

When? Holy shit. She was like nobody I'd ever been with, nobody I'd ever known. When? I was drawn toward her while wanting to run for the hills. The next statement coming from my mouth amazed me:

"After I talk to my sponsor. Saturday."

After I talk to my sponsor? Where did that *come from?* The truth was, as attracted to this woman as I was, I was terrified.

El was like no other woman I had ever been with. In the world of lesbian feminism, women (womyn? I didn't know what I believed any more, nor how to spell) would meet, exchange their life stories, their world views, their political and ethical beliefs, explore relationship with each other's pets to make sure of compatibility…and then bring the moving van. Someone would always move in with the other. Serial monogamy was the structure of the lesbian community that I had inhabited. I was operating in a brave new world. Was this the bridge back to life that AA talked about?

I did talk to Stephanie, my somewhat lenient sponsor, who suggested I go slow, practice my program, keep it simple, get to plenty of meetings, and take it one day at a time. I interpreted that all as: I do what I want.

El's apartment was a perfect reflection of her—gauzy and flimsy hanging materials covered the walls, beaded room dividers hung in every archway, thick incense filled the space, and deep piled carpets ate up my shoes. The general vibe was one of sensual opulence. Her bed was round and bedecked with a few dozen throw pillows. The sheets were blood-red and silky.

I was on those sheets. It was Saturday.

She was wearing a Madonna-like underwear contraption that baffled me, one that my lesbian feminist cohorts would scoff at, before declaring me traitor. We were of the flannel-sheet, flannel-shirt crowd.

Quite frankly, there wasn't much foreplay. There was some kissing, some rolling, some minimal sucking of necks. Very soon into the experience, El stopped, pushed me off of her, and breathily asked:

"Do you want me to come now?"

Nobody had ever asked me that before. I pondered the question for a moment, realizing I had absolutely no idea how to respond. I wondered what the right answer might be. My silence was prolonged, I realized. She looked expectantly at me.

"Sure," I casually offered, figuring I had a 50 percent chance of hitting the right response.

The rest of the evening was a blur of sensations, fumblings, and self-conscious attempts at connection. Hours later, slowly walking away from her 23rd Street apartment as I wandered home, I had enough sense to go the few blocks out of my way to attend the midnight meeting on Saint Mark's Place. Sitting in the room, still smelling El around me and on me, I sank into the swell of AA. I was perplexed. Perhaps lesbians were more into the journey of the sexual experience than the destination, as El seemed to be. And certainly feminism insisted that each woman have power over her own orgasm. But this was a new world. I was seemingly sober and got to sleep with a hot woman. There was nothing wrong here.

We had made a date for Thanksgiving.

A cloud of loneliness swept over me when I thought of the holiday. I missed my friends, my wacky and dysfunctional community. They were appropriately gone now, yet my new life was not formed. Going home to my family in Pennsylvania was not an option yet. It was too soon. Maybe El? Maybe she was someone I could be with up ahead? I needed someone to get through the holiday. I needed a place to go, somewhere to belong. El would cook the turkey, I would bring pies. That was our agreement, our distribution of tasks. There was talk of a friend or two of hers coming, too. And who knew what else might unfold?

Time tumbled toward Thanksgiving and my three-month anniversary. The kids at school were incrementally more wacked out as we approached the upcoming holiday, making focus and control, always an issue, even more of a challenge. My freshmen classes were beside themselves with excitement, in celebration of the holiday that honored the white men that stole the land from native people just like them. *Go figure*, I thought, busily passing out worksheet after worksheet to keep them occupied. It was officially the Thanksgiving countdown.

I planned and re-planned my pie contribution. After great and obsessive consideration, I ordered three pies from Balducci's, an upscale store in the West Village. Since I couldn't decide what kind, I would bring all my favorites: an apple, a blueberry, and a pumpkin. After all, opulence was the theme. The price was startling and outlandish. *But what is the price of connection?* I rationalized. I would pick the pies up Wednesday night after work, and have them ready well before 5:00 on Thanksgiving Day. El and I confirmed our date once during that pre-Thanksgiving week via voicemail. I didn't see her at meetings. I was excited and scared about the great adventure that day of gratitude might bring me.

Thanksgiving morning dawned with icy, sleety rain, everybody's favorite Macy's Day Parade weather. The morning was endless. I paced up and down the skinny strip of flooring that was my apartment, fretting about the day, trying to care about the parade quietly raging on my television set. I was anxious about the pies, her response to them, about what to wear, how to appear. Would there be sex again? Could I perform as she needed me to? It was a long and miserable morning.

I bundled up inside my raincoat and, as was my plan, traipsed the three blocks to the noon meeting. It was packed with familiar and not-so-familiar faces. I found a seat in the third row, settled into the infinitely uncomfortable yet familiar folding chair, and waited for the moment. The chairperson, a stunning, large black man wearing an outlandish red-and-black-checked hunting hat—the East Village was always full of surprises—asked for people counting days. I raised my hand proudly into the air of sobriety, found my voice, and announced, a little more confidently than usual, "Hi, my name is Nachama, and I have ninety days clean and sober." The place erupted with shouts and applause. I tried to soak in the waves of good cheer offered by perfect strangers rooting for my health and recovery. The chairperson gave me a purple medallion that said, "TO THINE OWN SELF BE TRUE." I clutched it in my sticky palm throughout the meeting, trying to remember my life three months ago. *It was so different then*, was the refrain that my mind was humming. *So different then.*

Was it? Did everything change? Or did nothing change? I remember lying on the floor of my apartment, banging my head. I remember the heat, the humidity of the day. I remember the headaches. What did three months even mean? Who am I now?

I had no idea, but I had a hot date for Thanksgiving.

The meeting ended with a scraping of chairs, a rush of fellowship, and a grasping for hands as we gathered in a large, irregular oblong circle for the Serenity Prayer:

Grant me the serenity
To accept the things I cannot change,
The courage to change the things I can,
And the wisdom
To know the difference.

Clumps of folks lingered; some dispersed, off to their Thanksgiving celebrations. Some people were staying here, helping with the buffet that was being offered, a free Thanksgiving meal for all. The AA meeting marathon was a holiday tradition for the Saint Mark's group. It lasted until Sunday evening—twenty-four hours of ongoing meetings daily. I thought it a bit obsessive, the buffet a bit below me. After all: I had a date.

I went home, looking for ways to pass the afternoon. I settled into my bed with one of the football games on television. It did not hold my attention. I tried to nap, clutching my purple medallion in hand. Time tiptoed forward.

I had a plan: I was going to take the train to 23rd Street to El's because of the crummy weather. In calculating the time it might take, I decided to leave extra early, due to the holiday. Dressed in jeans and a burgundy turtleneck, more work clothes than "hanging out" clothes, I assessed myself in my tiny mirror. I felt a little upscale and ready. *I can do this*, I thought. *A bridge back to life.* Wearing my pea jacket, a bit too lesbian-feminist but all I had, and carrying three pies tied carefully together and balanced cumbersomely in hand, I headed toward the subway. I had somewhere to go. This was good. My nerves were shaky. *Such a good time to smoke a joint*, I thought. *But not today. Just for today.*

To my surprise, as I walked up to the train track, the train came instantly, swooping down on me before I was ready for it. I wanted to wait. Nevertheless, I got in and took my seat: me and the pies. The train deposited us on 23rd Street in four minutes, sixty-five minutes before my date. *Oye, hopelessly early as usual.* I traced up and down the block, the rain a fine mist now, trying to still my nerves. The streets were quiet, most folks at their destination by now. I looked in store windows, counted the cracks in the sidewalk, tried to relax. The time would not pass. Finally it was close enough. *Time for the date!* Attempting to look cool, I sauntered toward the building, a modern, fashionable, three-story brick, and found the doorbells. I located El's name, and willed my trembling finger toward its bell.

I rang. There was no response.

I rang again. Again there was no response.

My heart started rapping even more loudly. I was incredulous. Of course this was the right day. *Thanksgiving, 5:00, you bring the pies.* I was lightheaded with disorientation. I looked at my watch. 5:06. I pressed myself flat against the brick of the building. *Maybe she's in the shower? Sleeping? Wait a few minutes. Wait a few minutes and ring again.* I felt paralyzed, overwhelmed with feelings, trying to disappear, pressed into the building. I had a great rush of shame burst into my face, flushing me, heating me. There was nobody on the street to see—it was a generic, inherent shame surfacing up on 23rd Street for release and healing.

Finally, after an endless amount of time, it was 5:15. I tried again. I rang the bell.

Nobody was home. Or at least, nobody was answering the bell.

I waited until 5:20. I rang once again. No answer.

I was stunned. *What did Stephanie say? Notice the feelings. Feel the feelings. The feelings won't hurt me. What I do is try to control the feelings, and that's the problem.*

I can outlive them.

What would I do? I felt panic build in me, like an avalanche gathering speed. I felt overpowered, aimless, emptied. The pies clanked against my side, mocking me. *I could drink now*, a voice inside me screamed. *I deserve to drink NOW.* I started to walk downtown, with nowhere to go and nothing to do. I felt as if I might die, disintegrate, melt into the sidewalk. My knees were weak, my face flaming with heat. What had happened? I had a date. The pies...

And then the thought that might have saved my life slid into me: *the meetings, the buffet!* I walked faster. I did have somewhere to go. *The marathon.* I thought of nothing else, trying to keep the swinging pies under control, trying to keep my thoughts focused on Saint Mark's Place. The faster I jogged, the more wild the pies became, dangerously undulating at my side. I resorted to hugging them against my chest, my run to safety more assured now. I willed myself down the block. Huffing, I jogged to Second Avenue, turned right, and sprinted the rest of the block to the meeting place, running for my life. I dashed up the steps and into the main room, which was transformed by a huge buffet table, lined with a paper tablecloth and literally cluttered with Thanksgiving food: turkey, stuffing, potatoes, gelled cranberry sauce, the works, spread out randomly across the table. A feast. People milled around the table with paper plates and plastic silverware in hand, eager, reaching, gabbing, laughing.

I plopped the pies on the table, liberating them from their string with one swoosh of a knife. Opening each box, I carefully placed each one ritualistically on the table: apple, blueberry, pumpkin.

They took their place among the other offerings.

"Far out," said a disheveled guy with rats-nest hair who

was standing next to me. He was wearing a long dirty over-coat, greedily ogling the pies, obviously a homeless guy there for the goodies.

"Far out," I said back to him, smiling, thankful to be home at last.

19

⁂

Johnny Appleseed
Fall, 1987

The fist of pain was a tiny fireball burning in the pit of my stomach, relentlessly churning inside me. No matter where I was or what I was doing, be it day or night, waking or sleeping, the pain burned and churned on. It ate into my physical being with teeth of hot steel. Emotionally I was exhausted, stretched into a brittle, thin layer of nervous reactions. Spiritually young, I felt flattened, exiled into that parched land of rote prayers, supplications devoid of feelings—that vast, arid spiritual wilderness.

I was lost. Being sober made the pain worse—there was nowhere to hide. I wasn't utilizing something in the AA program, something my new sponsor, Amy, called acceptance. I couldn't accept what was happening in my life? Of course I couldn't. It was wrong—it was unjust. How do you accept injustice? I couldn't let it be. The unfairness lived inside of me, a separate entity, eating away at the lining of my stomach.

Zena had been my lover, my partner, for two rollercoaster years: one sober, one in active addiction. We had struggled with commitment, the "C-word," and after months of frustrating couples' therapy, after pleading, bargaining, leaving her, coming back to her—we were at the same stalemate. She would not commit fully to me; she insisted on continuing her relationship with Alexis. It was the bane of my existence, this push-pull, this craziness. I had been sober for over a year, and still this issue dominated my life. Amy, small, petite Amy, a dancer and committed recovering person, would never specifically tell me what to do, in spite of all my pleadings and begging for an answer. "You will know," she told me, in her level, reassuring voice. "If it's time to leave her, you will know. And you will have the strength to do it."

While drinking and drugging, I had been obsessed with changing Zena's behavior. I knew I could convince her to see the light, to see it my way. It didn't work. But ever since sobriety, that focus seemed to have shifted inside of me. For the past sober months, I had been obsessed with the decision to leave her or not. It consumed me. The pain of staying with her as she continued her life with Alexis haunted me. Yet imagining my life without her seemed literally impossible. Simply the thought of it squeezed the breath out of my body.

Scheduling dates with Zena was a series of strategic negotiations. Bickering for holiday time was the rule of thumb, since she divided her calendar between the two of us. I was so vulnerable on the holidays. What did Amy mean, accept it? How could I accept something that was so…not acceptable?

Labor Day was coming, the end of summer, a three-day weekend. Zena divvied up the weekend—I would spend Sunday and Monday with her in her Park Slope apartment in Brooklyn. That was the decision. It upset me, because I preferred Friday night and Saturday. Monday wouldn't be good for me; it was the day before I returned to work, which meant probably a day of anxiety. I was annoyed, but gathered my things—sweater, book, change of clothes—stuffing them into my pack. I had figured out which Manhattan meetings I would attend before and after the trip, as Amy suggested I do, and would attend one before I left. I never went to meetings in Brooklyn, not wanting to sacrifice any of my precious time with Zena.

As I drove over the Brooklyn Bridge in Ruby, the morning light filtered softly through the steel latticework on the bridge, creating dancing diamonds of light on the roadway. The traffic was light, most of it headed into the City, creating a spacious and comfortable drive for me, always a New York gift. Ahead of me, Brooklyn looked stunning, almost surreal, stretched out in the new day. Summer was ending, school was beginning. Transition was here. I felt hollowed out, emptied yet still aware of my always-companion: burning stomach pain. I didn't look forward to this weekend, yet I couldn't wait to get there. My reactions didn't make much sense to me any more. Being sober made this craziness harder.

Zena met me at the door. Lithe and thin, her green eyes blazed her greeting. She leaned gracefully toward me, keeping her body away from mine, as she kissed me on the cheek—a chaste, virtuous embrace. She wore tight-fitting jeans, a fashionable cream t-shirt cut as she so perfectly did into a scoop neck. We sat at her wood table, her spacious, bright kitchen around us, and drank some tea. I felt jittery and exhausted. Why? Was it the upcoming school year? What was wrong with me? Being sober meant I got to feel my feelings—oh, great.

We decided to walk in Prospect Park, just a few blocks from her apartment. We ambled toward the Park, watching the families; toddlers in strollers, small kids on tricycles, the suburban population of Park Slope, so unlike the motley population of my East Village, filling the streets on this holiday Sunday and heading toward the Park. I was strangely uncomfortable, although the day passed amicably enough. Our conversations were easy, light, skimming the surface of our darker disagreements, as if we both unconsciously decided to wave a white surrender flag for the day. Even though the surface of the day appeared pleasant—walking in the Park, enjoying the takeout food from the Thai restaurant on the corner, watching a video on the couch—and all the right elements were present, I continued to be edgy, miserably uncomfortable inside myself. What was happening?

We crawled into Zena's big bed early, said goodnight—it was not a night for snuggling—and retreated to our own spaces for sleep. I closed my eyes, and began my own private descent into hell. My mind circled around itself, circumnavigating the situations with Alexis, with Zena, with the upcoming school year, with my sobriety. Around and about, in and out, the little thread of obsession wove itself bigger, first into a scarf, then into a suffocating blanket. The night passed as I lay sleepless. I felt utterly alone, while in bed with my lover. She was miles away in the other corner of the bed. The distance between us was obvious and insurmountable. I shivered, in spite of my burning belly. I shivered, and shivered again deeply in my soul. How could I possibly be so cold while in bed with my partner? How could she in God's name possibly be so unavailable to me?

In a moment of utter despair, something broke inside of me. I got it. A thought clicked into me, sliding into a physical and psychic opening, for the first time:

It's not about changing Zena. It's about changing myself. She will never change. Maybe that's the acceptance that Amy keeps talking about. Accept Zena as she is, and decide from there.

And I knew what that meant. For all the hours that I struggled to know, to create a knowing, now I simply knew. I knew I had to leave her. I knew that living sober should not and could not be this painful. I knew it. I got it. And I grieved. The rest of the night was a torturous journey of grieving. Knowing I couldn't stay, not imagining my life without her. But, as Amy predicted, the break was made. Something greater than myself created the split. It had ended.

Toward dawn, I napped a bit, cuddled up into myself, snuggling into the ball of throbbing pain, the Brooklyn air amazingly cold. My sweater was on the other side of the room, and an afghan on the couch in the other room. Yet I couldn't will myself to leave this freezing bed, this last night with my lover, my mirror, myself. A part of me was dying in that bed, over and ended.

My own, customized-by-the-universe opportunity to grow, Amy would say.

I awoke with a start a little after 6:00. The torturous siege wasn't over yet, since Zena always woke up so much later than I did. I willed myself to stay still and quiet, memorizing the contours of the ceiling above her bed. A gem of old New York architecture, the ceiling was a treasure—an old, restored tin ceiling, with beautifully crafted designs in it. Painted a pale lavender by Zena, I carefully examined and lovingly savored each of the squares that held a diamond shape within them. Recognizing I would not awake to these shapes again, I studied them and anticipated the loss of them. Time hung heavy.

Unable to stand the wait, around 8:00 I uncharacteristically got up, tiptoed into the other room, and shimmied into my clothes. I made some tea and sat by the window, watching the light in the morning change. I had steeled myself for her awakening, preparing myself for the words I might say.

About 9:30, she wandered in, sleep softly surrounding her. She wore a fleecy lavender robe, which she had bundled up around her face, her short black curls tussled in disarray. She sat down next to me in silence.

"I'm going to go." My voice was flat, remarkably unemotional.

She poured herself some tea from the white teapot with red flowers on it that sat on the table. She was used to my proclamations. Like the boy who cried wolf, I had depleted my ultimatums. She said nothing. I rose, scraping my chair on the floor, and reached for my backpack, which was packed and ready to go. I put on my corduroy jacket, heart breaking, and reached over to kiss the top of her head. Tickled by its softness, I breathed in for one final time the familiar scent of shampoo, of sleep, the accustomed smell of what was. I turned and walked away, heart exploding, toward the door.

"Call me later," she called nonchalantly over her shoulder.

I continued toward the door, knowing completely that there would be no calling. There would be no *later* for us. I knew the truth.

Once on the stoop, I burst into an explosion of tears quite unusual for me. I made it to Ruby, sobbing, and threw myself into the car. I fumbled her into gear, navigating our way out of the parking spot, away from Union Street, never to return. *Never to return,* I thought. This was different from my other proclamations of leaving. Inside of me, I had already left. There was no going back. Onto Sixth Avenue we turned, my sobbing making the driving harder. Traffic again was mercifully light, most people still hunkered down where they were for the final day of the three-day holiday. *Not me,* I thought, *I'm going home.* The Bridge awaited, stretching before us, as we made our way toward Manhattan and then effortlessly up First Avenue toward the East Village. In just a few minutes, the traffic lights on the street unusually green, my building appeared on my left, with parking spaces abounding. We navigated into one, Ruby and me. From door to door, it was a twenty-minute ride that spanned universes inside of me.

I sprinted up the four flights of steps and worked the several keys that unlocked the several locks on my door, shouldering the door open. I flung my pack down and threw myself onto the bed, exploding into a new layer of sobbing.

Never to return. It was over.

Now what? I reached for the phone to call Amy. She wasn't home, so I left a message:

"Amy. It happened. It's over now. For real."

I called my friend Cindy, a woman from the Saint Mark's meetings. I repeated the message into her machine.

It was 10:30. I had ninety minutes until the noon meeting. I decided to walk—moving seemed like the only way to deal with the pain that was flooding me. I found my keys, put on my jacket, and made my way down to the street. Which way, I wondered?

Mindlessly I turned left and began to walk up First Avenue. The sidewalks were light with pedestrians, creating an open walkway for me. I tried to relax, to invite my body to find its stride.

One foot down, then the other. One foot. Then. The. Other. The sobbing that had infiltrated me for the last forty-five minutes seemed to subside, to quiet a bit. One foot. Then. The other.

Maybe this is what they meant by one step at a time, I guessed.

My mind looked for a song, a rhythm. Out of nowhere, or perhaps out of everywhere, "Johnny Appleseed" flowed into me. A grace sung before meals at Archbald Camp, it found me again as I walked First Avenue:

Oh, the Lord is good to me,
And so I thank the Lord.
For giving me
The things I need.
The sun and the rain and the apple seed.

The Lord is good to me.

Its rhythm fit my walking perfectly, propelling me, moving me toward calm. I passed over the intersections of 6th Street, then 7th, then 8th. I continued north on my pilgrimage of healing, this old camp grace repeating itself over and over again inside of me, a balm to my soul. I found myself crossing 14th Street, heading north, heading toward calmness, heading toward a new beginning.

The words of the song settled over me, its meaning slipping into my body, through my cells rather than through my mind.

To have gratitude, even for the hard times, I pondered. *Even for the hard love, for the hole in my heart. Especially the hard things, they grow us. The sun's not enough to grow the seed. Gotta have the rain. It's been raining for a while now.*

At 11:15, I stopped and took account of my journey. I was at 42nd Street. I turned around, got my bearings again, took a deep breath, and began the return trip, heading south on First. "Johnny Appleseed," my mantra of healing, my mantra of recovery, carried me down the blocks. I headed toward the noon meeting, toward the sun, toward connection and wholeness. All the while a small, quiet voice whispered quietly inside, telling me I would make it. I would outlive the pain.

The Lord is good to me.

20

Seeking

O*h, the Lord is good to me.*

This prayer became the centerpiece of the first two years of my life without drugs or alcohol, without my actually realizing it. My sponsor, Amy, continued to tell me that life came to support and bless me. She emphasized that circumstance gave me exactly the situations that I needed to grow spiritually, continuing to harp on the theme of gratitude. *There is nothing wrong with this moment,* she would say, with infinite patience, her voice reassuring and level.

All in God's world is in its rightful place, even the things we don't like, she told me endlessly during our daily phone calls. I listened to her, phone receiver sweaty in my eager palm, trying to believe what she said. Life was much better without drinking and drugging, that was obvious. I had no hangovers, no blinding headaches, no wild shame attacks, and no abusive relationship to gnaw at me. The worst was surely over, behind me. Yet something—what was it?—something was missing. I felt hollow and emptied out. I continued to scan my life to identify the missing piece, the piece that would bring me comfort and solace.

The 12 Step meetings I religiously attended fascinated me with their simple catch-phrases for dealing with life and their fascinating cast of characters. I found real comfort at my local two-blocks-away-from-home meeting, filled with all kinds of people—the motorcycle bunch, swathed in their leather, bikes parked rakishly at the curb; the heterosexual women, hair a'teased, with matching sweater sets; the smattering of street people off the Bowery, in attendance for the cheap cookies and coffee. It amazed me that, amidst such different kinds of people, I could begin to relax and settle into my seat.

These people were literally new to my world. I had been so profoundly isolated in the final days of my active addiction, my lesbian-feminist-separatist beliefs rigidly separating me from straight or gay men, from heterosexual women—even from lesbians with other political leanings. Under the guise of my sophisticated political awareness, I had kept myself so righteously alone that my fear of people was iceberg-deep. But now that iceberg was slowly beginning to thaw as I found myself in my daily meetings laughing, relating to other people's sharing, beginning to raise my hand, and even managing little random conversations after the meetings' end with others. As Amy pointed out, this was all new behavior for me.

And yet, I was longing for something more. A vague, thick impatience hung over me. I knew my teaching job at Malcolm X High School, so much more painful without my daily noontime joint, was doomed. Without the fog of marijuana surrounding me, Newark's criminally ineffective system of education was almost intolerable to my newly sober sensibilities. Seeing the students' needs literally unmet by the system—the brighter, edgier students unengaged and doomed for drop-out, the docile, quiet ones rewarded with passing grades—broke my heart. Seeing the racism amongst the faculty, the inefficient administration, the emptiness of the curriculum—none of this stirred me to create new curriculum, but seemed to suck the energy out of me. By each Friday, my broken heart was aching. I somehow realized deep inside of me that I would have to leave this, my profession. But what would I do?

I had no clue.

In response to my daily whining, Amy continued to patiently offer me her favorite AA slogan: *more will be revealed*. But when? I wanted it revealed, now! What would I be? Where would I go? What work might I do, that would be a fuller expression of my soul? Amy was a dancer, and I so envied her creative, passionate source of expression and paycheck. Her response, although its truth rang true, annoyed me and grated on my nerves: *time takes time.*

Even my relationship to New York, my beloved city, the City, was morphing. Without the drugs and alcohol to "soothe" me, I found the endless flow of people, movement, and stimulation overwhelming and exhausting. Lying in my apartment on Fifth Street, the incessant whine of buses rumbling up First Avenue washed unremittingly over me. From room to room in my apartment, from bed to bath, from table to desk, the busses moaned on in my consciousness. There seemed no escaping the noise and vibration of their constant movement, as there seemed no diversion from the constant rumble of movement and sound, 24/7— the heartbeat of the City that never did sleep.

I was tiring of it. That which had once seemed to stimulate and excite me now drained me.

Freeing myself from the grip of my addictive relationship with Zena dropped me into a world of aloneness such as I had never inhabited before. My first weeks alone after leaving her were filled with aching physical suffering, as if some essential internal organ had been yanked from its rightful place inside of me. Slowly, those physical feelings began to ebb. Emotionally, too, I was learning to manage living alone—to wake by myself, to eat alone, to sleep alone. Sleep, the ongoing struggle, was still such a difficult state to reach alone and unattended by drugs. I needed to watch television at night after my meetings, allowing the light and sound to lull me to sleep. Yet I gradually managed to cobble together a burgeoning relationship to myself. Although I regularly felt myself attracted to women at meetings, I found myself too terrified to act on any feelings, and was supported by Amy to "just notice without acting." Being alone was possible, but where was my soul mate? Would I spend my life alone? What would happen?

Sobriety was the right path, I was certain, yet so many questions, so much longing filled me—wanting professional expression, a relationship of truth, a home in a sane and quiet place, a community of like-minded friends. I seemed to echo emptiness. I didn't know how to move forward in any of these arenas. Amy and my 12 Step friends encouraged my lack of action. *Live sober*, they told me. *Don't just do something, sit there. Put God in the center.*

Put God in the center.

People in recovery, who were really the only people in my life at the time, advised me that, by focusing on my spiritual connection, the margins of my life, the job, the relationship, the decisions about leaving New York—all would eventually and perfectly resolve themselves. I was drawn to this un-solution, both tired out by trying to solve everything myself and clueless about what next steps to take. But what was this God, this Power, this entity that had picked me off the floor of my apartment that hot summer night a few years before and given me this gift of living in an entirely different world of possibility and connection? I didn't know. And I wanted to. That's what I really wanted—to know God.

I really did want to know. I became dedicated to understanding the literature in the 12 Step meetings that described conscious contact with a God of my understanding. *Understanding?* I didn't have any. What did that mean? I wanted to figure out this concept of surrendering to reality, so I could grasp it and be done with it. At night after my meetings, I would play George Harrison's "My Sweet Lord" over and over on my tape deck, lying on my bed, and be moved to tears by the passion of his search:

> *I really want to see you*
> *Really want to be with you*
> *Really want to see you lord*
> *But it takes so long, my lord.*

It seemed the more I struggled to understand, the only insights I received were the fast track into my frustration.

When I considered the twenty years of my drinking and my drugging, I could begin to identify an underlying spiritual yearning. Smoking pot was my way to salvation, to grace, to becoming one with the cosmos, to being with God. The cosmic irony was that drugs became the way out of the moment, rather than the way into the moment—the moment that God inhabits, as I heard it said in the recovery rooms. I had been headed in the wrong direction. But what direction to head in now? I wanted to dive right in to something, but didn't know where or how.

I was befuddled, but kept going to meetings, and kept practicing living sober.

One day I was sitting on a bench in Saint Mark's Place, having a before-the-meeting talk with Nancy, a pleasant, chubby-cheeked woman from my home group. The sky was a gentle blue, the air a delicious finally-spring temperature. Nancy and I were casually discussing summer vacation options. She nonchalantly mentioned a yoga retreat center she had visited in New England:

"It's a great place—just a few hours north. Wonderful food, good people, and fun classes. It's an ashram. People live there and practice living a spiritual lifestyle."

Her three-sentence comment landed deeply inside of me, like seeds planted in my awareness. I couldn't stop thinking about it, as that day, and the next and the next, unfolded.

It's an ashram. People live there and practice living a spiritual lifestyle.

Summer was approaching. I had not yet been on a sober vacation yet, having spent the last summer in the City. *What should I do?* I wondered inside my head. *Maybe I should move to an ashram. What's an ashram, anyway?*

After much internal debating and external support from Amy, I decided to visit this yoga retreat center for a three-day weekend. I anxiously made my reservation with their overly polite reservations agent, and counted the days for my trip north. I was going to visit the ashram.

The last days of teaching before summer break unfolded with their typical chaotic intensity. The students were wildly unresponsive, my classes rowdy, we staff members even more disconnected and moody than usual. It wasn't pretty. I found myself hanging by a thread of hope through those long, hot airless days in May. *I'm going to visit the ashram.* It was a beacon of…of something I couldn't quite identify, as my professional world descended into humid frustration and despair.

School did, of course, end, and summer officially arrived. I left Newark and Malcolm X Shabazz High School behind me without looking back, as I drove away that hot June afternoon, my pre-dated summer paychecks tucked safely into my bag. I looked forward to a summer of spiritual discovery. I was anxious and excited about heading north to the yoga center. Amy sanctioned my trip with her reminders to *keep it simple*. We agreed: I would go to a meeting before and directly after my trip, and call her during the weekend. The plan was in place. Finally, on that quiet summer New York morning, my East Fifth Street block not yet awakened to activity, I packed my car, Ruby the Volkswagen, with hands trembling with possibility.

The trip north was uneventful. My anxiety about following the driving directions proved yet again unfounded. I was beginning to see how my fear and anxiety exhausted me and how my catastrophic thinking never became reality. New York State was beautiful and green, quite the change from the East Village in Manhattan. I slipped effortlessly across the border into Massachusetts, its welcome sign cheerily urging me on. The trip unfolded easily, which was not my general belief about things, I was starting to recognize. Expecting the worst was a filter through which I saw life.

Driving up the Kripalu driveway, I was taken aback by both the beauty and the strangeness of the building. It stood on top of a magnificent hill, overlooking the countryside with a 360-degree view of green hills and rolling woods. The building itself was long and peculiar, made of light brick, with a pointed white steeple atop it. It seemed so much more institutionalized than I imagined. What had I imagined?

I didn't know. I was entering a zone that was beyond my imagination.

I parked the car alongside the many others in the vast parking lot. With shaking hands I grabbed my pack, pulled myself out of the car, slammed the door behind me, and headed toward the door marked "reception." Walking toward it, I tried to breathe—it wasn't easy. As I put my hand on the door, I noticed my pounding, racing heart.

Little did I know: there really was a door closing behind me. The door I faced, hand steadied on its knob, would open into the next chapter of my life.

21

❧

Finding
1989

It was Thanksgiving Day, 1989, and I was an official member of the Kripalu ashram. My one Kripalu vacation the spring before had merged into another, and then into a two-month summer volunteer program. Enthralled with the excitement of living in an intentional community, captivated by the amazing range of Kripalu people, and mesmerized by its shared spiritual practices, I returned as a volunteer for a year, taking a leave of absence from Malcolm X Shabazz High School. It was a time of great excitement and much hope for me. I was surely on the fast-track path to God now, I was certain.

Thanksgiving Day began with early morning yoga practices in the darkened Main Chapel, hushed but for the muffled breathing of us supplicants. I struggled with the poses, and, whenever noticing, willed myself into relaxation. I so wanted to do it all right. I so wanted something—what was it? The community's approval? The guru's love? A cool work assignment, rather than the housekeeping, vacuuming, and bathroom-scrubbing role I now had? Yet underneath all that surface longing, because of the young blossoming of my spiritual insightfulness, I now knew that I just wanted to know God.

The final *om*, the chant done at the beginning and the end of every class that aligned the energy centers, vibrated through me. I quickly gathered my belongings, feigning mindfulness, and consciously hightailed it back to my shared dormitory, where fifty-six women lived in bunk beds and cubicles. Staying in "social silence," a practice that helped keep the internal focus, I changed into my whites for breakfast and our morning ceremony, satsanga, with the guru. We always wore white when the guru was present, to display our purity, our spiritual willingness. Satsanga was the Sanskrit name for "in the company of truth." It was a gathering that consisted of chanting, teaching, and voluntary dancing. Getting there early meant a better seat for me and greater access to the guru; hence, a more direct route to God for the day.

Breakfast was silent, another opportunity to keep the focus internal, the energy building. I attempted to gulp down with mindful awareness my brown rice and miso soup, practicing being present while anxiety about getting a good seat for the ceremony built. I feared that I would be obvious to the other spiritual seekers—a young, devout whippersnapper, obviously missing the moment's doorway to grace by eating unconsciously. But damn, I did so want to sit up front! I tried to still my excited mind as I attempted to chew consciously, the forty bites per mouthful (as it was taught) still an unfeasible goal for me.

Sufficiently finished with breakfast, bussing my dishes, I grabbed my shawl and wrapped it around me. Shawls were big on the spiritual path. I had a lovely blue Guatemalan scarf that worked well, cuddling me into itself comfortably. I practiced walking calming down the hallway, while my screeching mind was flying into the Chapel, grabbing the best available seat. Slowing down my body was an excruciating practice for me. I walked with awareness toward the Main Chapel, taking off my sandals and storing them slowly on the shoe rack. I made my way into the half empty chapel, filled with younger residents like myself seeking a good seat. I found a back-jack—the funny little on-the-ground seats we used—near the front rise, and claimed my spot. I sat down, with almost an hour to wait, happy to be freed from the routine of vacuuming and bathroom scrubbing for the morning.

How to appear calm and present? I was still so self-conscious, trying to appear the best little spiritual seeker.

After an eternity of my contriving a meditative stance, the satsanga launched itself with frenetic chanting, led by the guru, splendid in his dressy white robe with simulated gold embroidery, and wild drumming by over-eager, sweaty male disciples. The guru taught at great length that morning about gratitude and Christ and things I didn't quite grasp. He had a circular way of teaching and thinking which, when compounded by his thick Indian accent, kept my mind befuddled. I couldn't quite figure out what he was saying. But my body was so open and happy being there. I felt joyous celebration in my heart, a feeling of lightness and headiness infusing me. I liked this, whatever this was. It beat the Thanksgiving I would be having at home in New York—a turkey dinner in an expensive restaurant with a friend or two, followed by a cool, current movie. This was—I didn't have the words yet—real? Deep? I didn't know, but I liked it.

We ended with a bang as a long, continuous *om* seemed to blow the roof off both my head and the chapel. The guru left to sounds of our prayerfulness, "Bolo shri, shri Krishna Chandra," the traditional prayer of salutation. My heart was pounding, and, for no particular reason, I quickly navigated my way out of the chapel, and found myself skipping down the long corridor, down the steps taking two at a time, and, with a childlike exuberance, down toward the first floor lobby. Usually a hubbub of people and movement, the green tiled lobby was hushed in silence but for the pounding of my happy, thanksgiving heart.

Hopping down the second step onto the tile floor, I stopped in my tracks. Before me the glass doors looked out upon a long, spacious hill that dove down into the Stockbridge Bowl, Lake Mahkeenac. Unbeknownst to me, a light snow had been falling, covering the hills and trees thick with gloriously white blankets of beauty. The Lake gleamed in front of it all, silver and reflective, snow dabbling its mirrored surface. Several long seconds passed, while my body and my heart seemed to fill up with silent, thoughtless celebration. There really was nowhere to go, no roads to drive upon, no need to head elsewhere. And there really was nothing to do, no cars to dig out of snow-banks. Nothing was real but this moment, this never-ending opportunity to practice relaxing into presence. I was fully and wholly freed in this tiny slice of time, opened to energy and grace, fully alive and available to life's glory. I had never been this completely and thoroughly alive.

And then my mind returned, slamming into me with all its chattering busyness. *What's for lunch,* I wondered. *Something good, something special?* My mind excitedly and seductively sneered at me, luring me away from myself. The rest of the day swept over me in a wave of unconscious activity, as did the next days, with the mundane, the human dominating. Tiny intervals of awareness of grace would skid over me and I would grasp at them, wanting to attain them, to hold them deeply and lock them into me. Like little energetic gratitude attacks, they were fleeting and relatively far between. The more I grasped at them, the quicker they would flitter away.

I practiced noticing and not judging. I practiced watching and returning to breath. I practiced, so profoundly imperfectly—

which, my Kripalu friends all reassured me, was indeed the perfect practice. Nevertheless, I wanted more. More of what? Of myself? Of life? Of God? Yes, I wanted more God, goddamn it.

And the time passed. Days folded into months effortlessly, each day so rich and full, yet the time speeding ahead. Living in the ashram was compelling, exciting, completely amusing, edgy, heady, breathtaking, never boring, rich, painful, and ever and always growth-producing, to name just a few of the emotions that regularly whirled through me. I had enough sense, thank goodness, to keep going to AA meetings at night. The Resident Life people who managed the fleet of ashram cars didn't completely sanction 12 Step meetings, but there were ways around the guidelines. We were a small group of recovering people who worked through those loopholes and got to meetings regularly. I found the paths of recovery and yoga very compatible. I was growing spiritually.

Yet brahmacharya kicked my emerging spiritual butt. It was one of the keystones of our practice, this ancient art of the moderation of energy. Derived from the yamas and the nyamas, codes of ethics and behavior for spiritual seekers on the yogic path, it was the observance of sexual abstinence and was used to detoxify the old patterns of attraction and sexual acting out. Its mirror of growth was shiny for me!

Being gay in a community organized around brahmacharya was bizarrely counter-intuitive and hugely counter-productive. The men were separated from the women disciples during meals, yoga practice, satsangas, all gatherings—the left side always for the guys, the right for the women, in order to support the practice. That worked fine for me. Not unlike lesbian separatism, being without men offered me a gift of ease and freedom. And the women—oh, the Kripalu women were wonderful. Strong and soft, the workhorses and the leaders of the community, there was wisdom and beauty abounding. Of course, Brahmacharya didn't "protect" me from my sexual longings as intended. To the contrary—it tossed me into the pool of possibility without a lifejacket. Alone in the candy store of options, I was hungry and easily distracted from the inner journey.

Crush after crush emerged pointlessly and painfully. I found myself fantasizing about wildly heterosexual women whom I didn't even know, imaging our happily-ever-after post-ashram life together. Reality and fantasy blurred, as in my childhood, my pre-coming-out days. My mind was wild and unleashed, untamable in the realm of passionate fantasy. Another addiction! My 12 Step friends assured me not to worry—it was only one addiction with many different faces. Their comment did not comfort me.

Woman after woman appeared to be "the one." There was one crush, a serious one, to whom, after four months of intense fantasy, I told of my longings in "rigorous dialogue." We were encouraged to speak our truth, and so I did. I will never forget the look in her eyes, as we sat outside in that summer haze of heat, masking her disbelief, stumbling on her words of rejection. I was crushed, embarrassed, humbled, and startled by the power of my mind to make the unreal into reality.

I turned to the support of a 12 Step group whose focus was sexual and romantic addiction. I went to a meeting in that fellowship, driving the fifty minutes each way, once a week for sixteen months, practicing its tools in my daily life. I began to realize that I had a choice; if an invasive thought of romantic fantasy slithered across my mind, I could chose to indulge in it with more thoughts, which would result similarly to throwing kerosene onto a fire. More flames, more distraction, more thoughts. Or, at the first notice of this invasive thought, I could release it and return to reality, to breathe into the reality of what is, rather than creating the fantasy world of what is not. Another practice emerged. The training of my mind was beginning, ever so slowly, to take hold.

And so I practiced as the days passed. Officially resigning from my teaching job was another stepping stone on my path. After my year-long leave of absence, I left my tenured position with the Newark Board of Education for good—along with my dirt-cheap apartment on East 5th Street, New York City in all its wonderful madness, my pension, my paycheck, my health insurance, and Ruby the Car. And, to the horror of my remaining lesbian feminist friends, I left behind my gay community, too.

But good things were unfolding in my life. The intentional collective focus of the Kripalu community, the shared spiritual quest, was both stretching me into new growth while accepting me for who I was. I loved it. The ashram was like the best of Girl Scout camp—beautiful land, interesting people, an exciting shared purpose, and communal living, but this time with a spiritual flavor. The romantic fantasies loosened their grip on me. I had more choice in the dismantling of them. And in my very own wacky and imperfect way, I thrived and grew.

Several years down the road of my residency, I became friends with an older resident. We would carpool to the swimming pool together in the mornings with a few other regulars. Driving to the pool became our point of connection. Our friendship expanded into walks and good talks. She was vivacious, strong-willed, tiny and feisty, a deep seeker, and fully committed to the Kripalu practices. I was always so happy to talk to her, to feel her energy, to receive her bubbly spirit and deep insights. I felt my heart opening up to her, yet chose to not speak of my feelings. She was not gay, and she was practicing brahmacharya, of course.

Time passed. I "held the posture," watching my feelings come, surrendering them, seeing them peak again. I had support from several trusted friends in yet another practice—to feel my feelings, and to release my attachment to their results. Could I do this and not fantasize? Could I feel these things soberly and abstinently? I did my imperfect best.

After a few months, I did tell her of my feelings, and was dashed by her response. She didn't see me "in that way." Nevertheless, I continued to keep open to her, to my feelings, and to the process of trusting the feelings in my body. Our friendship deepened. After a long year, we had the "come to Jesus" talk. Once the words were spoken, once I told her of my love for her—and love her, oh, I did—she began to acknowledge the very real feelings she had for me in her heart. And she was the one.

She was the real one, the one with whom I would walk forward into life in conscious, mindful relationship. And she continues to be the one, the one with whom to practice, the one with whom I age, the one with whom I fumble, try again, and grow. I practice, I simply practice mindful, conscious relationship.

For so many years I looked wildly around me and grabbed at toxic relationships to fill the void inside. For so many years I wanted somebody to fill that emptiness and to distract me from my pain. And I was to find out that, even with a healthy and committed relationship, I still had to do the work. Even with a wonderful job, I still had to do the work. I still had to cultivate relationship inside of me with that internal silence, that internal stillness. There was nothing outside of me to fill that God-shaped hole. Even the pursuit of God could be a distraction from the process of being.

One breath at a time, I continued to practice finding my way home.

22

_≈_

Shopping With The Guru
1990

It was just another day in the ashram: rising before dawn, floating off toward yoga in the darkened, candle-lit Main Chapel, moving tearfully through the poses, and eating a silent breakfast of brown rice and miso soup, prayerfulness and intentionality launching my day. How different this was from awakening, leaping up, and sprinting to Malcolm X Shabazz High School to endure a day of noisy stress as I had done for the last fifteen years.

_Ah,_ I thought, striding down the long corridor toward my new work assignment. _This lifestyle works for me._

Life was good. I was living a spiritual quest.

And now my seva was changing and I was psyched. Seva, the Sanskrit word for service, was our work assignment, and yet it was about much more than simply work. Seva embodied mindfulness practices that emphasized meditative techniques rather than just the emphasis on the work. The practice was to be in the moment, rather than focus on the task's completion. Even washing the toilets was an opportunity to practice meditation in the moment.

After almost ten months in the household department— vacuuming rugs that weren't dirty, cleaning bathrooms that were, scrubbing shower stalls, and attending to massive amounts of garbage bags—I was moving from an entry-level function to one with more seniority. I was joining Educational Resources, which was the department that transcribed and archived all of the Guru's lectures. I was elated. It meant closer proximity to him, and, almost more importantly, a desk of my own. I was excited to put my scrub brush, vacuum cord, and rubber gloves to the side and pick up a computer mouse. It represented the evolution of my ashram life—I was developing.

The Guru was called Gurudev. He was a strikingly handsome Indian man, with long dark hair, high cheekbones, a piercing glare, and a relatively thick accent. He had started Kripalu from the attendees in his yoga classes, nursing it into both an ashram for 350 volunteer disciples and a multimillion-dollar guest center. I was drawn to him, finding his presence evocative and powerful in our satsangas, or community sessions. But mostly I was smitten with the community. I loved the Kripalu people, a cast of characters wildly interesting, widely diverse, and remarkably unusual.

I knocked on the office door of the head of my new department. A voice beckoned me to enter. Mena was sitting behind a desk strewn with papers, books, newspapers, rulers, envelopes, a clock, two tissue boxes, a picture of Gurudev, and wads of used tissues. She looked up at me and nodded toward a chair, preparing to launch into a sneeze. She waved me down with a fistful of tissues and blew her nose fiercely.

"I haff allergies." Her voice was thick. I felt anxious being in her presence. She was an "older resident" and had status and power within the system. She was small, blonde, and mousy, her pale skin accentuated by a red nose. Her hair was wispy thin.

I didn't know what to say. "Sorry," was all I could muster.

"So tell me about yourself, Aruni," she said, looking down at a stack of papers to reassure herself of my name—the Sanskrit name I had received during initiation the year before. She pronounced it "A-run-i," elongating the vowel sounds. Each syllable was enunciated explicitly, making each a complete name to itself.

Damn. What to tell her? What might be relevant? I didn't have a clue—my mind seemed to go on tilt. I thought longingly of my former household crew, who would be circling around to the third floor women's bathroom around this time. The anonymity of that function seemed appealing as I sat, withered beneath Mena's intense gaze.

"I'm a writer." It came out of my mouth effortlessly, flowing like honey off a spoon. "Yes, I'm a writer." I frightened myself with this proclamation. *Did I just say that?* Well, it was sort of true. I was a writer inside my mind, always and forever a writer inside my mind. Outside of my mind, I was more like a writer-wannabe. I did not specify that distinction for Mena.

She sat up a bit, pushed her glasses up the bridge of her nose, and studied me more intently. I squirmed and continued, rambling on more quickly about my teaching experience, trying to backpedal from the "writer" disclosure.

After our meeting, I was hustled into a boxy communal office crammed with five desks and four busy typists, given a shared desk, and trained in some basic methods of transcribing. My trainer was an intense, dark-haired woman named Trusha who had a big laugh, a loud voice, and a gruff exterior covering her kind heart. I was anxious about the computer functions, and fumbled through the long day. By its end, my neck hurt from sitting at such forced attention. I unbelievably found myself longing for the freedom of bathroom bowl scrubbing, but showed up the next morning at the transcribing office nevertheless, ready to give it my reluctant go. Trusha turned her head when I entered the room.

"Hey, Mena wants to see you in her office."

Oh, dear. What the heck was happening? I was deeply intimidated by the older residents who had been here for many years, imagining that my spirituality was of an immature and inferior nature compared to their many years of practice and deep devotion. I tried to stay away from them in the dining room and in the study groups they led for us. Now life offered me another encounter with Mena. *I wonder why?* I thought.

Again, I found myself staring at her office door. I took a breath and knocked. She beckoned me in. I found her sitting in exactly the same position as the day before, fiercely focused on her computer screen, with exactly the same accruements around her, used tissue piles highlighting the scene. I sat down in the same seat facing her desk. She seemed to ignore me for a long minute or two. My anxiety accelerated. Finally Mena looked up, as if to suddenly discover me sitting before her. Her nose was even more prominently red, the little patches of skin surrounding it on her cheekbones rosy to match. She cleared her voice.

"A-run-i," she said, repeating her particular pronunciation of my name, "we have a writing project for you."

A writing project? A Writing? Project? I was spellbound, holding onto the seat of my chair with full-squeeze.

"Yes, Gurudev is looking for a new writer to work with. We want you to do that for us."

I was riveted to my seat with disbelief. Write with the Guru? His experiences with his ever-changing team of writers were legendary, his inability to commit to the written word famous. He chewed writers up and spit them out regularly. *This would mean...this would mean...* my mind was still on hyper-tilt... *that I would* talk *with him? Like, one-on-one? Ride with him?* Writers always accompanied him places in the car, recording his teachings so as not to waste his time and to gather every syllable the man released. *What?* I thought, mind reeling. *There must be some mistake.*

Mena scanned over me, recording my response. I attempted to feign respectful nonchalance, as if being selected to write with the Guru was something to which I was entitled, something that matched my competencies, yet something I was tremendously humbled to receive. I clutched the chair more violently and attempted to keep my response neutral. My internal world was in shambles.

"Does this work for you, A-run-i?" she inquired.

Does it work for me? I wanted to either flee as far from Lenox, Massachusetts as I could, or fall down on the floor in supplication. My heart was pounding so loudly I felt as if I had to shout over it to be heard.

"I am honored." I kept it simple, trying not to betray my terrified elation.

And so it was done. I was officially part of the editorial team, those select few of us who were writers with the Guru. I, who hadn't really written anything outside my head for many, many years—inside was another story—was a writer with the Guru. I could correct papers. I could edit up a storm, given a red pen. But write with the Guru? I staggered out of Mena's office, the slamming door beckoning me toward a new reality.

I was moved swiftly to a new office, an office to be luxuriously shared by only one other person. Amma was my new office mate, a very senior resident and writer, who sat with upright dedication at her computer, eyeing my arrival in the office with a raised eyebrow and polite reserve. I anxiously plopped down my personal things—a picture of my parents, a feather from my cockatiel Buzzie the Bird who was in my room waiting for me, a dog-eared thesaurus that I had schlepped with me from New York and that I imagined would give me some credibility— onto my desk, not a shared desk, but my desk, all mine. I was claiming my space. After all, I was a writer with the Guru.

I had a new coordinator now—another senior resident named Arjun. Meeting with him that afternoon was unnerving to the core. He was a proper, humorless guy, who obviously took himself and his department very seriously. Sitting behind his desk, fingers intertwined, circling his thumbs around themselves, he seemed in his own world; just like Mena, he appeared to be unaware of my presence in the room. Was his thumb-twirling an advanced meditation technique? I waited patiently to get his attention. Finally he spoke to me, in another clipped, bizarre fashion, sort of a Bostonian accent with forced, nasal overtones. What was it with these people and their talking?

"You will conceive of your project after meeting with Gurudev."

Oh, my God. I would meet with Gurudev. And then I would…what? *Conceive* of my project? Again, my heart was thrashing so loudly, I could hardly concentrate on his words.

"You'll meet with him on Thursday morning…"

Three days from today! Holy shit.

"…and have a few sessions with him. We'll transcribe the tapes after you meet with him each time, and you can work off of the hard copy."

Hard copy? I'll be working off of hard copy? And I'll have a few sessions with him? Sessions, tapes, and hard copy?

"…and we'll then look at the body of work that has been generated and move from there. Any questions?"

Yes. What the heck? my mind was screaming.

"No, none, thanks." *No, none, thanks?* Did I just say that? I was completely clueless, without the faintest idea about sessions (What the heck happened? What was a session?), tapes (How? Who? Was I supposed to *do* something to make that happen? Plug something in? Turn something on?), and hard copy. Hard copy? My mind couldn't conceive of hard copy. There was absolutely no way to ask this strange man anything. I would have to make it up as I went along.

"And one suggestion." Arjun finally looked straight at me, his green eyes blazing with integrity, preparing to change my life.

"Read the *New Yorker*. We have a subscription. Get it from Trusha. Read it weekly. Read and notice the writing."

For some unknown reason, this I heard. His comment sank deeply into my awareness. Some of the best advice I have ever received, I have followed it loyally for most of the weeks of my life since that morning.

"Okay, then," he said, swiveling around in his rotating chair, obviously dismissing me.

"Okay, then," I unconsciously replied, getting another eyebrow raise from him. I nodded feverishly in agreement, got up, and released myself from the office.

I had one overriding thought: *get me out of here*. Since I really had no seva to do, I retreated to my bedroom—after ten months of shared dormitory housing, I finally had my own room. Here I began to "integrate," in Kripalu-ese, my experience. That meant lying on my bed with Buzzie the Bird walking up and down my chest saying, "Pretty bird," while my mind was saying, "What the heck?" Both Buzzie and my mind repeated their sayings in rapid-fire repetition.

That week I was the recipient of more eyebrow raises than in all the years of my life put together. Response from my friends, fellow younger residents, was incredulous. At the dinner table, where some of the older resident women sat, there was a general hubbub about my assignment. Obviously it was unusual for a "young" resident to have a guru-centered seva. I found myself assuming an attitude of feigned humility again, while my internal experience was one of sheer terror. I tried not to talk about it to people. It was almost embarrassing to me that I had been given such a gift.

The three days passed slowly. Since I had no work/seva, I sat at my computer and wandered the network—fortunately this was long before the worldwide web, which might have taken me under. I found some timed typing exercises that engaged me, and practiced them obsessively, my fingers skipping over the keys. My typing skills got sharper over those few days, as my self-confidence drooped. Perhaps I should have been preparing for my first encounter with the Guru. But I didn't know how, so I wildly typed, trying to type my anxiety away.

Thursday arrived, the day for my "session" with the Guru. Arjun would come with me, which made the untenable seem totally and fantastically impossible to bear. Then he would leave. With him or without him, the entire situation was unfathomable. I wore my white skirt, tights, white sweater, and mala beads. We writers were suppose to wear white when attending to the Guru, which made me feel even more out-of-place in the dining room for breakfast. I felt as if I were eating my last meal. Most residents would kill for time alone with him. Why was I so terrified? Was it because I felt so undeserving?

Arjun and I trudged up the hill to the Guru's house, which stood on the west hill overlooking the main building. Arjun carried the tape player (if I'd had a job description, the operating of said tape player would have been my responsibility). He opened the door and we entered Gurudom, the Guru's home.

The doorway opened into a spacious, open meeting room,

decorated simply with some Indian statues and prints on the wall, smelling of incense and his guru-scent, a pungent oil that was available in the Kripalu Shop for purchase. I must admit—I did purchase a bottle upon my arrival at Kripalu and daily dabbed it carefully onto all my particular personal spots. I shakily followed Arjun's lead and hung my coat in the hall closet. My mind screamed, "The Guru's closet!"

We entered the meeting room. Arjun began setting up the tape player, instructing me in grave detail as to its operation. I did not hear a word he said, which would return to haunt me in future sessions, when I was the solo audio operator. I could not possibly listen. My entire life's energy was directed toward stilling my screeching heart and crazy mind. I tried unsuccessfully to look around, to take in the surroundings. There was a set of glass sliding doors looking out onto a gorgeous view of the lake. My mind floated toward the lake, as a door opened into our room. Arjun jumped to his feet, and chanted the traditional greeting, "Bolo shri, shri Krishan Chandra...Jai, Gurudev." I attempted to chant along, mustering up some semblance of "Jai, Gurudev," as he walked, smiling, into the room.

The room filled up with his guru-scent a few long moments before he himself entered it. *He must use a lot of oil,* was my first conscious thought upon seeing him up close and personal. He was wearing his everyday velour (always velour) robe of light brown, what I imagined to be his play clothes. He seemed very tall. My second thought was: *Where does he get those robes?* He had a huge smile on his face, and had his hands clasped together in the traditional Indian greeting. I followed Arjun's lead and knelt onto the floor, forehead to the rug, showing our respect, or, in my case, complete mindlessness. He clapped us both on the back with a hearty thwack (another gift that everyone in that building behind me would have killed for) and we rose, kneeling before the Guru.

He was cute, cuter up close. Long nose, high cheekbones, grey hair peppering the sideburns at his temples, he continued to beam a huge, toothy smile down at us. Arjun introduced me as the new writer. The Guru's face got serious then; the smile instantly dissolved. His responses were childlike and whole-hearted.

"Oh," were his first words directed at me. "Oh," with a serious sigh behind it, as if the fun was taken out of it for him, too.

And so began my relationship with Gurudev. My up-close-and-personal writer's relationship with the Guru.

I walked up that hill to "work with him" twice a week, and spent the rest of the week recovering, reestablishing my balance on earth, and looking bleary-eyed at the "hard copy" generated from our sessions. My job was to engage him, to stimulate him, to get him talking—never the problem—to challenge his ideas, to tape the sessions (the ultimate trial for a techno-phobe like myself), and then to write and synthesize his ideas. Gurudev himself didn't write. He needed others to talk to, to teach to. Then we, his surrogates, would write up his ideas, return to him, reading it aloud, only to be interrupted after the first sentence or two, as he launched into an entirely new spewing of philosophy. Simply put, the Guru could not be contained to the written word.

We in the editorial department talked about this phenomenon as the Guru's prerogative, like the famous story of the disciple, Milaropa, whose life work was to build his Guru a house. He built it, stone by stone, in the spot so designated by the Guru. After its mighty completion, the Guru looked at it and instructed him to tear it down, and to build it ten feet to the left. And on and on the legend goes, with Milaropa constructing and deconstructing the house. And so did we in the editorial department, constructing and deconstructing the Guru's words. This phenomenon was the key to our spiritual growth, the destruction of our ego. It was about seva, selfless service, and yet there were no books by him, for this very reason. Years after his fall to the weaknesses of sexual and financial improprieties, it was bandied about that perhaps he very simply had an attention deficit disorder, making any linear, forward-moving project or discussion impossible. But that was years in the future. In 1990, our job as good disciples was to spiritualize his foibles. And spiritualize we did.

A few weeks later, sitting in front of Arjun for our weekly meeting, I felt hopelessly lost. I was there to present my "concept" for the book I was going to write with Gurudev. I had not been able to get a full sentence out in front of him, nor had I been able to write anything that he didn't just simply deny by fresh, rambling teachings during the next session.

Suddenly, out of nowhere, I had a wacky idea and blurted it out to Arjun:

"I want to take his morning meditations"—the easiest for me to stand—

"and distill them into verse!" There. I'd said it aloud. Arjun looked surprised for a moment. He then nodded his agreement and tilted his head toward the door, both sanctioning my wacky project and excusing me from further discussion about it.

Taking the Guru's words and putting them into verse form could be fun and achievable. But getting him to agree would be like the Bible verse he always misquoted—trying to get the camel through the eye of a needle. This was a man who would not be contained in a book. And I was claiming I could channel his teachings and energy in verse! I could not possibly have picked a more impossible task. Like Milaropa, I struggled. Although working through his voluminous teachings was excruciating, I did manage to eke out a few verses, which eventually made their way to another ashram publication.

Forever Free

That which
we hide from
haunts us.

That which
we run from
reins us.

That which
we avoid
creates a void
in us.

That which
we clutch
has a hold
on us.

But that which
we allow to flow
leaves us
forever free.

There was a second major obstacle in writing with the Guru. He was an energy-based kind of guy. The yogis called it shakti, or life force. Being with him was an energetic experience, as if consciousness around you had taken on a spin, a deepening. Sitting with him, alone or with the entire community, he might say, "The grass is green." It felt like the most profound thing one had every heard. *The grass is green! Oh, my good Lord, the grass IS green!* The energy was real and alive and one was, in that moment's insight, enlightened. However, the next day, looking at those words on paper, "The grass is green," was devastating. *The grass is green? What the heck? That's ridiculous.* It was empty, flat, and meaningless. Not unlike some of the poems I had scribbled at midnight on many a stoned, drunken evening on a slice of envelope, his words, too, did not land in the light of day.

His energy just didn't translate to writing. At least nobody had cracked the code yet to make that happen. I had absolutely no illusions that my poetry idea was anything but a death sentence to my seva. I just grasped at the form I felt safest in, the one I could control the most, shut my eyes to the results, and continued trudging up that hill. I felt as if I were headed toward my death. I guessed that was because it *was* my death: the death of my ego. I never told anyone this—not Arjun or Amma or any of my friends. I just schlepped my weaknesses, my self-doubt up and down the hill to the Guru's satsanga room twice a week to listen to him teach. And teach. And teach.

Eyes animated, fingers pointing, face alive with feeling, every cell in his body was pouring out philosophical wisdom. In general, I had no real idea what he was talking about. When I could momentarily relax, I enjoyed my fascination with him, his whole-hearted childishness. And I could grasp and appreciate his simple ideas, the ones that were so parallel with 12 Step philosophy, like surrendering to life—life on life's terms, as the program says. But mostly, I was on the defensive, trying to form the next question in my mind, to get him to be clearer, more specific, more understandable.

We writers would travel with the Guru when he went on

trips, to utilize his time well and to not miss an opportunity to document his teachings. Arjun informed me one afternoon that I would be driving to Sumneytown in Pennsylvania, the home of the ashram's first site, with Gurudev and Rupkanand, who would drive. Rupkanand was a renunciate, one of fifteen or so who had taken lifelong vows with the Kripalu order, a very high-up fellow and someone with whom I would never have had any interactions—up to that point we had traveled in different Kripalu worlds. We would be gone for three days. Frantically putting together bird-care for Buzzie, packing my travel case with whites, I faced these days with a grave and heavy heart. Yes, what a gift, yet, oye, so much unknown. Arjun packed a dozen audio tapes for me, and the portable tape player, which I had finally (practically) mastered. This was the first of many road trips I would take with Gurudev.

The six-hour ride was a blur of countryside. It was filled with their front-seat conversation, stopping to look at an unremarkable stand of trees on the parkway's edge that caught his attention, and several Guru bathroom stops. I was too anxious to pee. I sat absorbed, sunken into the back leather seat of this large car, seemingly triple the size of my former Ruby, as Rupkanand navigated us southward. The two of them chattered, their words like soft little bird calls floated above my head. Was I in a devotional bliss? Traumatic shock? Denial? I had no clue. I watched spellbound out the window as the countryside ticked by.

Once we'd arrived at Sumneytown, an austere yet lovely series of buildings, I was whisked away to my freezing dormitory. I attempted to settle in. The only other inhabitant of the huge room with sixteen beds was a warm, kind woman who unsuccessfully attempted to welcome me. I was too self-absorbed to appreciate her kindness. I had a sparse dinner with her, and spent a cold, shivering night cuddled in my cot, missing my Buzzie and my bathroom duties.

The next day dawned with glorious brilliance. Fall had not quite arrived in Pennsylvania, and the leaves were just beginning to shift their colors. I had breakfast with Vivian, my bunkmate, when Rupkanand came in all aflutter, giving me news of the day's agenda:

"Gurudev wants to go shopping. There is a sale on men's turtlenecks at The American Man, a store on Route 32. Please accompany him. Meet him in twenty minutes by the car."

The American Man? Route 32? Turtlenecks? Life was getting stranger and stranger. Vivian assured me wearing whites to The American Man was not required, so I rushed back to my dorm on shaky legs, to redress in my presentable slacks and crewneck sweater. I waited by the car, tape player in hand, trying to breathe.

He approached, his grin arriving before he did. Robeless, he looked stunning in charcoal pleated pants and a black turtleneck, carrying his trench coat carefully folded between his hands. As if remembering our task together, his face became somber.

"Jai, Gurudev," I shouted a bit too loudly, breaking the still silence, my hands trying to enter the Namaste pose but hampered by the very heavy tape player. He got into the car, sliding behind the driver's seat. I assumed I would drive and he would navigate. But no, life had a different idea. Fumbling with the passenger's door, I slid in beside him, tape player bumping my shin as I sank into the leather seat.

"Buckle up, buckle up," he affably instructed, suddenly an expert at driving. I wondered when the last time was he had driven. I surrendered. Truthfully, I wasn't sure what surrender really meant, so I just tried to relax. That was the best I could do. He skidded out of the driveway, taking too wide of a turn

255

and leaving the ashram screeching behind us as our road trip together took on new dimensions.

It was a long and memorable morning. Since my fumbling with the tape player annoyed him, we agreed I would put it aside and use the legal pad I brought. I felt freer without technological restraints, and continued my attempts at relaxation. Holding the pad on my lap, pen poised, I was there, I believed, to archive his profundity.

Five minutes away from the ashram, he turned down an unmarked road. Breath squeezed out of my body as I looked ahead. We were headed in the wrong direction on a fairly busy four-lane road. Cars were streaming toward us. I had a moment's glimpse of death, and calmed myself by imagining that dying with an enlightened master in a fiery car crash was an evolved way to go. His response was a complete surprise—when he had a feeling, it registered fully; his face, his body, his very being became that response. "Oh," he said, amazed at it. "Look, Aruni, the wrong direction!" I squeezed my eyes closed. We would surely die. But somehow he got us to the side of the road, and, without police arrest, got us heading in the accurate direction.

We drove past strip mall after strip mall. I was relaxed enough now, realizing that I was still alive, to begin to enjoy myself. Shopping with the Guru! We passed a Baptist church that was set back in a concrete mall, its marquee announcing, "Seize the day for God's purpose." Gurudev loved that, and launched into a ten-minute flow of teaching about seizing, about God, and about purpose. I attempted to scratch down notes but had long ago given up any hope for the writing aspect of my time with him. I just tried to hang out and watch. It seemed a smart strategy.

The American Man was on Route 32, but we seemed to circle around it for a long stretch of time. Finally the miraculous happened—we found ourselves in the right parking lot, and my driver, the enlightened master, found a parking place for us. Getting out of the car I was heady, stoned with the incongruity of it—my Guru in a strip mall. He carefully smoothed his turtleneck over his lean body and solemnly put on his trench coat. Together we walked, an unlikely couple, into The American Man. A bell chimed our entrance.

It was a large, upscale discount store that seemed hushed against the noise of Route 32. I stood starry-eyed next to my teacher, watching him as he began to scan with wonderment the tables of sweaters, the racks of socks, the hanging bins of oxford shirts. I was on a spiritual quest with my Guru. A very white, eager young salesman approached us. As his eyes flitted over us, I wondered his deduction about our status: young white woman with her sugar daddy? Unlikely. The salesman leaned forward into our space and carefully inquired, "Anything I can help you folks with this morning?"

Gurudev responded seriously in the negative, moving his head from side to side with profound conviction. There would be no helping this man. He would master this shopping process himself. So off we wandered, from table to table, as he fingered each item, studying each cut of shirt, examining each piece of material with all of the focus in the universe. I followed behind, trailing in his wake, now in bliss at the silly and perfect juxtaposition of this day: my deep, spiritual master, bargain-hunting.

We eventually found the table of reduced-price turtlenecks: two for $18, the sign announced. Gurudev was fascinated by the many options of color, size, and style. Finally, after much fingering of material, he selected a charcoal grey in two different sizes and two different necks, mock turtle and regular turtle. He took off his trench coat, passing it to me as he flowed with beyond-human grace toward the dressing room. I stood, hugging my Guru's coat close to my body, floating away on a cloud of guru-scent, absurdity, and sheer love. This guy was not of this world. I hugged the coat deeply into me.

Eventually he came out of the dressing room proudly modeling option number one, and stood innocently, almost shyly before me, beaming in his new sweater. He pirouetted around, so I could see it from all angles, smoothing it down over his taut belly. He was a turtleneck kind of guy. I nodded my head in sheer infatuation, as he retired into the dressing room to prepare option number two. This went on for a countless number of options, colors, sizes, and necks. A guru fashion show! I was giddy by now. He finally decided that the quality of workmanship was not of his standard, declining all options, and we worked our way through the other racks of clothing toward the exit, finally making our way into the Pennsylvania morning air.

"Ah," he exclaimed to nobody, "that was in-vig-or-a-thing." His accent added a particular ambience to him.

He was child/man, a channel of both fierce grace and pure innocence.

Our shopping extravaganza continued throughout the morning, as we sampled material swatches in a furniture store for an alleged couch, paint colors in a hardware store for the walls of his office, and tiling in the flooring store for no particular destination. At one point, we dashed across Route 32 together to get to the other side, easier it seemed than moving the car to the next store. We dodged traffic together, not literally holding hands, but dancing in soulful unison across the road.

We returned home without purchases, without text, yet fully victorious. I had witnessed the guru fashion show; he had explored the deep, spiritual essence of shopping.

Light-headed and over-stimulated, I curled into my bed in the damp, empty dorm. Visions of turtlenecks, material swatches, and multi-colored tiled patterns danced in my head as I squeezed my eyes tight. Exhausted, I slept for the rest of day, wrapped in dreams of delirious delight.

"Long nose, high cheekbones, grey hair peppering the sideburns at his temples, he continued to beam a huge, toothy smile down at us."
Yogi Amrit Desai

23

⚬

Recovering My Voice
1992

To live in the ashram was to see myself. To see my foibles, my limitations, the trauma from the past that still affected me, was inevitable—all the activities of a yogic lifestyle, from seva to conscious relationships to the contemplative practices of meditation and yoga, were geared to activate those old tapes, in order to release them so new ones could emerge. The damn place was a mirror, a shiny, bright mirror, reflecting back to me those parts of myself that were not integrated. It was a wacky and wild ride, and profoundly uncomfortable at times.

My relationship with yoga on the mat was a good example. Yoga was never my forte. I loved its silence, its depth, its permission to explore inside. But I continually felt so unskillful at it. I had such difficulty allowing myself to simply be at my level, to simply be where I was. To not compare myself to the residents—the other Kripalu volunteers, all around me on the floor—was very challenging. When yoga practice was optional, I eagerly awoke and made my way to the Main Chapel. I adored the early morning forays into my own longing heart, my body stretching in the dark, reaching toward inner grace, making the struggle worthwhile. But sometime in 1991, yoga became mandatory for all residents at 4:15 p.m. In the light of day, with the stigma of *compulsory* on it, my struggle ignited into the flames of self-rejection. It wasn't fun.

Wanting to be better than I was ate away at me, as I stood on the yoga mat, struggling in the standing postures. Never great with balance, both on the yoga mat or in my life, the balancing postures kicked my butt.

"Relax," reassured the annoyingly melodious voice of the Kripalu senior teacher, soft gentle music floating all around us. "Soften your gaze, and surrender to the energy." I, however, tipped; I toppled, I sweated, I struggled. Surrendering to the energy seemed like it would take me down, crashing into the earth. That would be unacceptable. I would have to fight with all my strength to keep upright. I thought of Gurudev's teaching about perfection, an ironic banner for my journey into my own imperfections:

Recognize that
you cannot be
any other way
than the way
you are
in this moment.

I didn't like it. I didn't like it at all. I didn't want to be un-skillful at yoga. I wanted to learn the poses and be done with it, once and for all.

But nowhere in the lifestyle did I confront my internal challenges as much as in groups, struggling to find my voice. Like on the yoga mat, I had such difficulty finding my balance in these activities. Our days were group-heavy. We had share groups before seva began in the mornings, study groups led by a senior teacher in the afternoons, and group activities in the evening. I loved these gatherings. They were fascinating, alive, dynamic—my interest in people began to emerge here.

However, at the same time, they brought out terror in me—terror of speaking.

I wasn't sure of what I felt about the topics of discussion, what my contribution to the conversation might be. I always doubted my understanding of the discussions. While others were sharing, I spent time considering and shaping what my input might be. My obsessing kept me from the moment, separating me from my innate ability to access my more authentic self. I was so propelled by people-pleasing. I wanted to say something that would generate approval. Being aware of these patterns was so excruciating. Also, I felt as if I couldn't trust my voice. Not just the content, but the mechanics of successful speaking still weren't guaranteed to me. If I opened my mouth, would sound come? Or would it be a burst of stuttering? I sweated my way through, one group at a time, loving and hating the experiences.

I was aware that my childhood/young adulthood stuttering issues were being re-triggered and re-traumatized in these situations. I felt like a child sitting in seventh grade, counting the number of students ahead of me, so I would be prepared to read my verse of poetry. Feeling that young and that vulnerable was horrifyingly hard for me, and so confusing. I had many reasons to feel comfortable about my place in the community: fourteen months writing with the Guru, a great seva editing disciples' stories for the Guru commemorative book, great friends who loved me. What was the problem? Why couldn't I trust my voice?

So when Varuna approached me one spring day in the Dining Chapel, where I was sitting alone, this issue took on a deeper resonance. She sat down in the empty seat next to me and launched into some superficial banter. She then stopped abruptly, looked me squarely in the eyes, and asked if I wanted to lead a workshop in Retreat and Renewal, the in-house program for guests. I was instantly elated and then, in the next breath, frozen inside. How would I do it? How could I stand both the pressure of it and the bliss?

Varuna was an "older resident," but she lacked the holier-than-thou gene. She was irreverent and spicy in her speech and presence, completely unintimidating to me. Her laugh was joyous and contagious, which served her well with the guests. Her mid-neck-length soft sable hair, her bright smile—she was easy for me to open up to, to talk with, to appreciate. But in that moment, I was speechless.

"Come on, what's the problem here?" She kiddingly kicked my foot with her sandal under the table. "I thought you would be thrilled."

"What if I can't do it, Varuna? What if I don't have anything to say?" This was my gravest fear. My voice sounded young and thin.

She laughed. "Where did you say you taught for fifteen years? Malcolm Who High School?"

"Malcolm X Shabazz."

She laughed again, her gusty, throaty laugh. "Honey, if you can teach there, you can manage our guests in the Forest Room." Seeing that I was still unsure, she got more serious. "Aruni, there is no problem here. You are full of his energy. Draw on his energy." She was, of course, referring to the Guru.

I was full of the Guru's energy? It was a strange yet mobilizing thought. It was enough to move me forward.

And so I began to plan my first workshop, searching for my authentic voice. Not the elusive Guru's voice. Not the voice of the disciples whose stories I was editing. Not the curriculum in Newark, N.J. What was my understanding of yogic philosophy? What was my curriculum? I realized I had free reign to completely make this up. There was nobody to check with, no principal, no department chairperson. I could create a workshop as I fully chose.

My little editorial office was hushed; only the sound of air hammering through the pipes filled the room. Amma was away, leaving all space and air for me, as I struggled, trying to focus myself. What was the topic that interested me? What was the one slice of philosophy that spoke to me? What was my hardest piece to grasp? Where did I fight reality?

I thought of the poem, "Perfection." I thought of my own struggle to stand on the yoga mat, of how difficult it was to accept myself as I was. The title breezed into my head: *The Gift of Self-Compassion*. I wiggled with delight on my office chair. That was it, the title. But what was the workshop?

Over the next week or two, I hammered away at an outline, looking for yogic principles that might support this title. *Perhaps I am working backwards*, I mused at my desk, pencil at my lips, *and putting the egg before the hen. Perhaps I should be starting with the workshop, and then create a title. Is it okay to have the title come first?* It was whatever it was. This was the journey.

I considered the yogic principle of *ahimsa*, non-harm. Surely when I beat myself up mentally, when I drove myself crazy during a group wondering what to say, I was violating this principle. I was doing harm to myself. And I also thought of Swami Kripalu's core teaching, "self observation without judgment," that urged watching our habits, witnessing the obstacles that blocked us from being fully alive, and then, without judgment, realigning to right action. Perhaps those two teachings could be the core of this workshop?

I worked long and hard, struggling against time, perhaps violating the dictates of this very workshop in its creation. Lying in bed, with Buzzie the Bird asleep in her covered cage five feet away, I pondered the perfect soft background music for the journaling segment of the program. *Oh, no. Will I become one of these Kripalu teachers who is addicted to soft, elevator music surrounding each aspect of the class?* And I obsessed about questions for the guests to journal about in their introspection, word-smithing myself to sleep. It was compelling and fully engaging. Like writing with the Guru, however, I felt not deserving to teach, and surely not qualified. But I kept that to myself. Residents with my few years in the ashram didn't teach. Teaching in this culture was something you had to earn through years of residency. It seemed I was on another track, and it was moving me quickly forward.

I was very concerned about *"om-ing."* *Om* was the chant that we used to begin and end classes. Supposedly it was the sound that aligned all the energy chakras or centers in the body. I, as facilitator of the group, would lead the *om*. I practiced quietly and obsessively in my bedroom over those weeks, with Buzzie dancing and chirping her critique. She was a bird who appreciated her *oms*. It was such a point of doubt. What if sound didn't come? What if I couldn't *om*? I had *om-dread*. I was *om-phobic. Oye.* I mean, *om.* What if I chanted *oye* instead of *om*?

The day finally arrived. As I awoke in my little room, mattress unfolded on the floor, Buzzie stirring in her cage, I felt annoyingly over-structured and completely unprepared. Okay, so I had a structure. But what would I say? Within the teachings, what words would come out of my mouth? I didn't know. I couldn't know. In the words of Sarah, my AA sponsor at the time, I was supposed to "suit up and show up." My dear friend, Eric, nice Jewish boy that he was, carefully recounted his version of Jesus and one of the disciples—he forgot which one it was. Paul? Matthew? Whoever. Jesus had told them to go out and teach. And this one disciple said to Jesus, "But Lord, what do we say? What do we tell them?" And not unlike Sarah, Jesus said, "Get there and I'll tell you." I appreciated the AA perspective; I smiled at Eric's Jewish paraphrase of the Jesus perspective. I was still terrified.

My dear friend Arpana insisted on ironing my clothes for the workshop. Ironing, a lost art! I dressed in freshly pressed khaki pants and a spiritual-looking-but-hopefully-not-overbearing gauzy top, and looked in the mirror. Buzzie was on her cage, chirping at the morning sun. I looked—heavy. Bloated. With bags under my eyes. I could not see the child of God the Guru talked about. I could not see divinity disguised as humanity. I could only see the pimple that erupted, taking over my left nostril.

Oh, well. Suit up and show up.

I got on my knees and sat before my altar, a make-shift milk crate from my NYC apartment, covered with a spiritual-like blousy scarf. On it was a picture of the Guru, a Buzzie feather, a picture of my parents, and a mirror. I sat there, trying to notice my breath as everybody told me to. And I prayed. It was a simple prayer, all I could muster: "Help." The prayer didn't stop my pounding heart, but it did slow me down a little bit.

Finally it was time. Getting up from my altar, escorting Buzz back in her cage despite her reluctance, gathering my notes and my flipchart, I made my way toward the Forest Room, to launch The Gift of Self-Compassion. I scurried down the back hallway and down the less-traveled stairs, precariously balancing tapes, notes, and flipchart.

I yanked the door onto the third floor landing, and almost bumped into Gurudev. He was never around this early in the day. Wearing his everyday tan robe, he was all meditation in motion, moving through that doorway with the grace of movement that still took away my breath.

"Jai, Gurudev," I managed to blurt, offering him the traditional welcome. My flipchart fell from my hands in my disciple's eagerness. Why was I always so clumsy around him? I didn't see him individually anymore since I had been dismissed from Guru-writing detail. It had been a while.

He laughed, beamed a hello, and reached down to get the flipchart for me.

"Where are you going with so many in your arm?" he asked with his typical accent and innocent, mangled grammar. I knew he had forgotten my name. He always forgot names. He stood, holding my flipchart.

"Gurudev, I'm going to teach my first guest workshop." I gulped.

"Oh, very good. Very. Good." He stood for a moment, smiling at me, then handed the flipchart back, managing to wedge it under my arm. He tapped me on my right shoulder, an auspicious blessing. As stealthily as he came, he so disappeared, sauntering down the steps and gone from my sight.

Did that just happen? Did Gurudev just hold my flipchart and bless me? Did I just make that up? I could smell his guru-scent lingering in the hallway all around me. Shaking my head in disbelief, I gathered myself and continued.

I made my way toward the Forest Room, my gait a little looser now. The room was empty but for the already arranged back-jacks, little on-the-floor seats for the guests, in a tidy circle. I set up my flipchart on the easel with shaky hands. *Breathe,* I told myself. *Breathe.*

Guests entered one by one and found their seats. I managed some easy chatting with them and put on my favorite, New-Agey instrumental soft music in the background, fine-tuning the volume to slide in right behind one's awareness, to not overpower. I turned to face the crowd. The room had filled up with twenty-five or so guests. Rasmani, a cute, silver-haired elflike woman and member of the faculty, had come to support me. She twinkled her support. I looked away and tried to breathe.

"Hi, everybody. My name is Aruni. This workshop is called The Gift of Self-Compassion. Let's start our time together with an *om*."

I took a deep breath, exhaled, and the sound of *om* released itself from me. It wasn't a perfect *om*. It was kind of shaky and weak, a bit off-key. But it was my *om*. The guests sounded their chant, our voices coming together in wacky and remarkable harmony and perfection, compensating for my pitch.

And then the miracle emerged, mid-*om*. The miracle-prayer emerged. It came forth within me:

Help me. This is Yours. Give me the words.

And each and every time that I have chanted *om* before a class during these past two decades of teaching, this prayer has emerged for me. This prayer of request. This prayer of connection.

And for all of the times that I have chanted *om* after a class during these past two decades, this prayer of completion has emerged, too:

Thank you. This is Yours. I offer it back.

And within the pillars of those two prayers, words came to me that day. I was able to speak my understanding of the teachings, and encourage the guests to pursue their own. The class went well enough, my feelings somewhat leveling out through the guests' kindness. But it went too quickly. After the final *om*, I regretted that I hadn't savored it more. I didn't know then that I would have lots of opportunities to savor the brilliance of Kripalu workshops; that I would facilitate thousands of them over the coming years.

And within those prayers, my voice continues to emerge. It is not a process in which I am exonerated from preparation. By no means—preparation is my responsibility. And yet, when facing the many who have sat before me, I continue to learn, perhaps by sheer terror; to remember that I am not alone in the creation and in the offering of this voice.

During the workshop that day in 1991, I learned some basic tenets about the offering of my voice:

> ➤ *That what I have to say is really not all that important.*
> ➤ *That keeping the guests relaxed and feeling safe is.*
> ➤ *That there is nothing before me that needs fixing.*
> ➤ *That as I teach, I practice.*
> ➤ *That I have the words—all I do is suit up and show up.*
> ➤ *That the participants have words, too. My only job is to facilitate their listening to their own voice.*

This very morning I taught the same workshop, The Gift of Self-Compassion. Eighteen years later, with as many revisions as I have had, the same pillars of prayer hold me strong. I am still warmed by the kindness of the guests. These same lessons emerge for me, time after time, *om* after *om*.

Years later, sitting at my computer, beginning to channel this voice that I have been given onto the written page and into my books, the prayers continue to carry me. And through all of the teaching and all of the writing I have done, these prayers are the riverbanks through which I swim:

Help me. This is Yours. Give me the words.
Thank you. This is Yours. I offer it back.

Part Two: What Is

24

Body

I was once at a 12 Step meeting on Cape Cod. A little man in a blousy yellow seersucker shirt in the back of the room raised his hand. Obviously a local, unlike so many of us tourist-types—we were the ones with burnt noses, googly-eyed at the natural beauty all around us—he was straight-forward, a typical New Englander in his sharing. His voice echoed with that familiar flat twang. He offered great practicality, as he described his newest sober challenge, something relating to a propane gas tank, blocked pipes, and the like:

"If you have a home, you'll have home issues. If you have a propane gas tank, you'll have propane gas tank issues."

I was profoundly struck with the simplicity of this brilliance. My entire drinking and drugging career, twenty years of hell, was about trying to control life so issues did not arise, and then trying to control my feelings when issues did inevitably emerge. With this simple sentence, this living scripture, this anonymous fellow offered me a guideline for living. *Shit happens*, the bumper sticker instructs us. I always thought that our job as humans was to prevent the shit from happening. And surely, as adults, we were commissioned to not have feelings about the shit when it did occur.

This philosophical maxim from the yellow seersucker man has served me well. I have used it successfully in the realm of dogs and their soft tissue injuries, cars and their failed transmissions, bosses and their eccentric personalities, and in a multitude of other "life on life's terms" kinds of situations. Yet as I age, there is nowhere I need to utilize this spiritual brilliance as I do in relationship to my own aging body. Six decades later, this body of mine, although blessed with resiliency and wellness, has places of weakness and breakdown.

If you have a body, you have body issues.

This invitation diffuses emotionality, guilt, blame, and judgment. Separate from the mind's wild reactions, we can simply respond to our bodies and their needs. Quite simply, we are encouraged to get over ourselves and to just simply deal.

So many of us live from our earlobes up, without any awareness of our disconnection from our body. Even the pursuit of healing, grace, and spirituality can all take place in our heads! There is so much activity constantly going on in our minds— couldn't we just light up our cities from the released energy of our busily firing brain circuits? Yogic philosophy and the contemplative practices can, however, interrupt our disconnection from our bodies and bring us awareness—not always a comfortable perspective, but an essential one for change and growth.

Yoga teaches that we are born with an inherent balance between body, mind, and spirit. In our culture, it appears that the mind gets out of balance, and becomes the center of all, severing connections to the body, let alone the spirit. This has certainly been my experience. In those famous words of James Joyce—who knew he was a yogi?—"Mr. Duffy lived a short distance from his body."

In my younger years, it wasn't safe to feel. What I was feeling was illicit and needed to be hidden. I hid so well from you that I lost myself to me. Hence the cord of connection and awareness was severed. This is one aspect of the human dilemma that raises such essential questions: How do we quiet the mind enough to reconnect to the signals of the body? How do we begin to hear the faint whispers of the spirit? One response to these questions is consistently reliable—the contemplative practices and mindfulness practices are avenues of union, of reconnection with these divorced aspects of ourselves.

Although all of us inherit both the oneness of body, mind, and spirit, along with the inevitable separation from that harmony, addiction is an attempt that some of us make at an ultimate check-out of the moment, the creation of the definitive split between body and mind. The mind will kill off the body. Yet again, we can count on yoga and mindfulness practices as a check-in to the moment, the healing reunion of body, mind, and spirit.

At the age of sixty-one, I have the beginnings of a relationship with my body that I intend to cultivate during these next years of aging. I believe this is a generic formula that, when applied specifically to your body and your needs, can help us all continue cultivating health and wellness for our aging bodies.

We need to find ways to return to our bodies for physical, emotional, and spiritual health. For many, yoga is the road home. But others among us have found great release and profound sanctity in moving with mindfulness. Bike-riding in the early summer mornings, hiking with dogs in the woods, swimming laps in the pool, even the elliptical machine in the gym—all can become meditation in motion for us, venues in which our minds can relax enough to allow our bodies' signals to be received. Returning to that place where spirit is available, where intuition is effortless, where relaxation is constant, is essential. Motion is the lotion for body, mind, and spirit. As we practice moving, we practice feeling. This allows our minds to quiet down and our bodies to come forth. And all we need is a perfectly imperfect commitment to mindful, meditative movement. This is pillar number one in the tripod of body awareness.

Pillar number two is nutrition. Food is medicine. What we put into our mouths determines mood, energy, attitude, capacity to interact with others, ability to sleep, self-esteem, and wellness, to name a few. When we choose to act against this knowledge and eat that which is not nutritional food—which for some of us might run the gamut of processed foods, artificially sweetened food, and foods heavy with empty carbohydrates—we pay the price. However, when our actions are in alignment with this core belief, that food is medicine; when we are able to eat less processed, more natural foods, we are rewarded with energy, balance, and hope. Right nutrition spreads its healing tentacles into the realms of body, mind, and spirit.

The final pillar of body awareness is a commitment to balanced sleep habits. To go to bed consistently at an early enough time to wind down, to not activate ourselves later in the evening through the stimulating temptations of television and internet, to allow ourselves to unload and integrate the day's events rather than consuming more intake in the evening, to follow natural body rhythms, to wake early and consistently—all these actions keep us connected to our bodies.

So many clients sitting in my office complain of their struggles with food, their resistance to exercise, their inability to get off of prescribed medications for blood pressure and cholesterol. As we unravel these issues, at the center of the conundrum for so many is a single issue: disturbed sleep.

Working on the computer, watching television, taking on more stimulating activities when integrating the day is essential, yet it takes us out of balance. And to save us from this imbalance, caffeine comes to the rescue of exhaustion. Sweets come bearing their merciful yet artificial spike in energy. Sleep often needs to be the first thing that is addressed, to begin to restore rest and renewal. Behind that balance, the body returns to stasis and health.

This tripod of body-centered practices—mindful movement, conscious nutrition, and balanced sleep—can maximize our energy and offer us lives of wellness and possibility, no matter our age.

Beginning my journey through the sixth decade of my life is an entrance into the most unknown of terrain. My body is simply different. Eyesight taken for granted for decades is now fuzzy and out of focus. Driving at night is stressful, lights haloed and distracting. *How could this be?* screams my mind, which appears timeless in this cavalcade toward the grave.

Perhaps you could join me in this mantra: ***We do not like aging.*** In a perfect world, perhaps we would have it abolished. Aging looms terrifying with its unknowns, which hover like whispering, invisible ghosts just around the corner of my mind's eye. *What will happen to you? What disease will take you down? How will you ever afford health care? Who will take you to the urologist?* This unchartered territory is rife with unknowns, not comfortable for us recovering-or-not control freaks. It is simply not comfortable for us humans! We think we don't know the way through this uncharted terrain.

But, in fact, we do. We get to pick from the entire range of health care options to keep fit, from the most allopathic to the most woo-woo of New Age possibilities, to create our specific plans of response and healing to all that life has to offer our aging bodies. And life will indeed offer us plenty to deal with. That is simply life doing its job.

The New Age philosophy that encourages us to take responsibility for our bodily ailments can be helpful, when utilized appropriately. But it can also be a potentially slippery slope of self-blame and over-analyzing. When dealing with an eye issue, a friend recently asked me, "What are you afraid to see?" I considered her well-meaning question deeply, and found myself coming up short with responses. Perhaps my eye just simply had a pre-disposition to this specific condition? Traveling too far down the path of "What is it that we don't want to see?" might result in our blaming ourselves. Blame is useless in healing. This perspective could be disastrous and could serve to take us further away from wellness.

According to the yellow-seersuckered man, if you have a cornea, you just might have a cornea issue. Or not. Period. Deal with yourself.

So this is what is possible today: Rather than making giant proclamations about the next years of our lives, we can break it down to this single day. What do we choose for ourselves today, in relationship to our aging bodies, these temples of spirit, these containers of mind, these ultimate of homes in which we dwell?

I choose to walk into this bright brisk morning of my life with eyes wide open and as fuzzy-less as possible, with feet on the ground. Today I choose to be an energetic, active, vital woman. I will do that, as best as I can today, by walking with the dogs, by picking up the endless apples (to which Lucy Doodle the Dog is addicted) that continue to fall from our apple tree, by going to the gym and affirming life with Michael Jackson, by eating sane and whole meals, and by getting to bed before the 10 p.m. re-run of *Law and Order* that will inevitably activate me and leave me empty. I will find home inside, as best as I can.

And when I cannot, I will continue to practice.

And you? No matter your age, no matter your body issues— what do you choose for yourself?

25

☙

Practice

The concept of practice is both misunderstood and under-utilized in our culture. Our Western minds set us upon a new endeavor as a task, like a dog with a bone. *Go get it! Gobble it up. Finish it. Do it and complete it. Check it off your list of to do's.* We certainly are a linear and goal-oriented bunch. This Western approach does not necessarily lend itself easily to an attempted lifestyle change or spiritual development.

The word practice, as it implies, is an invitation into a consistent, long-standing relationship between you, the practitioner, and It, the thing to which you are committing. To practice mindfulness, to practice prayer, to practice a sustainable plan for healthy weight loss, to practice an exercise regime—all demand release from the idea of "completion" or "perfection." Practice encourages us into a conscious experiment to watch without judgment, to allow the natural evolution of the process to unfold. Like in the expression "two steps forward, one step backward," we notice, we watch without judgment, and we continue to realign to our commitment. We can continue moving forward, strengthened and informed by our "backward" steps.

If you were teaching a toddler to walk and the child fell, your response probably would not be, "Get up, you loser of a baby. Walk right, or I'm leaving." Of course not. Even the mere sound of this response is ludicrous. You would say something like, "Oh, good walking, you smart baby, you. Great falling. Try again! There you go, one more step, great." And yet, aren't we terribly harsh and self-rejecting with ourselves, without patience for our own falling, or our human failings? Don't we reject ourselves and sabotage ourselves, in response to the times we fall?

How can we begin to develop a relationship with ourselves that encourages experimentation, that allows imperfection, that releases attachment to the results, and that supports ongoing involvement in the process of growth? This is the practice—of practice!

It seems we have limited tolerance for the process of change. We just want to be done, damn it. However, change is a process, not an event. Change can engage us in the spirit of conscious experiment where there is no right or wrong, no complete or incomplete, and certainly no good or bad. It is a fluid evolution, filled with rich emotional and spiritual data. It is a journey of self-discovery, the ongoing practice of being present in the moment.

In my world, my foundational spiritual practice is the trusting of reality. This offers me powerful grounds for conscious experimenting. There are moments, perhaps even chunks of time, in which I am certain, in my body, mind, and spirit, that all is exactly as it should be. Usually this happens when I am teaching or coaching. I simply know in my core that nothing is askew. That woman in the third row in the red turtleneck is exactly where she needs to be, emotional and open. The tall, lanky guy in the Harvard baseball cap is as he should be, sitting perfectly still, seemingly untouched by my words. Energetically it is not my role to change these folks. My role is to let it be as it is, to be a conduit through which change happens. Life works, I am positive, and I am relaxed and certain.

And yet there are so many other moments, perhaps most of my life, in which I am uncomfortable, doubting, struggling, and pushing reality away. My partner is frustrated, and I believe it is my job to change her. The dog is injured, and I must solve all resulting problems. I want to get in there, to mastermind reality, and make it right, according to my version of life. Inevitably—I suffer. Wanting life to be different is surely the fast lane to suffering. There are certainly actions to take, plenty to do, but two prerequisites exist for successful action: to take it in the spirit of ultimate acceptance of what is, and to let go of our attachment to the results.

This is the muscle of practice. We all could so benefit from this flexibility, this fluidity, the acceptance of the forgetting as well as the remembering. Forgetting and remembering are both essential parts of the puzzle of sustainable growth. Swami Kripalu taught that the highest spiritual practice was "self-observation without judgment." Noticing and realigning, that is my job.

I have learned to respect and to explore the vast power of incremental steps in creating change. Tiny actions lead us successfully in the right direction and have the inherent capacity to sustain. Generally our inclination is to over-commit, to over-extend. We believe so fully in the outcome we hope for that we leap over tall buildings to get there. Yet our actions are unsustainable, resulting in internal defeat and potential emotional despair. Without step-by-step cumulative actions, we are often ultimately ineffective in creating change. As a coach, my job often is to simply talk folks down from the ledge of over-commitment and over-extension.

In working with Beth, a client of mine who was fiercely committed to losing the forty pounds she gained through the physical and emotional stressors of menopause, job loss, and a divorce, this human foible was never so obvious.

"I commit," Beth said passionately, sitting in my office in a posture of such determination, "to go to the gym every morning for the 7 a.m. Boot Camp class." She pumped her hand into the air for emphasis. "I will do that for however long it takes."

I shuddered. Clearly Beth was fully committed, ready to do whatever it took to begin to shed the pounds that now compromised the quality of her life. But seven days a week? After not moving for years? She was setting herself up for failure, physical injury, and an emotional roller coaster.

After much debate and negotiation, Beth decided to begin her morning BootCamp class with two mornings a week, and to walk a third morning. She did this for two weeks, after which we assessed, and added a second walk and a personal training session on weekends. After several months of assessing and tweaking the plan, she is doing fine, losing her weight at a slow, steady, and sustainable rate.

People resist, not wanting to hear the suggestion of moderation. No matter what your mind says as you prepare to commit to a practice, give yourself the gift of starting small. Assess your progress, tweak your plan, and recommit to its essence, while you continually create your revised structure of practice, responding to the data you are being given by your body and spirit. We want the end result so fully—the weight loss or the exercise program, the yoga practice or the healthier nutrition. We have little tolerance for the tiny steps that increasingly build up, moving us in that direction. As we said so regularly in the '60s: the destination is useless and improbable without an embracing, a relaxing into the journey.

Another element of practice emerges—the need to be, to do

nothing, to be passively receptive. Strangely enough, this is another difficult component for Westerners.

Even Albert Einstein, that famous yogi, cautions us as to the limits of the mind. "We can't solve problems by using the same kind of thinking we used when we created them," he warns us. This is pretty "heady" stuff, coming from one of the world's most notable intellectuals. Einstein invites us into the heart as the complementary problem-solver and partner, to work alongside the ally of the mind.

What is this heart that Einstein and others encourage us to explore? The heart of being opens us up to deep relaxation. It is the portal to divinity, to the silence, the intuition, the essence of our own souls. This journey is an essential component in any practice you intend for yourself. Since our lives are so saturated with never-ending stimulation, data, input, noise, and to do's, we are in a constant fight-flight alert, the parasympathetic nervous system ever-vigilant in its firing of adrenalin and other hormones of response. We are exhausted. Being flings open the doors to that cosmic pause, where the mind assumes its rightful place amidst its equally compelling companions, the body and the spirit.

What might "being" look like? Being is simply prioritizing and implementing a practice of that which you love. My clients often look at me with disbelief when I offer this comment. Shouldn't being, obviously a spiritual practice, be something that we *don't* do? Isn't that the definition of a spiritual practice—that which we don't do, avoid, know we should be doing, talk ourselves out of doing, and beat ourselves up for not doing?

But being doesn't have to look like sitting on the yoga mat with your leg wrapped around your neck for two days, unless that is something you adore. Being must be that which you fully enjoy, like biking, swimming, hugging a dog, taking a bath with lavender oil and candles, or watching the birds in the morning before you jump into action. We must start with where we are, with what we love, and build it into our lives. Certainly the time will come for us to commit to doing that which is difficult, that which we don't want to do. Getting sober for me was a major example of that principle. Yet we must start where we are, and give ourselves back the things we adore.

Are you a painter who doesn't have the time to paint? Are you a writer who crawls home at the end of the day, giving to everyone but yourself? Are you a gardener who lives in a high-rise with no access to land? How could you begin to incorporate elements of these activities into your life?

Of course we must expect inevitable resistance, and from an unlikely source: ourselves. The self-sabotaging parts of our psyche will show up to undermine our forward movement. These emotional responses are both essential to and inevitable in the momentum of growth. As soon as we commit to a practice, we can be sure that our resistance to that process of growth will surface. Yet somehow we see this resistance, these obstacles as something "wrong," something to be battled into submission. And we can do that—we can override them, but just for a while. That attitude of push will not and cannot sustain a practice.

However, relaxing around the obstacles, getting to know them, drawing them into the light of our conscious awareness will contribute to sustainable forward movement. Befriending these resistant parts of ourselves, getting to know them, literally entering into dialogue with them, takes us into a deeper, richer understanding of ourselves. The real gift of the commitment to a conscious practice is not even the obvious benefits of the It, the practice you are committing to. The meditation, the exercise, the healthy eating are actually by-products. The real benefit of a conscious commitment to a practice is learning more about ourselves, learning how to navigate the somewhat stormy waters that swell between commitment and resistance. This practice of practice is one of self-discovery. That is how change happens.

Change happens by bearing the process, by tolerating the missteps and knowing they are gifts sent from above. Change happens within the arms of radical self-acceptance of all the different aspects of ourselves, the *yes*, the *no*, the *maybe* all precious along the path. In the words of Rumi, the 13th century Persian Sufi mystic:

"Out beyond ideas of wrong doing and right doing,
There is a field.
I'll meet you there."

In that field, on this path, all our steps are sacred, and all our attempts are victories. We can literally do no wrong, as we are infinitely carried by a grace larger than ourselves.

26

❧

Mind

I have a mind that tells me to expect the very worst from life, to prepare in every moment for the worst-case scenario to unfold. This is in spite of decades' worth of evidence that nothing "bad" or "wrong" has happened or could happen to me.

Do you identify with this?

I have a mind that tells me to expect the very worst from myself, that personal failure and self-disappointment are inevitable. This, too, is in spite of decades' worth of evidence that shows me my development and my startling growth of competencies.

Do you identify with this?

I have a mind that tells me there isn't enough. Not enough money, food, love, attention, stuff, possibility, etc. And again, this is in spite of decades' worth of evidence that shows me that I have wanted for nothing, no matter what was happening around me.

Do you identify with this?

I have a mind that tells me that other people, you guys out there, know something I don't—you have memorized the instruction book that I never received. And again and again, this is in spite of decades' worth of evidence that shows me that I am fully able to navigate competently through whatever situation I am given.

Do you identify with this?

I have a mind that needs training. This is the only hope I have to live a life of relative sanity and calm.

What about you?

The yogis and ancient sages teach us that we are born in balance, with harmony between the body, the mind, and the spirit. It seems that in our "advanced" culture, our minds have gotten out of control. We become big-minded. The mind gets revved up, forgets to stop, overrides the messages of the body, and plunges wildly forward, ignoring the whisperings of the spirit. To believe the unexamined messages of our minds and to act without observation can cause us suffering, chaos, and potential ruin. Here is yet another human dilemma, since our minds are also our best ally, a collaborator of unparalleled abilities. The right use of will, finding and following the appropriate direction for our focus, is essential for mature and effective functioning in the world, and essential for our sanity.

A few years ago I had a profound job change that was not my idea. I deeply knew that the universe had always carried me forward to the next, best thing, and that, if something wasn't my idea, it just might be a good one. But nevertheless, this was a big letting go—I was in pain. After running the department for ten years, building it up, creating its curriculum, and dedicating myself to it, I was going to be released from that position. After a year's fearfulness about the potential change, which was very uncomfortable because it spurred me to more action and even more action, the inevitable did happen. Someone new was brought in to run the area. I was officially demoted, or, in the parlance of organizational restructuring, my job was "eliminated." In truth, I didn't really like many aspects of the job—the budgeting, the endless meetings, the political navigating of upper management. But I was attached, and profoundly identified with the role.

My new boss was a woman from "the outside," new to our organization, and she began running "my" department. Our initial relationship was rocky. Because of personality differences, my prideful response to my demotion, and a significant and sobering salary cut, I found working with her challenging. She undoubtedly would have said the same about me, and probably much more. Several months of internal struggle resulted. I found myself having wacky discussions with her inside my own head, debating and disagreeing with her, even though she was not there; she was having a fine life elsewhere. This obsessive thinking focused on what I had said, on what I wished I had said, on actually saying with great emotion what I hadn't said, on questioning what she had said, and so on, down the rocky road of compulsivity. My mind got carried away with this. It felt as if I didn't have a choice. I couldn't stop—I didn't have a choice.

This continued on. And on. The quality of my life was quickly diminishing.

One lovely summer morning a few long months later, I was biking down a beautiful dirt road, sun just rising over the mountains. I happened to notice that I was having a full conversation with this woman inside my head, this woman who was not, in fact, with me. I'd had enough of this. I hadn't even noticed that I was biking! I made a decision in that moment to commit myself to training my mind, in order to dismantle this pattern. Here was the plan I conceived: whenever I noticed myself talking to her, I would say to myself, "Not right now." This would be my mantra that would interrupt the compulsive pattern. Then I would take a good breath to relax and focus on one positive thing, in order to distract my mind. My commitment was to practice this for as long as it was needed.

So, in that moment, I said my mantra to myself, "Not

right now." I took a breath. I looked around and said to myself, "Wow, the corn is really so much taller than it was last week." And I continued biking, obsession-free.

Whether I was obsession-free for ten seconds, for two minutes, for ten minutes, I do not know. I do know that I was on the same dirt road when I happened to casually notice again that I was having yet another fevered internal chat with my new boss. So I repeated the process. I said my mantra and took a breath. I looked around for a positive thing, and I said to myself, "Oh, the sun feels so delicious on my arms." And I practiced.

This was not an instantly shifting cure-all, nor was it a magic bullet. It was a practice that I undertook, to begin to claim freedom from the craziness of my mind. It was not fast, but at least I now had a response, a healthy methodology to utilize, to buy space for myself. Over the next few weeks, it felt easier; life felt lighter. Over the next few months, the pattern disappeared. And over the years that followed, after being clear enough to speak my truth to her, I have developed an effective and working relationship with this woman.

I have dubbed this system of training the mind away from compulsive or unhealthy thoughts as "N-R-R": Notice, Relax, and Realign. To distract the mind away from those corners of craziness, to buy space and time away from the old, non-useful responses, to create new neuro-pathways—nobody is going to do that for you but You. It is not important how many times one has to notice and realign. It isn't about getting it right and being done. It is about having the willingness to practice. The commitment to the practice changes everything.

In offering this practice of N-R-R to clients over the years, I think of a dear young woman named Ree. Ree was in her mid-twenties when the first significant partnership of her life came to an unexpected end. As she replayed the loss over and over in her mind, she became increasingly frustrated at her inability to make sense of what had happened. No matter how much she tried to extricate herself from these obviously unhelpful patterns, she sensed herself becoming a revisionist—always going back in her mind, reexamining history, trying to arrive at the ultimate "truth" of why the relationship had ended and the mistakes she might have made. She journeyed endlessly through the hamster wheel of her own mind, round and round, working herself into deeper and deeper grief. She found herself getting angry, then sad, then sadder yet, constantly replaying conversations inside the wacky tape player in her head. "Why did it really happen?" she would ask me. "What did his words actually mean?" She was exhausting herself. Worse yet, all that she'd gained within the context of the relationship—her faith in herself as a partner, her knowledge that she had much to give—was getting lost in the frenzy.

When I initially shared with Ree the practice of noticing-relaxing-and-realigning, she told me she felt as if a giant weight had been lifted. For the first time, she felt as if she could give herself permission to breathe, to notice the negative patterns that insidiously slid into place, and then relax and realign to a more positive, more realistic perspective. Simply breathing was a major tool for Ree. For her, she said, it changed everything. The breath offered her an always-available response, a tool to rely upon to energetically and physiologically interrupt the pattern.

Ree is still practicing her N-R-R, and will be forever, she happily reported during our last session. She has risen from the ashes of her loss and is looking toward the future with new hope and energy. This stepping stone of walking through the negative thoughts has opened up wonderful possibilities for her. It has, in her words, transported her "from darkness to light."

All that we need to do is practice. Importantly, we must find ways to relax. Quieting the mind, relaxing its straining, returns it to alignment with the body and the spirit, where things emerge organically. What is intuition but the emergence of right knowing without the frantic busyness of the mind? Relaxation can come from a hot bath before bed. It can come from hugging a handsome dog who sits at your feet, or from a walk in the woods. It comes from a workout at the gym, from watching the mountains magically emerge behind the awakening morning sky, from pulling the weeds in your garden. There are so many ways to keep our minds in alignment. Each one of us has to discover our own, and then commit to that practice as a spiritual journey.

In my coaching practice, this principle of "do what you love" as a spiritual practice baffles folks. Spiritual practice has to be, we think, something we are not doing enough of, something we are not doing well enough, or simply, something we are not doing. What if the relaxing of the mind, the essence of spiritual growth, was the embracing and the prioritizing of the things you love the best? Gardening, biking, dancing around your living room, chopping vegetables? It counts. It all counts. When the mind quiets down, miracles emerge. When the mind quiets down, we are available for the miracles that are already all around us.

Swami Kripalu taught about "the nobility of retreat." Some of us might have thought of retreat as an unlimited amount of Chinese take-out food, the shades drawn, the phone disconnected for the weekend. This qualifies as a check-out, rather than a check-in to the moment. The concept of the nobility of retreat encourages us to release the push, to relax around what is happening rather than to banish it, to take a breath, to trust the process. To feel and release our human responses and feelings is the practice. And to remember the perspective of the bigger spiritual picture—that life does indeed work.

Couldn't our minds, if given a moment, identify plenty to worry about? But why bother? In the words of that AA saying, "If you worry, why pray? If you pray, why worry?" It just does not pay to go down that tunnel. But if we do find ourselves courting negative thoughts, straining and pushing at life, at any moment, we can return to this moment's grace. In the words of Rumi, the ecstatic poet, "Whether you've broken your vow a hundred times, come, the door is round and open."

I sit at my desk. The dogs are playing in the front room, their sounds of tussling floating down the hallway toward me. I can sense the excitement between them over their new soft white piggy-toy. Lucy's toy style is to lick the baby and cuddle with it, to carry it around with her, to have it forever. Zac Joey's style is to mutilate, to eviscerate, to tear it asunder as soon as possible. The life of our dog toys has been greatly compromised.

I smile to myself. *Not a bad moment*, I think. *Not a bad moment at all.*

Perhaps there are several things that, if it were up to me to choose, would be happening right now. But as I slow down and notice what is, all is beyond-perfect. Life could not possibly be better than it is in the moment. In this moment, there is nothing we could do to be closer to the grace and the goodness of the universe. And that is the truth of us all, right here, right now.

27

Heart

I spent much of my life worrying about not having a romantic partner. I deeply believed that my aloneness would somehow publicly display my deficits. The only people who were alone, I believed, were unattractive losers, malfunctioning humans missing the gene that would allow them to open their hearts to another person while that person reciprocally opened their heart back. From little girlhood forward, I knew this gene-less loser was me. Compounded by the gay issue and my family of origin dynamics, I spent much of my life energy until my forties searching unsuccessfully for "the one." The desperate voice of desire got louder as I got older. The relationships I was drawn into were far from paradigms of emotional wellness, since I was motivated by a lack of self, rather than a fullness of self.

When I quieted down as I began my spiritual practices in the days of the ashram, and as I committed to brahmacharya, the practice of not acting out my desires, change in my patterns subtly and eventually occurred.

I find myself today comfortably and happily married—not without issues in relationship, both with my partner and with friends, but with a different viewpoint. The perspective I now have shows me that opening my heart to another, no matter the form of relationship, is possibly life's greatest gift. Swami Kripalu once said, "The key to my heart lives in the heart of another." I know this to be true, not in a dependent, reactive, and grasping way, but in an independent, accepting, and relaxed way.

But first, let's rethink the illusion that there is something inherently wrong with being alone. I have some profound role models in my current life, strong and independent women who are traveling their life paths without a romantic partner at their side. They are whole and complete entities, creating lives of meaning and value. There is nothing "less" about the solo path.

When I was younger, my struggle for a mate seemed almost life-threatening. I now know that not everyone ends up in relationship. It seems incumbent upon all of us, no matter our relationship status, to focus on the positive, to care for ourselves, and to practice being with life as it is, be we partnered or alone.

During my struggling and grasping at relationship, life had an obvious message. It was requesting of me to create my own life first, before I shared it with another. Life asks us to focus on self-care, to respond to our own needs, to have a practice that we return to no matter what we are feeling, be it yoga, walking, writing, sitting, reading—all of these actions establish the platform of self, upon which relationship is planted. I know now that I wanted relationship in order to avoid my self. That high octane fuel of desire propelled me forward from one dysfunctional situation to the even more dysfunctional situation around the corner, constantly looking for someone to fill that God-shaped hole inside. *Find yourself first*, life was loudly insisting in my ear. But I was too busy searching outside myself to listen inside. The spiritual practices at Kripalu literally quieted me down enough to hear that internal voice of self. From that voice and from that source, things began to shift.

I currently have several coaching clients who struggle mightily in their aloneness, in their quest for a partner. My work with them focuses on encouraging them to pursue their own delights and interests, not to wait for another to make their equation complete. Do what you love to do; pursue the interests that fill you up. Imagine your life today as complete—there is nobody or nothing out there that can fill you up. It is already done. My clients and I also work with prayer and mantra, too, imagining the perfect person flowing into their life. And, paradoxically, visualization is a powerful tool when done with a specific and open heart. Our work typically centers on building patience and tolerance for the process. We create a plan to take right action, to get the client out there amidst like-minded others, while letting go of the results of those actions. Within the contradiction of *Be comfortable where you are, and from that place, imagine what might be*, we practice.

What a contradiction! How can we be present with life as it is, while preparing for change? Transformation needs to happen in the groundwork of deep relaxation. I think of my friends Joe and Cindy, who for many years attempted to get pregnant, to no avail. After much struggle and suffering, they adopted. A glorious little baby joined their family after several years of effort. Sure enough, within the next six months, they found themselves pregnant! Once the struggle was released, once presence was established, change organically emerged.

Patience and tolerance is a huge key here. As I look back on my healing in the realm of relationship, it was a slow and subtle shift of attitudes that steered me away from the compulsion to "take a hostage" to being ready and able to partner with another who was available. My earlier ambivalence about sharing myself always played out in my selection of love interests—if you were not fully available, I wanted to get You to be Mine. The shift away from this destructive pattern was gradual, almost unperceivable. Time takes time. Healing has its own timetable. We have responsibility in the creation of right relationship—to take healthy actions, to focus on ourselves and our self-care, and to get ourselves out into positive environments where like-minded people might be. Yet we do not do the healing. We create the circumstance in which we become ready, in which relationship is given to us. And this is a process, not an event. It takes the time that it takes.

Once in right relationship, one does not simply float away on a cloud of endless bliss. Hopefully there will be bliss—bliss is wonderfully God-given. Yet there is conflict, too, and work to do, internal doors to open in order to get closer to ourselves and this other person. Simply said, right relationship is sadhana, or spiritual practice. I always thought relationship was about enrolling my partner in my perspective and living happily ever after. Needless to say, I was not terribly successful at partnership as I held my emotional ground, digging into my perspective of the moment like a little bulldog with a bone. *My reality, my reality, join me over here!* my mind would shout.

I am ever so slowly learning that in relationship, it is incumbent upon me to build bridges from my view of the moment to my partner's, and vice versa. We grow closer to each other, by developing the parts of ourselves that are untouched, the not-yet-integrated parts of our personality that our partner most perfectly triggers. My wife is exactly the right one to heal my issues with anger. She is comfortable and easy with hers; it comes, she feels it, it lessens and releases. I, on the other hand, come from a family where anger was subterranean, not exposed and not released. It festered under the surface. I am new to feeling anger, and its power frightens me. So who do I perfectly end up with? What cosmic lottery do I draw in the arena of relationship? The exact one I need to grow and develop. Instead of trying to change Ras, trying to talk her out of her feelings, I am practicing allowing her to feel it. My cage is rattled, my comfort zone expanded; I become able to feel it, too. She moves through it as I touch into new emotional ground. I grow. We become closer.

Here are some cardinal rules for healthy, growth-producing spiritual relationships. Have enough time for yourself. How easy it is to merge into the other, and to forget about your own needs. Make sure you prioritize self-care and activities that bring you connection to the self. Look to other people to supplement and compliment your relationship. Nobody can or should be everything to you—that is just not sustainable. Have fun! It's easy, as time passes, to get complacent, to settle into a rut. Go on surprise dates, different vacations, cook wonderfully out-of-the-ordinary meals together, and supplement the habitual with the seasoning of uniqueness and fun.

Surely, and perhaps most importantly, find ways to communicate. Each one of us needs time and space to express our different perspectives. A simple and elegant method of conscious communication is a twelve-minute process that you can do with the agreement of your partner and an egg timer as a prop. Decide who is going to speak first and who is going to listen. First speaker: what do you need to say to be present in this moment? It could be as commonplace as reporting the day's activities, or as extraordinary as an insight or a dream. The speaker uses the first person, "I," to assume full ownership and power over the situation and the communication. This might sound like, "I'm aware of," "I feel," or "I notice." The second speaker listens in silence, holding the space of the non-judgmental witness. When the three minutes end, the roles are exchanged, and the second speaker begins downloading her communication. There is no need to respond to the content of the first speaker's words. This is about downloading our own experiences, so each can feel present. Repeat this so each speaker has two rounds. Twelve minutes later, notice how you are feeling. Do you feel more relaxed? More connected to yourself? More connected to the other? Just notice.

Several things happen in this conscious exchange. The speaker has full reign to unwind her experience. Without interruption, even well intended ones, the speaker has spaciousness and freedom to disentangle the thoughts and feelings of the day. Being truly listened to is all we really want—*to feel felt* is a profound psychological and spiritual gift, offering a connection deeper than words can give. An intimacy and connection can be effortlessly established.

Opening your heart is as simple as relaxing and noticing without judgment what is around you. Such rewarding heart connections are those I feel today with strangers. They seem easier to access than family and close friends, with their loaded emotional ammunition. As I notice and pay attention to the check-out boy in Stop and Shop with the long bony fingers and curly blond hair, the Kripalu guest so touched by her partner in the communication exercise, the stranger in the department store, looking for the right size of jeans, connection can be made so effortlessly. I can be so touched. Seeing the graciousness, the goodness, the God-ness in strangers is a profound spiritual practice. We only think we are different. We only think we are alone. Attending to the similarities in us all, reaching out with a smile and a kind word or gesture, diffuses the assumed separation between us.

Get out of your own emotional way. Don't take yourself too seriously. See who is around you, standing, walking, waiting, hurting. The Gujarati greeting of *jai bhagwan* is a powerful tool in the practice of opening your heart. It translates as, *I recognize the divinity within you.* Look around you. Allow your heart to be opened.

28

Calling

We all deserve to work in an arena that fills up our hearts. We are all entitled to pursue the kind of work that resonates inside, that echoes with satisfaction and delight. We all need work that gives to ourselves and to others on levels deeper than the practical, deeper than the financial. But for so many of us, it doesn't work like that. We get lost in the external professional shuffle and lose our internal way. We miss our calling; our life mission alludes us. Hence, when our actions veer us away from our core beliefs and core values, we suffer. Nowhere is this split more endemic than in our world of work.

How can we reconcile this, and begin to return home to ourselves in our work environment? How can we move toward work as the outer expression of our inner selves?

Dharma is a yogic principle that means one's righteous duty, one's virtuous path. It is the path we are born to walk, the work we are born to offer to the world, the conduct and conformity we each practice in relationship to this ordering principle of the universe. In my understanding of dharma, it is that place, that zone, into which we walk, and the universe responds. The doors of ease open, the obstacles resolve themselves. A sense of timelessness may ensue. Focused relaxation comes forth without effort. Work is done, yet ease and depth are available as simply as breath.

We all know this feeling of mindful presence. Consider what you love to do—is it gardening? Sketching? Walking with your dog? Remember the ease of those moments, the focused, timeless deliciousness of quieting the mind. This zone of presence is available to us, as we walk toward our calling. Work, too, can offer us the ease and satisfaction of one-pointed awareness.

Yet we often seem to get corralled into professional fields that don't speak to our heart, fields that only suit our financial needs, our mind's projections, or other people's expectations of us. So many of my coaching clients over the years have faced this daunting question: how do we begin to listen inside to our heart's longing, to bridge the gap to right livelihood that suits our authentic selves more comfortably?

Knowing what you don't want for yourself offers us a glorious beginning. I had a client who was so "over," in her words, her corporate role that she had held for eighteen years, that she was able to walk away—not without trepidation for the future, but with certainty about the past. Corporate was surely over. Yet she then found herself in that hallway we speak about, where one door has closed and the next has yet to open. Hanging in the hallway is a powerful, formless, energetic time. Not defined by what was, open to what might be, we are powerfully present in the moment. In that formless reality, devoid of our habitual identity and usual defaults—get up, go to work, punch the clock, work, work, work—life is more immediate, more raw, more vibrant. It is not necessarily a comfortable place, that hallway, but it is a place where grace and God and energy are available.

How do we move out of the hallway toward the first door? Right action is, of course, necessary. Both being and doing are needed to create sustainable change. The right use of will—taking small, incremental steps that move us toward our heart's calling—is essential. Mindy, my no-longer-corporate client, had a deep love for yoga, but never thought of it as a source of right livelihood. During the last year of her corporate job, she began taking advanced yoga workshops and trainings, and found both delight and possibility. Could she become a yoga teacher? The idea terrified and thrilled her.

After leaving her corporate job, she had planned to take a month-long yoga teacher training program. After that month, she had some limited consulting work set up, and a hope to begin teaching in her local yoga studio. By downsizing her standard of living to create a more sustainable and manageable way of life, she would be able to move into a new world, still secure on her savings and consulting income. She had a plan. Mindy still had many feelings of doubt along the way, but found such joy in her yoga teacher training program. She knew she was on the right path.

In discussing with clients this phenomenon of right livelihood, they often define their struggle like this: "But I don't know what I want. I just know that what I'm doing now is not it." For some people who have no inkling as to the next direction, I recommend journaling as a way to prime the pump of inspiration, responding to questions like:

What would the elements of a perfect work day be?

Describe that perfect day at work.

What do you love to do?

What are your greatest hopes for yourself in regard to work?

Not everyone responds well to journaling, but for many people, this is a way to begin to intuit next directions.

Trust your intuition. Move toward what feels good. Listen to your internal passion. Right livelihood captures the essence of what we love to do. If one of my clients is unable or unwilling to walk away from their current income source—an understandable position in these economic times—I suggest finding other ways to investigate their passions. Take an art class at night; find a writing coach. Look for weekend trainings to become a certified fitness instructor. Wiggle around your current work schedule to bring in the elements and the essences of interest, creativity, and self-expression that are missing for you. In spite of not walking away from your current job, it is still possible to weave in threads of dharma or points of passion into your existing life. Ways to express ourselves are infinite. Your existing job need not block them from you.

Relax into the process. My client, Mindy, was so certain of leaving her corporate job. Yet after being so plugged in, so structured in an A-type world for so long, she began experiencing the world of yoga freelance teaching as too unstructured, too unchallenging. After considering her options, she decided to step up her own personal practices of yoga and meditation, bringing more challenge and depth to her home practices. She also started taking more yoga classes in her area, consciously critiquing each teacher on a grid she created, and learning from them. She needed to continue to trust her inner guide, and allow herself to shift down to a different pace in this very different world of work. Not right, not wrong, this is simply Mindy's personal path, the journey she has needed to take.

Mantra is a tool that can guide some people in their search for work that matters. Mantra can function as a mind protector, an energetic springboard to transformation. If you are open to mantra as a supportive tool to potentially move you in your heart's direction, consider this question: What is a first-person, energetic proclamation that captures your intention? Keep it strong, specific, simple, and short. You can discover your mantra by quieting your mind, journaling, or simply asking inside and listening—there are many, many ways home.

Mindy's mantra eventually revealed itself as: "I, Mindy, am a holder of sacred, healing space as a teacher and a guide for others on their yogic path." Once she had the mantra, she repeated it to herself in the morning upon awakening, at night upon going to sleep, as she began her yoga practice, and at any other time of the day when she felt anxiety or stress. It gave her a positive place of strength to go to, to automatically distract the mind away from the more negative, self-doubting thoughts. It is our responsibility to train our minds, and mantra is a strong training tool for some.

You might also use prayer in this search for meaningful work. We know prayer is an earnest request or wish. In Sanskrit, the word prayer or *prarthana* comes from two words: "pra" and "artha," which means to plead fervently. Also inherent in this word are the elements of love and faith in the requester. Expressing our humbled position and request for support demands that we supplicate ourselves. To acknowledge that the real creator of right work is someone or something else larger than our human willpower—to remember that our job is to create the circumstances in which the miracle of right livelihood is manifested, by aligning ourselves with something greater than our own minds—we are again petitioning an energetic partner for support. We cannot do this alone. Coming into relationship with that which is larger than our minds opens the doorway to possibility, healing, and change.

If this prayer perspective interests you, write a prayer for yourself. What are you wanting and needing? How can you humble yourself to request support in this very human arena of work? Once your prayer is revealed to you, weave it into your day, using it at specific times or anytime that your stress level increases. Mindy's prayer was, "Show me the way. Walk with me." She found great solace in using it as both a way to train her mind away from the negative, habitual thoughts, and to open her heart to that which is greater than herself.

Looking back on my work history, I am awed at its rambling and perfect course. Working for fifteen years in Malcolm X Shabazz High School in Newark, teaching kids about nouns and verbs, was a frustrating, effortful, energy-draining experience. I dragged myself home at the end of most days, sapped and emptied of both liveliness and hope. Once I got sober, I knew I had to leave that job, that there had to be more for me professionally. But where would I go? And what would I do?

A few painful years ensued, during which I knew I had to leave Shabazz but was clueless as to my next steps. It was by volunteering at Kripalu several years later that I was able to walk away from my paycheck, my pension, and my definition of myself as "public school teacher." Learning about seva, selfless service at Kripalu, working on the household crew, the editing department, managing the kitchen—all these departments taught me the same possibility: taking action and letting go of the results of those actions. Write the best story I could, and let go of its outcome. Vacuum the floor as a meditation, and release my attachment to its end result. Karma yoga taught me how to imagine that act itself was the practice, the results literally none of my business. Writing as a meditation, teaching as a way to connect to the power of the moment—embracing the journey opens us to the power of now, to the depth of the present moment.

Teaching, coaching, and writing are now my spiritual practices. They are the places in which I am most connected to grace, and most free of my mind's limiting beliefs about myself and the world around me. This has happened through patience and through time, from one simple, incremental step leading me to the next. I am aboundingly grateful, awed, and fully aware that, although I had "things" to do to get here, so much of this process was not my idea and completely out of my control. I fully believe that right livelihood is our birthright, that each and every one of us is both worthy and able to walk its path.

One step at a time, may we be led home to ourselves.

29

Spirit

What do I believe in the depths of my soul, at this moment of my life? What are my spiritual truths, my safety nets of belief that catch me as I tumble, amidst the everyday struggles of my life? How do I navigate my way through the potential sludge of suffering that regularly awaits me?

I believe there is a spirit, a power, a grace in my life that is greater than I am and greater than my mind. It is greater, I believe, than the human experience. This power is running the show, determining my reality. Call it God, call it spirit, call it intuition, call it grace or evolution, call it the great reality, or call it nothing. There is something going on here with which I partner. That's the good news—I'm not alone.

The bad news is: I forget this regularly. I think I am in charge and attempt to control my reality. When this happens, the results are generally not pretty. When I am operating on self-will, when I am forging forward with my intended plan for the moment, I suffer. When I relax into what is, there is freedom and breath and ease. It's profoundly simple, yet it is the imperfect practice that will carry me to my final breath.

The ancient yogis and sages described this power as positive life force, as evolutionary urge. Humans have wrestled with an understanding, a description of this energy for thousands of years. In this moment, I have no need to embody this spirit in an entity with a name, a personality, or a visual appearance. For me, after all I have experienced, I simply see this flow of grace manifested as reality. *God's will is what's showing up in this moment*, I heard a woman say, early in my sober journey. Her insight continues to guide me, a flashlight on my path.

What is our role in this relationship with reality? How do we begin to accept its relentless and continual onslaught of experiences? How do we balance the real need for right action, the right use of will, with the need to surrender to this force of life, this inevitable unfolding of events? How do we keep ourselves open and connected to this sense of spirit? So many questions evaporate down to the concept of practice, an imperfect dance between remembering, living in alignment, and forgetting, slipping away into self-seeking and attempted control.

I need a set of tools, a structure of practice that I use no matter what I am feeling. For me, the continuity of a structure to reconnect to this spirit is essential. Without a ritual or routine of re-connection, I lose my way.

My "kit of spiritual tools" has morphed as the years have washed over me. Today I keep my practices low-key and simple. Instead of the verses of prayer that I used to repeat religiously (forgive the pun), I now simply ask for help in the morning, and offer thanks at night. And in between, during whatever moments I can muster, I remember that I am not alone. This remembrance can flood into me on the flow of a breath, on chanting *om* with guests in a workshop I am leading, on watching the sun set over the hills in a blaze of orange streaks, on playing ball with Lucy Doodle—the doorways back home are infinite and all forgiving. No matter how long I have been disconnected from spirit and living in my head in my attempts to direct the show, I am welcomed effortlessly back into silent grace. That is a pretty good deal—to partner with a positive life force that, no matter how many times you betray it and attempt to overtake it, will offer absolutely no retribution, just a welcomed depth of reunion.

Prayer works for me. I have certain ones that act as a special balm, an ease to my soul, that reconnect me to spirit. They offer a shifting of my cognitive understanding—"I am safe"—to an openheartedness that is viscerally felt in my being. The journey really is from the head to the heart for me. I find that repeating prayers aloud comforts me greatly. I don't believe prayers alter the reality around me, but they certainly shift my relationship to that reality, by relaxing me, by helping me to soften my grip on what I think should be happening. While driving alone in my car, with the glorious Berkshire land unfolding around me, I practice repetitive prayer. It brings me depth and ease, my car such a perfect container of sanctity.

The prayer that most resonates today in quieting my mind and opening my heart is the Third Step prayer from my 12 Step program. It encourages me to:

Offer myself to Thee,
To build with me and to do with me as Thou will.
Relieve me of the bondage of self, that I might better do Your will.
Take away my difficulties such that victory over them
Might bear witness to those that I might help
Of Your power and Your love and Your way of Life.
May I do Your will always.

The simple, repetitive lines of this prayer remind me that I am not in charge; that there is a plan here, greater than anything I could imagine. Relaxing into that plan, I am able to show up to the moment and serve others. My intentions are suspect, but when I "get out of my own way," as this prayer urges me to do,

I become helpful to others, the most satisfying position of all. During my ashram days, I loved the guru mantra, *om namo bhagavate vasudevaya*, which translates as, "I invoke and surrender to the Great Reality." The two prayers are such a compliment to each other.

I use lines of the Third Step prayer as a mantra, to relax me. Before a program, an intense meeting at work, or any stressful situation, I may write it out, substituting the words to be appropriate: *I offer this program to you.* Before I work on my writing projects, I invoke the spirit of this helpful verse. Simply put, it manages my anxiety, relaxes me, shifts my perspective away from myself, and frees me up.

Exercise and movement are another avenue for connection to spirit. In the words of simple 12 Step wisdom: "Move a muscle, change a thought." I try regularly to think my way to grace. It doesn't work very well. But if I quiet my mind through walking, a workout, swimming or biking, the feeling of connection to spirit is often restored to me. The ease that settles over me—the woosh of resulting energy—is a gift. My mind has quieted and my spirit has been urged forward.

Most remarkably, teaching, coaching, and writing are vehicles of restoration to grace for me. I have practiced these forms enough to know that, although my will and my mind are surely needed for forward movement, the container of their creative and healing process is one of being, one of grace. I need to create the structure, do the planning, come prepared to the moment. Yet, by then relaxing into what is happening, my creative self is freed. I am profoundly blessed that my work is a spiritual practice.

I think of a coaching client of mine named Rose. She is a minister who had to leave her congregation due to chronic illness. Leaving was not her choice, and her heart was broken by her bishop's decision. A sense of failure, of disbelief, of premature endings filled her. She needed to connect with the God of her understanding to begin to bring some solace to her broken heart. We talked of ways, of structures, in which she could begin to reconnect, to gain spiritual support in walking down this painful path from congregation to self, from outward focus to inward healing. She balked at going to a formal church—too soon, too much shame, too much ambivalence. But at the idea of walking, her eyes lit up!

Rose agreed—her body could use the gentle movement, and her heart could use the opportunity to be quiet, to connect with grace. She agreed to three gentle walks a week, which did function as an emotional, physical, and spiritual balm. The structure and commitment to those walks held her as she began her healing journey.

Inspiration is essential. How can I keep my heart open? How can I continue to inspire myself through the routine, the humdrum, the stressful inevitabilities of my imperfectly perfect day?

For me, my participation in a Shabbat service at my temple functions as a rocket to inspiration. The ancient Hebrew melodies tug at my heart; the English translation seems to inexorably mirror my current moment and current struggle. I often find myself releasing tears for no cognitive reason, as if the blessedness of the place itself encourages their healing flow. Nevertheless, I struggle with my resistance about going, often choosing to hunker down at home on a Friday night rather than generate the effort it takes to get myself to temple. Another bizarre dilemma of the human condition emerges—the difficulties in doing the very things that so sustain and feed us. Watching the Friday night DVD sometimes wins out.

This leads us to ask the question: If I am a human partner to this divine energy, how do I interact with it? How much action should I take? Do I just sit at home and expect divinity to create a perfect world around me? What exactly is my role?

The 12 Step programs talk about "becoming right-sized"— discovering the balance point between willful action and surrender. To understand this, and to continue to remind myself of this, I think of the last five years of my drinking and drugging. I could not get sober on my own. No matter what rules I imposed on myself—*I won't do This until after work, I won't do That until Saturday night, etc.*—I had no choice. I woke up and did It, no matter the pledge or commitment I had previously proclaimed. It wasn't until I was fully beaten, fully surrendered, finding myself on the floor of my apartment, emptied of my own willfulness, that a power greater than myself could enter. In that instant, I was given a lifelong partner in living. Something shifted. I was literally guided to my first meeting, led down the street and walked into that non-descript church.

Yet I have "stuff" to do, footwork to take, actions to initiate in order to realign myself with this benevolent power. After my moment of powerlessness on First Avenue, I had to pick up the phone to figure out the location of the meeting. I had to find my keys and my shoes and make my way there. Yes, there was something guiding me, but I had human and willful actions to take. And on a daily basis, I must take right action. I must head in the direction of God's will for me. For example, I am positive that God's will for me is to live free of drugs and alcohol. I know that without question. I am aware of the daily footwork I need to do to get in alignment with that energetic intention. I must talk to my sponsor, get to a meeting, talk about what I am feeling, give myself the hour of the meeting to slow down, and get in touch with myself. And I need to not pick up that first drink or drug. And so the partnership continues.

The concept of passionate non-attachment is active in my life today. To me this dictate means to take action, and to release the outcome of that action. My life coaching practice is a wonderful example of this. When I sit with a client, I fully intend that that person receive support, help, connection, a tool, a plan—something that can move them forward. Yet I am powerless over "making" that happen. I can create the circumstances to encourage those conditions, by helping the client to feel relaxed and safe, by mirroring back their experience, by offering threads of forward-movement. But ultimately, the outcome is not in my control. It is a humbling position in which to sit.

Some miracles manifest in strange ways, as that which I do not want or that which I do not choose. But inevitably, if I stay open and keep available to their unfolding, seeds are being planted for future flowering in my world. The greatest traumas in my life have been the most remarkable open doors to healing, to oneness, to possibility. My stuttering, the most shame-filled aspect of my earlier years, has morphed into one of my strongest tools: my voice. The very place I ran from, the spoken word, is one of my greatest professional strengths. Another example is my addiction, the most life-threatening and despairing aspect of my middle years. Yet it opened the door to recovery, to an understanding of a working God as partner, and to a community of like-minded and like-hearted souls, whom I never would have met if left to my own devices. Life works when I let it. Life works when I participate with it. Life works when I remember that I am not alone, managing all.

I believe that, for me, suffering is a self-inflicted choice. It is a forgetting of the perfection of what is around me, a negating of my energetic, spiritual partner, and a demand that life show up differently. I slide into this human trap dozens of times each day. We all do, I am certain. Yet when I am able to notice my forgetting, relax and realign with the truth, I am home again. I practice remembering that all is well as it is, that life is unfolding perfectly, and that there is a grace walking alongside of me—carrying me when necessary—unfailingly and consistently making everything all right.

There really is nothing wrong with this moment.

30

🖋

Home

And now it is today. The early morning light shifts slowly on this November day, sunrise still a distance from us. The house is still and quiet. Zac Joseph the Dog, my staunch supporter in writing endeavors and secret muse, sleeps serenely on the floor by my side, curled up in a ball of soft black, contented fur. Lucy the Princess Dog inhabits her throne on the couch, supporting me from afar with her blonde, sleepy love. Only the soft hum of the refrigerator floats on the silence of this moment's stillness. There is nowhere on earth I would rather be than here, in my home.

I never imagined that I would have a home. My childhood house, so full and yet so empty, was an unreachable model. So much love and so much angst filled it, so much caring and so much turmoil surrounded it. It seemed impossible that I could duplicate such a place. Maybe all children feel that the only real home is the one where Mommy fed them, where Daddy held them. Perhaps the always-looming trauma of my father's potential dying made this place, even in its richness, a place of vulnerability and hovering loss. I simply knew that I was deeply doomed, that I would be exiled from this source of nurturance and torment, never to recreate it.

Try to recreate it I did, emulating heterosexual America with my upscale marriage apartment, to no avail. Despite its color coordination and trendy comfort, it was empty. Later I tried to rebel against middle class values in my funky, furniture-free walk-through railroad flat on East Fifth Street in New York—again, to no avail. It, too, was an empty, hollow place. I hadn't yet landed inside myself, hadn't yet created an internal home.

Since then, I've explored the spectrum of living accommodations. My travels have taken me far, both outside and inside far, and, because of my internal journey, my understanding of home has changed. It no longer hinges on another's presence, on visual objects, or on a certain neighborhood. It starts inside each one of us, and works its way out.

Home is a place where your heart can relax, where your body can rest, where your mind can quiet down. It is a place that offers shelter from the humdrum and the habitual, a place to take off your shoes and hunker down. It is a place of spiritual retreat from the intensity of the day, a place of safety and warmth apart from life's conflicts. It offers us the safety to let down our guard, our pretenses, and to simply return back to ourselves. It is a clear and obvious extension of our inner world, manifested around us.

Although solace cannot rely on externals, attending to the visual aspects of your home is nevertheless both necessary and helpful. Finding a color of paint for that wall might soften the room perfectly. Hanging just the right picture there might open your heart. Displaying knick-knacks that hold positive emotional memory within them—all of these choices can relax our minds and open our hearts. A comfortable chair and a snuggly throw can help create a sacred and relaxing place. The externals cannot be the only thing—that focus will be doomed—but they can be part of a tapestry that weaves together relaxation and ease in your home.

Human nature seems to encourage crowding and hoarding. What are those things in the basement? Where did they come from? Does this closet have a magnetic pull? Clothes of different sizes hover in the back of closets. Possessions gather around us, in spite of ourselves. Make a commitment each year to look around your space with fresh eyes. Are the things that surround you currently living in an emotional present tense for you? Are they relevant? What can be tossed, offered up to that great recycle machine in the sky? Our outer space reflects our inner space, and vice versa. Keeping your surroundings tidy and current helps to keep the home space clearer.

It took me many years to realize that I deserved to live in a beautiful place. Before moving to the Berkshires, it never dawned on me that natural beauty had anything to do with home. I lived in the suburbs; I lived in the city. The country, with its solace, natural rhythms, and slower pace was somewhere you visited or vacationed. It was only through the pull of the Kripalu ashram that I discovered the glory of living in a place where sunrise and sunset shined in their fullness, where winter and summer were untouched by sidewalks, crowds, and traffic. Without Kripalu, I might not have learned that the land upon which we walk, upon which our homes sit, has a huge impact on our lives. Do you resonate with the natural surroundings in which you live? If you live in a city, do you have access to nature, to trees and grass, to earth and unencumbered sky? A connection to nature, to the earth beneath us, can bolster the potency of any home.

Whatever your living space, you can begin to cleanse its energy and make it yours. Energetic ownership can begin by burning sage, which can clear negative energy, influences, and feelings. It can purify the energy that is present, and give you a sense of participation in making the space yours. Ritual can have a strong impact on the person enacting it; like prayer, which may not alter external reality, the supplicant might feel touched and changed. Ritual can function similarly, as an invitation for the doer of the ritual to recreate relationship with her surroundings.

You can't do ritual wrong. It is simply an expression of yourself—feel free to take wild liberties in creating one. When my partner and I moved into our first shared housing in the post-ashram Kripalu, we were given a set of rooms where the very deceptive, wrong-doing CEO had lived for years. She had just been exiled in disgrace. It was a wonderful living space, relatively speaking: a suite of two rooms with an aging yet dignified bathroom. It was a far cry from the tiny, bathroom-less, closet-like housing we were used to in our earlier ashram days. But Krishnapriya's room? At that moment, living in that space was like inhabiting the devil's discarded condominium.

It was too good to turn down, certainly, but how could we make it ours? We tried burning sage in seashell ashtrays on the windowsills, its smoke drifting in sweet little tendrils toward the heavens. That felt way too passive. We needed the big energetic guns, so we consulted with some of the energy workers from our Healing Arts department. One suggested using dampening Epson salts with rubbing alcohol, lighting it, and offering prayers of clearing.

We tiptoed into the emptied rooms, an old frying pan filled with Epson salt, alcohol in hand. It still felt a bit like enemy territory, very much not ours yet. We saturated the salt with alcohol, lit a match, tossed it into the frying pan, and helplessly watched as a giant blue flame leapt toward the ceiling. "Old energy out, new energy in," we feverishly chanted, speedily guiding the flame through the room. Ras followed me with the plant mister, ready to attack any rogue flame. We hastily yet hopefully infiltrated each nook and cranny, put the fire-pan out in the sink, and sunk onto the floor laughing. Energy changed in those once-tainted rooms: a good coat of paint covering the Ultra Carnation Pink that had plastered every surface, the bright flame dancing, and our shared laughter began to mold these rooms into our first home together.

Animals can make a set of rooms into a home effortlessly. They settle in, claiming territory without guilt, discovering spots to call their own, offering permission for our claiming of comfort. They exude being. Silence and goodness tumble out from them. Many years ago, well before my entrance into 12 Step program, two of my friends returned from a trip to Greece. Several of us sat around their kitchen table as they recounted their tales on the islands of Lesbos and Mykonos. Cindy opened up a bag of shells that she had gathered there, to give us mementos. The shells came in all sizes and shapes—they covered the table in a tapestry of texture. Then, to our disbelief, one of the shells started moving!

The shell was inhabited, it seemed, by a snail who had snuck its way through customs at Kennedy Airport and was crawling across this kitchen table, attempting its return to Mykonos. Cindy scooped up the tiny refugee into a glass jar labeled "Nettles," an herb that she was using for medicinal purposes, and shoved the jar toward me. Nettles came home with me, and became, strangely enough, an unlikely companion for the next several years of my life. Living in her round fish tank, little North American shells her new landscape, she provided comfort, companionship, and a point of focus for me. Despite the emptiness of my life, at that point riotously run by addiction, this little snail was a companion on the path, and offered me solace. I wasn't alone, in a time of such rampant self consciousness. There was something, someone I could focus on, besides my own breaking heart.

Consider creating a heart center in your home. It can be as ambitious as a yoga room, or as humble as a spot on a windowsill for a candle or a flower. Returning to this spot daily, renewing your commitment to yourself, can unfold as a sustaining and sustainable home practice. Often we are easily lost in the possessions that clog our homes. To declare a spot for your altar, a focus for spiritual renewal, transforms both the person and the home in which the practice occurs. And remember, practice does not have to be wrapping your leg around your neck and sitting for an hour. It can be the lighting of a candle, the repeating of a mantra or prayer, the gazing at a picture of beauty or a reminder of a teacher or a loved one. We often block ourselves with complications and expectations. Simple works really well. In the words of that 12 Step slogan, "Keep it simple, sweetheart."

The house is softly quiet now, morning light streaming through the skylights. Only the occasional canine snore can be heard. I snuggle on the people-couch, the dogs on the dog-couch, and wrap a blanket around me. I feel wrapped also in the silence, the home-ness of this place. Inside of me, a tiny child's voice whispers:

"I am safe here.
I am home here.
I am me—here."

Part Three: What Might Be

Epilogue: Articles of Faith

How can we navigate the future? No matter our age, unknowns lurk in the shadows. Whether it's financial security, romantic desire, the quest for healthy aging, or whatever your specific obstacle, we can be potentially plagued by that which is undefined. How can we see ourselves up ahead as healthy, vital, and dynamic, no matter what we might face? When the picture of the future is so vague, how do we imagine it, prepare for it, and even envision whatever it brings us as a time of grace and goodness? Non-judgmental retrospective evidence can guide us.

If I could rewind the movie of my life twenty years and see myself as a new initiate in the Kripalu ashram, I could never have imagined the life I have today—one full of meaning and dharma, right livelihood and ease of purpose. I was so disguised to myself that this path upon which I now so gratefully walk was invisible to me. The time was not yet right for it to be revealed.

If I could rewind the movie of my life forty years and see myself as a twenty-one year old entering the Peace Corps, I could never have imagined the life I have today—one of service and value, community and connection. I was blinded by fear of my differences and frantically searched for someone, something, to take away my pain.

If I could rewind the movie of my life fifty years and see

myself as an eleven-year-old, never could I have imagined the personal freedom I have today. To be legally married to a woman, to have a home, dear animal companions, ease and safety surrounding me—all of that was inconceivable. This life I now live did not exist as an option. My life today is stunningly freed of the internal and external homophobia that terrified me and kept me invisible for so many years.

These past years, one day at a time, one episode at a time, one trauma and one opportunity at a time, each and all have delivered me to this moment and to a life beyond my wildest dreams. The evidence is tangible. There is protection and care around us always. Despite our feelings, as more is revealed, we are moved forward. There is some force, some energy walking with us, carrying us to the next, best moment, the next, best expression of ourselves.

How can we utilize the lessons of the past, the evidence of our yesterdays, to show us our growth, to mirror our possibilities, to strengthen our faith? How can we put worry to the side of our minds, and move forward into life's mysteries?

Oh, worry, I do. At 3 a.m., I worry. I wonder who will get bananas for me when I am an old, constipated woman. Who will die first, Ras or me? Who will shovel us out after the snowstorm when I cannot? Who will help me navigate our tragically dysfunctional health care system? Will my dying be sudden and untimely, or will it be a protracted, delayed process? It's not being dead that I find so frightening. It is the process of dying that sends shivers up my spine, especially in the middle of a long, winter night. Loss of capacity, mental breakdown, inevitable physical weakening— who will help me get through it and find my way to the other side?

There is no picture of what might be, no image of what form

my aging might take. Without children to give color to that empty mural, it truly is a blank picture, a colorless, formless void of unknown.

All of this does terrify me—when I let it. The practice I now choose has to be utilizing my faith and distracting my mind away from the unanswerable questions. I must continue to remember where I come from, and how much I have been offered. These next years, for as many as I am given, be they one or forty, must be grounded in a practice of a faith that works, a faith that reminds me to look in my rearview mirror for spiritual evidence.

I must consciously remember what was—where I come from—the loneliness, the trauma, the pain. I must remember what is, the transformation of those obstacles into the gifts I have been given in these almost twenty-four years—the gifts of community, of right livelihood, of love. Like with each situation in these past years of healing and sobriety, more will be revealed to me in its right timing.

Surely there was no picture for me as an eleven-year-old for the life I live now. No picture existed as a twenty-one-year-old, or a forty-one-year-old. The pictures have emerged through time, through willingness, through prayer and presence, through practice and radical compassion for myself in the process. I must trust the process and continue the spiritual journey of self-observation.

We can learn how to consciously age as we age.

We can learn how to face whatever we are given, and relax and grow through it.

We can learn how to respond as we find ourselves in unknown situations.

We can trust the process of aging, of financial, professional, health-related challenges, in living life "on life's terms."

We can also allow our mistrust of the process.

And we can continue to realign with the imagining of the best of what might be.

We can live in gratitude for all we have been given, even and especially the challenges. We can rely upon the practice of gratitude to appreciate what is, to keep our minds away from what is not, away from those compelling worst-case scenarios.

We can live in possibility—for the continued healing of our bodies, minds, and spirits, even and especially in our aging. We can imagine a future, no matter what it brings us, of physical activity, of mental stimulation, of emotional satisfaction, of spiritual connection. We can choose the possibility of healthy food, a vigorous lifestyle, and a mental attitude that is positive and affirming. I believe in the possibility of our own choosing.

We can live in hope that, be it twenty-four hours or twenty-four years that we continue to live, we offer ourselves to that which is greater than our minds, surrender to the grace of reality, continue to discover who we really are, and relax into this moment of perfection.

In the here and the hereafter, we shall be blessed, as long as we continue to remember that we are not alone.

There is nowhere to go, nothing to do, and no one to become.

We are already home.

Aruni Nan Futuronsky

Writer, teacher, and mindfulness coach, Aruni Nan Futuronsky finds life is best experienced with compassion, gratitude, and a whole lot of humor. She lives in Western Massachusetts with her wife, Ras, and canine teachers, Lucy Kay Doodle and Zac Joseph Doodle. A dynamic guide on the path of healing for body, mind, and spirit, Aruni is the creator of the innovative CD, *Life-Works, Meditations for Mindful Living*, and the author of *Recovering My Voice: A Memoir of Chaos, Spirituality, and Hope*.

You can visit with Aruni at her website:
www.coacharuni.com

Breinigsville, PA USA
29 March 2011
258626BV00001B/5/P